MW00607479

Eighteenth-Century Brechtians

Eighteenth-Century Brechtians looks at stage satires by John Gay, Henry Fielding, George Farquhar, Charlotte Charke, David Garrick and their contemporaries through the lens of Brecht's theory and practice. Discussing the actor mutiny of 1733, theatre censorship, controversial plays and Fielding's forgery of an actor's autobiography, Joel Schechter contends that some subversive Augustan and Georgian artists were in fact early Brechtians. He also reconstructs lost episodes in theatre history including Fielding's last days as a stage satirist before his Little Haymarket theatre was closed, and the 1740 staging of Jonathan Swift's *Polite Conversation* on a double bill with Shakespeare's *Merry Wives of Windsor*.

'Joel Schechter may have written the perfect book for this historical moment. 'Eighteenth-Century Brechtians is part history, part exegesis, and part polemical manifesto. As we enter a period of political uncertainty, the satirical voices that Schechter celebrates here may prove useful once more. Readable and concise, the book is accessible enough for an undergraduate but with enough sophistication for more advanced students.' *Journal of Dramatic Theory and Criticism*

'Not every book about the eighteenth-century theatre alludes to Chelsea Manning, Occupy Wall Street and Bernie Sanders, or concludes with a chronology that jumps from 1763 ("James Boswell visits Newgate Prison") to 1928 ("Brecht and others adapt Gay's *The Beggar's Opera*"). *Eighteenth-Century Brechtians* makes these contemporary references and goes further [. . .] there is much here to prompt further investigation, not least for any post-Brechtian producers who happen to open the book.' *Times Literary Supplement*

Joel Schechter is Professor of Theatre Arts at San Francisco State University, where he teaches courses in theatre history, dramatic literature and popular theatre. His books include *Durov's Pig, Satiric Impersonations, The Pickle Clowns, Radical Yiddish* and *Messiahs of 1933*.

Exeter Performance Studies

Series editors: Peter Thomson, Professor of Drama at the University of Exeter; Graham Ley, Professor of Drama and Theory at the University of Exeter; Steve Nicholson, Professor of Twentieth-Century and Contemporary Theatre at the University of Sheffield.

From Mimesis to Interculturalism: Readings of Theatrical Theory Before and After 'Modernism'
Graham Ley (1999)

British Theatre and the Red Peril: The Portrayal of Communism 1917–1945
Steve Nicholson (1999)

On Actors and Acting
Peter Thomson (2000)

Grand-Guignol: The French Theatre of Horror
Richard J. Hand and Michael Wilson (2002)

The Censorship of British Drama 1900–1968: Volume One 1900–1932
Steve Nicholson (2003)

The Censorship of British Drama 1900–1968: Volume Two 1933–1952
Steve Nicholson (2005)

Freedom's Pioneer: John McGrath's Work in Theatre, Film and Television
edited by David Bradby and Susanna Capon (2005)

John McGrath: Plays for England
selected and introduced by Nadine Holdsworth (2005)

Theatre Workshop: Joan Littlewood and the Making of Modern British Theatre
Robert Leach (2006)

Making Theatre in Northern Ireland: Through and Beyond the Troubles
Tom Maguire (2006)

"In Comes I": Performance, Memory and Landscape
Mike Pearson (2006)

London's Grand Guignol and the Theatre of Horror
Richard J Hand and Michael Wilson (2007)

Theatres of the Troubles: Theatre, Resistance and Liberation in Ireland, 1980–2000
Bill McDonnell (2008)

The Censorship of British Drama 1900–1968: Volume Three, The Fifties
Steve Nicholson (2011)

British South Asian Theatres: A Documented History
edited by Graham Ley and Sarah Dadswell (2011)

Critical Essays on British South Asian Theatre
edited by Graham Ley and Sarah Dadswell (2012)

Victory over the Sun: The World's First Futurist Opera
edited by Rosamund Bartlett and Sarah Dadswell (2012)

Marking Time: Performance, Archaeology and the City
Mike Pearson (2013)

Singing Simpkin and Other Bawdy Jigs: Musical Comedy on the Shakespearean Stage
Roger Clegg and Lucie Skeaping (2014)

Ancient Greek and Contemporary Performance: Collected Essays
Graham Ley (2014)

The Censorship of British Drama 1900–1968: Volume 4, The Sixties
Steve Nicholson (2015)

Performing Grand-Guignol: Playing the Theatre of Horror
Richard J Hand and Michael Wilson (2016)

Forms of Conflict: Contemporary Wars on the British Stage
Sara Soncini (2016)

Eighteenth-Century Brechtians: Theatrical Satire in the Age of Walpole
Joel Schechter (2016)

Eighteenth-Century Brechtians

Theatrical Satire in the Age of Walpole

Joel Schechter

UNIVERSITY
of
EXETER
PRESS

First published in 2016 by
University of Exeter Press
Reed Hall, Streatham Drive
Exeter EX4 4QR
UK

Reissued in paperback 2018

www.exeterpress.co.uk

British Library Cataloguing in Publication Data
A catalogue record for this book is available
from the British Library.

ISBNs
Hardback 978 0 85989 997 0
Paperback 978 0 85989 335 0

Cover image: etching showing *The Stage Mutiny*, from the Harry Beard Collection
© Victoria and Albert Museum, London

Originally typeset in Plantin by
Kestrel Data, Exeter

Original jacket design by
Bettina Newman, www.bmld.uk

CONTENTS

     on Yoko Ono

20   Brecht Praises Garrick's *Hamlet*   231

21   A Portrait of the Artists as *Beggar's Opera* Disciples—   237
     Including David Garrick, Epic Actor

22   Walpole in America   251

23   The Future of Eighteenth-Century Brechtiana: 256
     Polly Exonerated

24   Conclusion: The Future Promise of an Earlier Age   258

     Eighteenth-Century Brechtians: A Timetable of Events   262

     Bibliography   265

     Index   270

The Cast of Brechtians in Order of Appearance

Brief first entrances in Chapter One are followed by longer scenes featuring:

George Farquhar (1677–1707)	Chapter Two
John Gay (1685–1732)	Chapters Two to Six
Jonathan Swift (1667–1745)	Chapters Seven and Eight
Henry Fielding (1707–1754)	Chapters Nine to Sixteen
Theophilus Cibber (1703–1758)	Chapters Fourteen to Sixteen
Charlotte Charke (1713–1760)	Chapters Fifteen to Eighteen
David Garrick (1717–1779)	Chapters Nineteen to Twenty-one
William Hogarth (1697–1764)	Chapters Three and Twenty-one
James Boswell (1740–1795)	Chapter Twenty-one
Robert Walpole (1676–1745)	Chapter Twenty-two
David Hare (1947–) and Caryl Churchill (1938–)	Chapter Twenty-three

Illustrations

Foreword

It was his book *Durov's Pig* (1985) that alerted me to Joel Schechter's idiosyncratic insight into the scope and potential of political theatre. This new book has been written as a challenge to the twenty-first century, a bid to jolt the anglophone theatre out of its political doziness.

My own exposure to a drama engaged in the Brechtian quest to change the world began in the 1950s, in Coventry (where I saw the premieres of the Wesker trilogy) and in Cambridge (where I was stunned by Arthur Miller's exposure of McCarthyism in action in *The Crucible*). The sheer inventiveness of Joel's study of eighteenth-century Brechtians has stimulated my reading (and, in some cases, rereading) of politically assertive plays of the past. The one that has most vividly affected me is Maxwell Anderson's *Both Your Houses*. It opened in New York on 6 March 1933, on the third day of Franklin D. Roosevelt's first term as President. The Depression required action from the government, but Anderson confronted audiences with corrupt Congressmen feathering their own nests at the expense of the nation at large. The criminal legacy of Warren Harding, unredeemed by the Presidency of Calvin Coolidge and Herbert Hoover, has clearly identified 'great' men as 'great' rogues. The dialogue might almost have been lifted from *The Beggar's Opera* or *The Historical Register for the Year 1736*. Government is in the hands of 'placemen', and policy is contingent on bribery and concealed chicanery. The fact that *Both Your Houses* (the Senate and the House of Representatives) earned Anderson the Pulitzer Prize suggests that his angry satire was widely endorsed by his countrymen.

Despite the determination of our politicians *not* to learn from the past, we tend to take it for granted that the present is an inheritance of that past, from which it ought to follow that the insights of Gay, Fielding, Swift and the other satirists at whom Joel invites us to look again are of some relevance in the whirringly changed world of today's global politics. This book is written in full awareness of the Marxian warning that history repeats itself at least twice. It treats its dead authors and actors in the present tense, and is unafraid of supplying them, on occasion, with splashes of dialogue that they neglected to provide while they were alive. Scholars too rarely write with this kind of relish. 'What if' and 'why not' are questions that recur in the text and in its context. What if Gay had read *The Threepenny Opera*? Why not add to the *Messingkauf Dialogues* in the light of eighteenth-century dramatic satire? Why not follow Brecht's example and rewrite *The Recruiting Officer* again? What if the past could learn from the present? It was Brecht's realization that we don't notice things we take for granted, which is convenient for the politicians who lead and mislead us. The *Verfremdungseffekt* was Brecht's device to trick us into noticing the strangeness of the all-too-familiar. This book in its entirety operates like a *Verfremdungseffekt*, an antidote to inertia.

Peter Thomson
June 2015

Introduction

The history of eighteenth-century British stage satire has been incomplete for three-hundred years. Essays collected here add new chapters to that history, as they consider the Brechtian contribution to theatre made by Henry Fielding, Jonathan Swift, Charlotte Charke, David Garrick, and their contemporaries. For some time it has been known that Bertolt Brecht (1898–1956) turned to Augustan and Georgian stage satire when he adapted George Farquhar's *The Recruiting Officer* (1706) and John Gay's *The Beggar's Opera* (1728), plays that mocked the state of theatre and representatives of the state. Farquhar and Gay could be called early Brechtians, as they anticipated the German playwright's political and self-reflexive theatre; or perhaps Brecht can be considered a late Augustan. Carl Weber, who served as a play director at the Berliner Ensemble when Brecht oversaw it in the 1950s, recalled the playwright asking assistants to look for other English plays from the eighteenth century, and propose them for new projects. If Brecht had lived longer, he might have adapted writing by Charke, Fielding, or Phillips for the stage, and made them part of his tradition, if they were not already creating the tradition before he arrived. Plays by these and other eighteenth-century authors anticipated Brecht's Epic theatre practices, at the same time as they rejected heroic tragedy and corrupt government in the age of England's first Minister, Robert Walpole.

Numerous essays and books have been written already about this period's leading playwrights and actors. While interpretations of the plays and their performances vary considerably, few earlier readings look to Brecht in assessing eighteenth-century British political playwriting and stage satire. The 'early Brechtian' perspective would, for example, lead to disagreement with a statement by Robert Hume that 'Fielding's "shifts" of theatre were entirely beyond his control and have nothing to do with politics. Fielding was a freelance writer who peddled his scripts where he could in the midst of rapidly changing conditions' (Hume 255). On the contrary, Fielding's political and artistic differences with his contemporaries shaped his plays, as he cast and directed his own playwriting for the Little Theatre in the Haymarket. His later satires anticipated Brecht's advocacy of theatre 'demonstrating with a view to fixing responsibility', having 'a practical purpose, [as it] intervenes socially', and moving 'from representation to commentary' (Brecht 1964: 122–26). A Brechtian view also would require objection to Hume's one-sentence dismissal of *The Stage Mutineers* as 'a silly little afterpiece', since the remark entirely overlooks that play's connections to the rivalry between Fielding and Theophilus Cibber, and its link to a labour dispute when first staged (Hume 162). The 1733 play refers to a 'combination', an illegal union of actors that might have been welcomed by Brecht. Other neglected satiric plays from the period, such as Gay's ballad operas *Polly* (1728) and *Achilles* (1732), Garrick's afterpiece titled *Lilliput* (1756), and Miller's adaptation of Swift's *Genteel and Ingenious Conversation* (1740) constitute a small repertoire of early Brechtian theatre.

Although few modern playwrights have selected the dramatic literature discussed here for adaptation, Brecht showed how the old texts could be renewed through his reutilization of Farquhar and Gay. Theatre of the period differed from Brecht's work in language, politics, and humour; still, some of the plays attracted his interest, and more than a few ballad operas and comic afterpieces anticipated his politically engaged, wry theatre about social struggle. Also, performances of these eighteenth-century plays involved direct addresses to the audience, self-referential commentary, and quick switches from speech to song that discourage the illusions of fourth-wall realism much as Brecht's theatre did.

Brecht himself noted:

> When our theatres perform plays of other periods, they like to annihilate the distance, fill in the gaps, gloss over the differences. But what then comes of our delight in comparisons, in distance, in dissimilarity—which is at the same time a delight in what is close and proper to ourselves? (Brecht 1964: 276).

Toward that end, when comparisons are made here between Brecht and eighteenth-century authors, their differences need to be honoured. If staged today, the older plays should be seen as distant and dissimilar from our own theatre and society; but their strangeness and distance also can make them 'early Brechtian' theatre. The call for change voiced by activists in recent rallies might be read into these older texts too, as we see our society has moved on to other scenes, and 'another world is possible'.

Much as Gay resituated his own characters from *The Beggar's Opera* in his sequel, *Polly*, Brecht rewrote *The Beggar's Opera* and set its criminals and law officers in a later period to discuss new social conditions. Gay's *Polly*, his third ballad opera *Achilles*, and other plays by eighteenth-century Brechtians deserve to be reconsidered and reutilized, as their responses to war and empire-building, theft, bribery and changing gender roles provide a basis for sequels that address current issues and ongoing social developments. New scenes and songs could turn a play by Henry Fielding or Samuel Foote into a twenty-first century satire suitable for stage, street theatre or screen. What follows can be regarded as a mapping of paths to future theatrical satire and activism, through a survey of earlier routes explored by Brecht and his precursors in England.

Besides surveying earlier routes, I have started to extend them in this collection, with a few chapters that employ historical fiction—my own additions to Brecht's *Messingkauf* dialogues about theatre, and speculative reconstructions of theatre events for which historical facts are scarce or missing. (This is done in Chapters Four, Six, Seven, Eight, Fourteen, Fifteen, Eighteen.) Borges in his creation of lost books and fictive encyclopedic entries rarely discussed stage art. But Henry Fielding provided a model of theatrical satire that fused fiction with history in his play *The Historical Register for the Year 1736* (1737). He also may have anonymously collaborated on another fictive history, the counterfeit memoir titled *An Apology for the Life of Mr. T . . . . C . . . . .., Comedian* (1740). The fictions and 'personations' offered here, inspired by Swift's and Fielding's satires, Mr T . . . . . . C . . . . .'s memoir writing, and Brecht's dialogues on theatre, should not be mistaken for historical record. The speculative reconstructions imagine Fielding's last days at the Haymarket, Charke's performance as Macheath in *The Beggar's Opera*, Woodward and Clive's acting in Swift's *Polite Conversation*, Brecht's meeting with Swift in Hollywood.

Although I hesitate to discuss Brecht in terminology that limits the reaches of his open-ended, experimental approach to theatre, his rewriting of plays by Farquhar and Gay (not to mention Shakespeare and Molière) might be seen as a form of intertextuality. Old texts are appropriated and revised to make new ones in a number of Brecht's projects; more than that, the sharing and appropriation of texts in this manner represents a step away from individual authorship toward collective forms of creation that attracted Brecht, and are still an integral part of theatre collaborations. Theatre productions frequently 'appropriate' past literature by performing it, giving old texts new actors, new readings, even new lines. Before these essays placed Brecht 'back' in the eighteenth-century, he did so himself, by finding characters and social situations there, and adapting their stories. Brecht looked at aspects of the past, particularly underclass and radical history, neglected by other writers. Looking at earlier playwrights through his sensibility changes the way we see them.

In *The Covent-Garden Journal*, Henry Fielding once asked if:

The World itself is commonly called a Stage; and, in the Eye of the greatest Philosophers the Actions in both appear to be equally real, and of equal Consequences. Where then is the mighty Difference between personating a Great Man on the great Theatre, or on the less?

Much as Brecht asked over whom the Caesars triumphed, and whether Alexander conquered India all by himself, Fielding mocked the off-stage performances of 'Great Men' such as Walpole by 'personating' them and their representatives in a small playhouse. In doing so he created a popular arena for opposition to government corruption. This 'smaller world' and its opposition to 'Great Men' had a recent counterpart in the Occupy Wall Street movement, whose takeover of a public park near the New York Stock Exchange Mike Davis described as 'Wall Street under siege by the Lilliputians' (Davis 2012: 2). But we find other forms of 'smaller world' opposition to Great Men in Augustan and Georgian playhouses, particularly in Fielding's *Welsh Opera* (1731), his *Historical Register for the Year 1736*, and *Eurydice Hissed* (1737). Such theatre followed from and enlarged political developments at a time when, as Peter Thomson has observed, 'Bolingbroke (high Tory) and William Pulteney (disaffected Whig) would sustain a campaign that created the concept of political opposition as an *activity*' (Thomson 2006: 82). 'Early Brechtian' theatre supported and responded to that activity.

Stage mutiny, a Georgian practice paid tribute by several plays of the period, also might have been countenanced by Brecht. 'From all the struggles waged', he advised in a poem addressing Danish actors, 'make pictures / Unfolding and growing like movements in history. / For later that is how you must show them on stage. / The struggle for work, / . . . Resignation and rebellion, Trials and failures, / All these you must later show as / Historical processes' (Brecht 1961: 18–19). Actor rebellions against management took place several times between 1733 and 1743. Plays about actor mutiny, and the rehearsal play format employed by Fielding provided occasions for acts of rebellion, too, only these rebellions took the form of topical satire directed at leading politicians, theatre managers and artists. While those performing *The Stage Mutineers* and satires by Fielding were only playing around with dissent, joking and not storming barricades, some of their scenes greatly displeased first Minister Walpole and his supporter, the poet laureate Colley Cibber, frequent targets of the ridicule.

Discussing particular episodes and sieges of the period, I have not attempted to offer a complete or chronological survey of Augustan and Georgian drama. Chapters focus on a few embattled artists, mostly satirists, their rivalries, and their place in the Epic tradition.

John Gay's beloved Polly Peachum appears in several sections of the book because Gay, Fielding, puppeteers, a duchess and Brecht kept returning to her. Theophilus Cibber, actor and son of Colley Cibber, also receives attention more than once in these pages since Fielding and other eighteenth-century satirists kept returning to him, mocking his ambitions in their plays and in *An Apology for the Life of Mr. T . . . . C . . . . ., Comedian*. One entry in the counterfeit autobiography attributed to Theophilus Cibber sums up his comic embodiment of the period examined here. The author who was not Cibber, but impersonated him, confesses:

> I was resolved, young as I was, at a Time when the whole Nation was in a Bustle, to make my share of it. In the Year 1720 when all Men thought of raising Estates, and bubbling the World out of what Money they could, I had a violent Ambition of getting Money . . . were I a South-Sea Director, that I would do—Ye Gods! What I would do? But as I was, resolv'd I was to act something adventrous within my Sphere. . . . As all were commencing great Men, I was resolved to commence Author, and accordingly alter'd a Play of Shakespear's.

Rather than profit from shares of South Sea stock (which precipitously fell in value when the famous South Sea Bubble burst in 1720), this young actor would invest his future in playwriting, or at least in rewriting Shakespeare, and become a Great Man. It is possible Fielding wrote these lines for Mr T . . . . C . . . . . Similarly satirized ambitions surface in Fielding's 1734 version of *The Author's Farce*, where Marplay Jr, a character based on Theo Cibber, vows he will alter someone else's tragedy, 'let a play be never so good, without alteration it will do nothing'. Fielding and the memoir counterfeiter both expressed doubts about minor playwrights who think they can improve Shakespeare, and politicians who bubble (that is, cheat) the world in the age of Bustle. Shakespeare later was linked to 'getting Money' and the business of literature by Brecht in *The Threepenny Opera* (1928), where Polly Peachum speaks of retiring 'to a little country house just like that Mr. Shakespeare father admires so much'. The age of Bustle in which Fielding wrote, and the business affairs mocked by Brecht in his plays and in novels about Julius Caesar and Macheath have passed; but new economic bubbles and Great Men deserving satire are still with us. We could use another Fielding, C . . . . ., or other Brechtians in their tradition, at a time when stage satire is nearly an extinct species.

A few of the essays collected here first appeared in different form in *Studies in Theatre and Performance* and that journal's website: htty://www.tandfonline.com (Chapters One, Fourteen and Seventeen), and on the *Hunter Online Theatre Review* website HotReview.org (Chapters Six and Seventeen). I want to thank Peter Thomson and Jonathan Kalb for their prior publication of the material, and permission to reprint it. Thanks also to Simon Baker for publication of this volume by University of Exeter Press; to Helen Gannon, production editor; to San Francisco State University for a sabbatical leave that gave me time to complete essays; to Robert Brustein, Lawrence Bush, Bill Christmas, R. Crumb, R.G. Davis, Larry Eilenberg, Joan Holden, Nadine Holdsworth, Carl Grose, Ron Jenkins, Brewster Kahle, Stanley Kauffmann, Mohammad Kowsar, Graham Ley, Eric Schechter, Florentina Mocanu-Schendel, Diana Scott, Peter Thomson, Carl Weber, Michael Wilson, Susan Walker and Kristen McDonald at the Lewis Walpole Library for their encouragement and advice; and to the theatre casts and crew at San Francisco State for not rebelling when I directed *Polly* and *The Stage Mutineers*.

San Francisco
June 2015

CHAPTER ONE

Eighteenth-Century Brechtians

A spectre is haunting political theatre, and that is the spectre of Bertolt Brecht. His radical theory and practices brought a transformative political consciousness to modern drama. Brecht chose not simply to interpret the world through theatre, but to change it. For his innovative exploration of economic and social conditions through stage plays, Brecht today might be regarded as a Marx of modern theatre. Following his death in 1956, the playwright's endeavours to align theatre production with movements against oppression and empire continue to provide an exemplary model of politically engaged artistry.

Post-mortem, Brecht enjoys and suffers from the classical status he once described as an inhibiting factor in creative work. His political playwriting is now singled out for special recognition and praise ('a modern classic') despite repeated efforts he made to create theatre collectively. Throughout his life he entered into creative collaborations, long periods of rehearsal with assistants, other writers, resident actors, designers, dramaturgs and co-directors all contributing to stage production. The author of *Mother Courage, Galileo, The Caucasian Chalk Circle* and *The Threepenny Opera* also depended on others for translations, musical scores, readings of works in progress. Originality or a highly personal statement was not the primary goal in such productions as *Die Dreigroschenoper*. His 1928 adaptation of John Gay's play benefited greatly from collaboration with others, notably composer Kurt Weill, and some song lyrics came from the satirist and critic Karl Kraus.

The collaboration included other artists, deceased; and here in Brecht's drawing on the past we can begin to sense how he was part of a larger theatre movement (a collective as it were) that went back to the eighteenth century, and has continued beyond the life of its writers. Eighteenth-century plots, characters and musical innovation became his, with variation, through adaptation. *The Threepenny Opera*'s libretto was based on *The Beggar's Opera*, a ballad opera John Gay wrote in 1728. Gay himself received encouragement and an idea for his play from Jonathan Swift, and a musical score from Johann Pepusch, who based his tunes on existing popular ballads. When Brecht's new version opened in Berlin two centuries later, he emerged as its popular and financially successful author; but he did so with considerable help. His play in which a gangster named Macheath dreams of founding a bank began with a German translation of Gay's text by Brecht's assistant, Elisabeth Hauptmann.

Brecht's 'collaboration' with eighteenth-century writers Gay and Swift for *The Threepenny Opera* extended and renewed (or in his term, reutilized) attempts by the earlier authors to intervene in political and social discourse through their art. If political theatre history is now haunted by Brecht's spectre, that is partially because he went back in time for co-authors as well as forward in his collaborations. 'Every writer *creates* his own precursors', Borges once observed (Borges 72). Brecht created not just his precursors, but also his collaborators; they include a number of other radical eighteenth-century authors—more than Swift and Gay—some of whom have yet to be acknowledged as his comrades.

Late in his career, Brecht adapted Farquhar's 1706 play, *The Recruiting Officer*. His reutilization of such classics was part of a new direction in theatre, but it had a retroactive impact on older plays as well, as Brecht reframed both the theory and practice embodied by Augustan and Georgian plays. These plays now can be seen as early forms of Epic theatre. When the German playwright began to develop his concept of Epic theatre, he distinguished his kind of plays from the 'Aristotelian' model. According to Aristotle theatre offered a tragic hero with whom spectators could identify emotionally, and see as their own representative on stage. Brecht preferred to offer spectators an anti-hero, someone like *The Threepenny Opera*'s gangster Macheath, or Captain Plume in *Trumpets and Drums*, Brecht's version of *The Recruiting Officer*; these characters may be likeable scoundrels, but they cannot be called tragic heroes. Their anti-heroic careers began in the eighteenth-century plays of Farquhar and Gay, and Brecht extended their run.

Brecht's Epic theatre concepts are well known by now; but their antecedents in eighteenth-century theatre practices deserve more attention. John Gay disrupted his anti-hero's action with songs long before Brecht. An induction scene featuring a beggar at the opening of Gay's ballad opera was not quite the same as Brecht's projection of intertitles on a half curtain, or the prologue opening *Caucasian Chalk Circle*. But these three forms of preview encouraged the audience to relax and see human conditions in all their unvarnished and varied motivation, which was social and economic as well as psychological. For Brecht this meant actors had to go beyond psychological motivation, beyond the so-called Stanislavsky method through Epic acting, and understand the social conditions and relationships that affected far more than their individual characters. The actors who first created the roles of Macheath and Captain Plume also employed techniques different from Stanislavsky's, and in some regards were closer to the acting Brecht sought than to other modern methods, as prologues and other direct addresses by the English actors to their audience acknowledged no imaginary fourth wall between actor and spectator.

It would be absurd to argue that all the theory and practice of Epic theatre existed in eighteenth-century plays such as *The Beggar's Opera*, or in their performance; but significant anticipations of Brecht's political theatre can be discerned in satiric and comic plays of the period. Other authors besides Gay and Farquhar were writing what could be called eighteenth-century Brechtian plays. The German author did not adapt or even admire all their works; but these artists (including Brecht) shared concerns given to them by history itself—particularly events related to wars of the period, to a stock market scandal of 1720, ongoing bribery and questionable banking. Brecht's friend, the critic Walter Benjamin once observed that Marx 'became a teacher of satire' as he illuminated 'the debased and mystified relations between men in capitalist society', and 'it is with Marx that Brecht has gone to school' (Benjamin 1977: 84). But Brecht the political satirist and anti-capitalist also learned from Swift, Gay, Farquhar, and the history of banking in England. Henry Fielding, Charlotte Charke, David Garrick and Samuel Foote also became eighteenth-century Brechtians without knowing it, to the extent that their plays anticipated Brecht's concerns with empire, conquest and capital accumulated on the backs of the poor and the oppressed. This eighteenth-century group's self-reflexive humour and mockery of theatre conventions also preview components of transparency Brecht would later consider features of Epic theatre. When E.P. Thompson called for 'more studies of the social attitudes of criminals, of soldiers and sailors, of tavern life [in the eighteenth century]', he did not have Gay's criminals or Farquhar's soldiers in mind. He was asking for more labour history and sociological studies, but ironically he added 'we should look at the evidence, not with a moralizing eye ("Christ's poor" were not always pretty), but with an eye for Brechtian values' (Thompson 1966: 59). Those Brechtian values can be found in some of the period's plays.

The eighteenth-century writers and activists who initiated comic, public forms of resistance to empire, patriarchy and plutocracy contributed to a larger, continuing series of protests that extends from their day to the recent satire of the Yes Men, Kneehigh and Michael Moore, and to the theatrical activism of the Ruckus Society, Reclaim the Streets and Occupy Wall Street. Equally important, the vision of resistance promoted through Brecht's art can be seen as a crystallization of historical developments that began with eighteenth-century responses to newly created banks, stock exchange scandal and military recruitment; prophetic Augustan and Georgian artists questioned these developments and their harmfulness, through humorous and innovative theatre.

Misery as a Commodity from Swift and Gay to Brecht

Brecht set *The Threepenny Opera* in the London of Queen Victoria, not John Gay's eighteenth century. The play's 'Cannon Song' ('The troops live under / The cannon's thunder / From the Cape to Cooch Behar . . .') evoked colonial war in Kipling's India. Costumes for the 1928 *Threepenny* premiere made the characters look like Berliners. Kurt Weill's music at times made Macheath and his cohorts sound like cabaret artists. The production was not simply a respectful tribute to the 1728 version; although ostensibly setting it in London's Soho district, Brecht and company showed Berliners of 1928 their own corrupt society in distorted comic form. Leading the charge onstage was a criminal who wanted to become a banker.

In Brecht's version the early capitalism of John Gay's England is gone; the industrial revolution has arrived, and Jeremiah Peachum's firm mass-produces beggars. The five basic types of misery his employees replicate are displayed in Peachum's showroom. Outfit B in the firm's collection costumes the victim of war and Outfit C garbs the victim of industrial progress; the latter represents a form of misery not yet well-established in John Gay's time. These crises are sources of profit for Peachum, an early beneficiary of what Naomi Klein has called the 'shock doctrine' of 'crisis capitalism'. Human misery is regarded as economic opportunity by the Peachums of the world, as long as they can trade on it.

Brecht may have derived Peachum's cynical attitude toward beggars in his play from another source besides *The Beggar's Opera*. Few beggars appear onstage in Gay's play; but they fill the pages of Jonathan Swift's essays, which propose new methods of control over the men, women and children begging on the streets of Dublin. The Swiftian hordes seem to merge with Berlin's unemployed of 1928 in *The Threepenny Opera* to form the army of beggars Peachum commands. Peachum threatens to disrupt a royal coronation by filling London's streets with poor people including his employees, but not only them.

If Brecht did not read Swift's essays himself, perhaps Elisabeth Hauptmann, who read English well enough to translate John Gay's play, first noticed that Jonathan Swift urged Dublin beggars to wear badges. Whether or not she found it for Brecht, Swift's 1737 proposal for giving badges to Dublin beggars has a counterpart in the opening of *The Threepenny Opera*, where Peachum berates a young scamp named Filch for begging without a licence. All of London's street life becomes property of Peachum's firm, as it parcels out territory to beggars and costumes them in outfits that win empathy and alms from passers-by.

Swift: 'My first question to those who ask an alms, is, Where is your badge?'

Brecht's Peachum to Filch: 'Any man who intends to practise the craft of begging in any of one of [our fourteen districts] needs a licence from Jonathan Jeremiah Peachum and Co.' (Brecht 1979: 7).

Brecht imbues his Peachum (as opposed to John Gay's) with a heightened awareness of the poverty and misery present in London, because his business requires it. While Brecht's Peachum 'regards misery as a commodity' (as Walter Benjamin suggested), Swift, or rather his pseudonymous stand-in writing 'A Modest Proposal', called for the commodification of beggars' industry through the sale of their infants for dinner delicacies. Peachum is no butcher of beggars or their young in Brecht's play; more a master of theatrical arts, he trains his employees to win pity as actors might. The Beggar King knows that well-to-do spectators will pay small coins in response to effective portrayal of personal suffering, while the sight of unadorned, artless poverty merely repels them.

Jonathan Swift's 'Modest Proposal' to slaughter infants stands as an early, grimly humorous contribution to debate on international trade, or a mockery of it, as he claims the succulent flesh of Ireland's children will add 'some thousand carcasses in our exportation of barrelled beef'. Peachum's business in a later, more enlightened era brings no gourmand's harm to children, who could be kept alive and employed at a young age, given the lack of child labour laws—one difference among many between Brecht's industrial-age satire and Swift's.

Swift provided inspiration for Gay's version of the play as well as Brecht's. In a letter of 30 August 1716, he proposed that his friend Gay consider writing 'a Newgate pastoral among the whores and thieves there'. A mere twelve years later, on 29 January 1728, *The Beggar's Opera* premiered scenes set in the Newgate prison district of London; while not terribly pastoral or idyllic in its conversations about murder, theft and hanging, the play periodically parodies dreams of brotherhood.

Macheath Reads Marx

Both playwrights refer to banking as well as begging, but their references reflect very different stages of capitalism. Gay's famous highwayman and his interest in bank business are introduced when Peachum asks his wife: 'Was Captain Macheath here this morning, for the bank-notes he left with you last week?' Such banknotes became widespread after 1694, when the Bank of England was founded to raise funds for England's war against France. In *Capital* Marx found that 1694 date tremendously significant; the opening of a bank to fund a war and create national debt (war debt to a large extent) provided the foundation for the modern doctrine that a nation becomes the richer the more deeply it is in debt . . . At their birth the great banks, decorated with national titles, were only associations of private speculators, who placed themselves by the side of governments and, thanks to the privileges they received, were in a position to advance money to those governments (Marx 1975: 920).

By 1728 notes stolen from the Bank of England or its patrons had become a source of income for Macheath. In Brecht's 1928 version, Macheath no longer wants to sell stolen banknotes; he wants to run a bank. He knows huge profits from banking are legitimate, even if they exploit clients to the limits of the law and beyond. 'What's breaking into a bank compared with founding a bank? What's murdering a man compared with employing a man?' asks Brecht's aspiring banker, who seems to have read Marx, or at least shares a Marxian concept of bankers and factory owners (Brecht 1979: 76). If Macheath read Marx's description of bankers as 'bandits' and 'gamblers' in Volume III of *Capital*, he would have found additional confirmation that his background was suitable for banking (Marx 1981: 600).

All this might be past literary history, and no more than an amusing link between Swift, Gay, Brecht and Marx, except that in our own age, bankers have become beggars. With great finesse, heads of some of the world's leading financial institutions secured huge government-financed bailouts in the past decade. While their accomplishments are not often described as begging, like Brecht's Peachum modern bankers have learned to profit from human misery, and employ the appearance of poverty to accumulate wealth. U.S. Senator Bernie Sanders said in a December 2010 speech on the bailout of American banks, 'the American people have learned the incredible, jaw-dropping details of the Fed's multi-trillion dollar bailout of Wall Street and corporate America', and they learned it from the Senator among others (Sanders 29). Sanders revealed that secretly trillions, not just the publicly disclosed billions, had been loaned by the Federal Reserve to distressed American banks and investment firms in their hour of need. (Banks in other countries were bailed out, too.)

In Brecht's *Threepenny Novel*, written after his 1928 play, Macheath becomes a banker. Instead of stealing his way into a bank, he informs his reluctant partners: 'For this purpose, it would be best if I entered the bank as, shall we say, Director of Business Investments'. Brecht also wrote some wry lyrics for a 'Song to Inaugurate the National Deposit Bank'. Not used in the *Threepenny* production of 1928, the song (in a translation by Willett and Manheim) gives advice on

. . . getting capital to start.
If you've got none, why reveal it?
All you need to do is steal it.
Don't all banks get started thanks to
Doing as other banks do?

Here it seems quite possible that Brecht remembered Marx's description of bankers as bandits. Macheath also enters the world of high finance in Brecht's *Threepenny* screenplay (partially realized by a Pabst film in 1931), where Peachum, police chief Brown and the Knife all become bank directors before the film ends.

If a sequel to Brecht's play and novel were written today (and it should be) in light of recent events, members of the new Macheath firm would not need to steal—they could simply announce their insolvency and secure a government bailout of billions. Prominent bankers of our era have become wily beggars. As they receive enormous loans to keep their businesses afloat, they can say they are serving the public—building on public trust as it were, or at least public financing, although their profits remain private. Of course these beggars, like the one who claims to be the author in the opening of John Gay's ballad opera, also are actors (and not necessarily financially impoverished ones) in a scenario of their own devising. Moreover, they are far more successful than Macheath in evading arrest; as of this writing (in 2015) not one director of a large American bank has been convicted of a crime, although Bank of America, J.P. Morgan, Chase—all leading banks—have been fined billions of dollars, and then returned to profitable business, after negotiating (an advanced form of 'begging') a settlement with the Department of Justice and the Attorney General. Macheath and Peachum could learn a great deal from these modern businessmen. (John Gay's Macheath seemed to know where the money was when he counselled his gang to steal from money lenders—'Have an eye upon the money-lenders', Act III, scene iv—but the banking industry was young and inexperienced in those days. Now it has considerable expertise in crime and criminal investigations.)

The transformation of a beggar into the author of opera, the conversion of a gangster into a banker, followed by the turning of bankers into wealthy beggars and actors, three episodes of theatrical and social history, were set in motion by the 1694 founding of the Bank of England and its issue of banknotes, followed by the first crash of England's stock exchange with the South Sea scandal of 1720. South Sea stock rose quite high and then fell fast, as a result of which John Gay lost a fortune, £20,000 by his estimate, after some stock had been given to him by a benefactor. In 1721, Gay's friend Swift commemorated such losses in a poem, 'The South-Sea', one stanza of which read:

> Thus the deluded Bankrupt raves,
> Puts all upon a desperate Bet;
> Then plunged in the Southern waves,
> Dips over Head and Ears—in Debt.

Fellow-satirist William Hogarth responded to the debacle with 'An Emblematical Print on the South Sea Scheme', an engraving that displayed a merry-go-round of financial speculation, along with a London monument—a pillar 'erected in memory of the destruction of this City by the South Sea in 1720'. The City survived the financial scandal, and John Gay was not exactly turned into a beggar after the crash; but he was more aware of financial malpractice when he wrote *The Beggar's Opera* in the years that followed.

Gay, like Hogarth, was no friend of those who benefited from the South Sea Bubble. One of the greatest beneficiaries, Robert Walpole, became England's first Minister, and his corrupt government, strengthened by its handling of national debt, bribery and deals with the Bank of England, was a prime target of satire in *The Beggar's Opera*. Song lyrics were directed at Walpole, especially when he sat in the audience on opening night and heard Lockit, the ballad opera's Newgate jailer, sing:

> When you censure the age,
> Be cautious and sage,
> Lest the courtiers offended should be.
> If you mention vice or bribe,
> 'Tis so pat to all the tribe
> Each cries—That was levelled at me.

Walpole heard the lyrics, and joined in the refrain to the delight of the audience watching him watch *The Beggar's Opera*. 'Does Walpole think you intended an affront to him with your opera?' Swift asked Gay in a letter dated 26 February 1729. 'Pray God he may', Swift added. Gay got his wish. The Minister endured the indignity of being associated in public with vice, bribery and the highwayman Macheath in 1728, but by December of that year his government had banned production of Gay's next stage play, *Polly*.

Regrettably neglected by theatres ever since, *Polly* brings Macheath back to the stage as a black-faced West Indian pirate at war with colonial British settlers; he takes on the British empire—or part of it—while the title character is sold into slavery. (Both Polly and Macheath escape slavery while in the West Indies.) Would the play have provoked more government repression if staged? It became victim of some new censorship without being staged in 1737; when Henry Fielding tried to adapt Gay's *Polly* and open it that year, his theatre was closed. (Details are provided in Chapter Fifteen.)

The Historical Register for the Year 1736, Fielding's next-to-last play before censorship took hold in 1737, featured a corrupt politician announcing his position on money: 'All we have to consider relating to money is how we shall get it' (Fielding 1967: 20). How those with influence secured their wealth is suggested by historian A.L. Morton, who writes that during this period votes of Parliament members

> were not (often) actually bought for cash down. Instead they were secured
> by sinecures, jobs, contracts, titles, favours to the family or to friends of
> members. The vast government patronage was freely used for party pur-
> poses (Morton 1968: 303).

'For of all Beggars, I look upon a Minister's Follower to be the meanest', one of John Gay's characters said in his play, *The Distress'd Wife* (1734). Then again, cash was not forgotten in the politics or culture of the time. The character of Sterling observes in Garrick and Colman's comedy, *The Clandestine Marriage* (1766): 'What signifies your birth and education, and titles? Money, money, that's the stuff that makes the great men in this country.'

Gay, Swift, Fielding, Brecht (and sometimes Garrick and Colman) chose to contest inordinate wealth, empire, illegitimate authority, capitalist cronyism and widespread injustices within their society by writing satires; their pamphlets and plays promoted public discourse on greed and power. Swift in several essays and *Gulliver's Travels*, Brecht in his *Threepenny Opera* and *Threepenny Novel* and screenplay based on the novel, explored theft, poverty, patriarchy and political corruption. All these themes were also addressed in *The Beggar's Opera* and *Polly*. To the degree that Brecht's theatre shared such concerns with Fielding, Gay and Swift, some of his satire could be called Swiftian, or Fielding-like; but it also can be said that Swift, Gay and Fielding, while very attentive to the follies of their own time, were early Brechtians.

The German author's association with the eighteenth-century Brechtians was not entirely welcomed by the critics who first noticed it. When *The Threepenny Opera* opened he was accused of plagiarism in Germany (stealing from Villon and others); but as Lotte Lenya noted, it was always 'Brecht's procedure' 'to adapt, reinterpret, re-create, magnificently add modern social significance; or in his detractor's eyes: to pirate, plagiarize, shamelessly appropriate' (Brecht/Bentley 1964: v).

Besides German critics crying theft in response to *Die Dreigroschenoper*, English critics responded adversely to Brecht's adaptation of George Farquhar's 1706 comedy, *The Recruiting Officer*, first staged under the title of *Trumpets and Drums* by the Berliner Ensemble in 1955. Some ink was spilled in a war of words over Brecht's Farquhar adaptation, in an episode that deserves to be reconsidered, along with the practices of political theatre and stage satire under dispute. Brecht's theatre, his eighteenth-century precursors such as Farquhar, Swift and Gay, and prospective audiences for their radical stage art who are still with us today might benefit from the spilling of a little more ink on this subject.

Brecht and Farquhar Take Over the National Theatre

The first foray in the battle over an eighteenth-century Brechtian named George Farquhar began when British critic Kenneth Tynan (favouring the Germany party in the dispute) praised Brecht's production of *Trumpets and Drums*. The play based on *The Recruiting Officer* was performed in German by the Berliner Ensemble when it visited London in 1956. 'Farquhar's text has been surveyed by cool new eyes, against the larger vista of England at war . . . As a corrective [Brecht] is indispensable', wrote Tynan (Tynan 1961: 453).

Adapting Farquhar's play, Brecht engaged in reutilization (*Umfunktionierung* was his term for it, as noted by Hans Mayer) of a classic, an activity he practised earlier without the special terminology when transforming *The Beggar's Opera* into *The Threepenny Opera*. Brecht relocated Farquhar's 1706 play in a later period during which England was beginning to lose its war against the colonial rebels in America. This made Farquhar's British recruiting officers counter-revolutionaries at the same time as it made their war a lost cause. The revised play glimpses the start of the end of British colonialism, and firmly historicizes the senselessness of recruiting and misleading young Englishmen into a losing battle. Although no one in the play is completely ready to admit the British are losing their war, resistance to recruitment and evasions or disloyalty of military duty in this version take on new significance.

Brecht's appropriation of *The Recruiting Officer* continued when director William Gaskill staged the original Farquhar text at the National Theatre in 1963. Tynan served as Gaskill's dramaturgical advisor—he was now collaborating on the production, offering advice at rehearsal instead of writing about the work on opening night as he had for *Trumpets and Drums*. A number of other British critics, rivals of Tynan, if you will, objected to the Brechtian qualities of the National Theatre performance of Farquhar's play. 'Brecht looms over it', wrote Harold Hobson of the production and its theatre house. Hobson and other critics questioned Brecht's presence in a once thoroughly British play. It was as if the German playwright had recruited leading British theatre artists to his cause. Sir Laurence Olivier, artistic director of the National Theatre, performed a role (Captain

Brazen) in the same production about military impressment; had he too been impressed by Brecht?

Gaskill explained why he chose Farquhar's original version over Brecht's adaptation:

> I saw no reason to put on an English translation of a German adaptation of a perfectly good English play. It is more pertinent to ask why Brecht should have chosen to adapt a comparatively little-known English classic . . . [Farquhar] saw that the Act of Impressment, which gave the final say in forcible conscription to the Justices, was a mockery because they were in league with the army. He saw the ruthlessness of the officers who were sent to beat-up for Marlborough's army. He saw all this accurately but he was not indignant . . . Brecht took Farquhar's observation as the basis for his own indignation at the exploitation of the working class. He substantially rewrote the play in his own terms and set it in the War of American Independence. It would be false to impose on Farquhar Brecht's statement of the social situation but we cannot ignore in Farquhar those elements which excited Brecht to make his version (Tynan 1965: 11).

In this sense, Farquhar became a Brechtian, or Brecht became one of Farquhar's recruits; and a new battle over Farquhar began long after the eighteenth-century wars had ended.

Brecht's Spectre Arrives

Harold Hobson praised the National Theatre's production of *The Recruiting Officer* in his review, but as noted already, he ended with an odd expression of

> one doubt about the National Theatre. Brecht looms over it. Brecht was a considerable dramatist whose value lay in the tension between his genius and his theories. It will be sad if at the National Theatre we get the theories without the genius (Tynan 1965: 142).

Here it is—Brecht's spectre has arrived, it 'looms' large; the year is 1963, less than a decade after the German playwright adapted Farquhar, and his spectre haunts England's new national theatre. Or perhaps it only haunts the critics; the National Theatre's artists are not so troubled.

Another critic, David Pryce-Jones, also sights Brecht's spirit in his review in the *Spectator*. He announces that the German author had chosen to 'counteract' the 'mannered' original of Farquhar 'by rewriting the play, making it into something it is not by assuming that its action arbitrarily suited other circumstances'. While acknowledging that Gaskill has directed Farquhar's text, Pryce-Jones sees the director making concessions to Brecht. 'Mr. Gaskill has been unable to resist showing Farquhar's "progressiveness", and in the so-called comedy of manners he has discovered a social moral' (Tynan 1965: 142). Here we go again, that Brechtian social consciousness descends like a pall, or so the critic suggests. Pryce-Jones wants his comedy unadulterated by Brechtian tenets (or is there a political consciousness already present in the 1706 text?) as he argues: 'The two countrymen [in the play] who are pressed into the army were clowns, not victims to Farquhar, and the justices' bench was a riotous satire and not a revelation of military and legal iniquity hand-in-hand.'

Perhaps the text of the play can offer more evidence than the critic to help readers determine the validity of such an interpretation. At one point in the play's courtroom scene, Silvia Balance tells the judges that instead of forcing working-class men such as a collier to go to war they should send their 'own lazy, lubberly sons . . . fellows that hazard their necks every day in pursuit of a fox, yet dare not peep abroad to look an enemy in the face'. Her accusations of class bias, written by Farquhar and not Brecht, are followed by a reading aloud of the Articles of War for mutiny and desertion (written by British legislators, not by Farquhar), meant to precede her own forced enlistment into the ranks:

> No man shall presume so far as to raise or cause the least mutiny or Sedition in the Army, upon Pain of Death. And if any number of Soldiers shall presume to assemble amongst themselves for the demanding of their pay or shall at any time demand their pay in a mutinous manner, the soldiers shall be punished by Death . . . If any Inferior Officer shall refuse to obey his Superior Officer, he shall be punished with Death.

No revelation of 'military and legal iniquity' here? Death sentences meted out to those who demand their wages? There was cause for sedition, or contemplation of it, at the time. Early in the eighteenth century, laws enabling British conscription of the unemployed turned the army into a compulsory labour force, and the law itself may have abetted conscription of men ill-suited for service, or at least unwilling to serve. Farquhar witnessed such recruitment, and then wrote about it in his 'riotous satire'. It was humorous, if not riotous, as the play mocked British law, order and military conscription.

Irving Wardle also argued with Gaskill and Brecht in his review of Farquhar's play, noting that when Brecht rewrote the text he 'gave it a strong element of social protest. But Farquhar, himself a former recruiting officer, saw the corruption and cruelty of the trade, and used it as comic material without advancing any moral conclusions'. The implication is that such conclusions were advanced by the director and his German source of inspiration. Wardle finds the scene in which two illiterate fellows are duped by recruiters going 'far beyond the regions of comedy', a foray 'untypical of the remainder of the production which is, first and foremost, riotously funny'. (Again the critic clearly would prefer a riot of comedy without interruption.) At the same time Wardle himself admits that the original script 'is not a typical Restoration piece. Its provincial setting, its breadth of social characterization, its sexual realism all set the play apart from the charmed circle of fops and wits which dominates the work of Farquhar's contemporaries' (Tynan 1965: 140). Might this 'untypical' writing by Farquhar be a factor contributing to Gaskill's discovery of social protest in the 1706 play?

The debate suggests that Brecht was not the only one who turned eighteenth-century authors into Brechtians. He had notable assistance from Tynan and Gaskill in 1963. *The Recruiting Officer* and its critique of militarism once may have influenced Brecht's plays, but today those who know Brecht's mockery of recruiting officers in *Mother Courage* and *Trumpets and Drums* can read more into Farquhar's lines, too; the English author's text begins a dialogue Brecht continues. Some of the ironic statements about war and cannon fodder written for recruiting officers in Brecht's *Mother Courage* might be suitable for delivery by Plume or Kite in Farquhar's play.

Margaret Eddershaw, tracing the impact of Brecht on British authors and directors over forty years, notes that after two visits by the Berliner Ensemble, first in 1956 and again in 1965, theatre artists in London became more familiar with Brecht and he was 'appropriated' by their theatres (Eddershaw 1996: 5). Brecht himself appropriated British theatre earlier, as noted already. His affinity with some eighteenth-century plays might be seen more fully if the texts were staged today with a sensibility similar to Gaskill's and Tynan's, with their appreciation of Brecht's attitudes toward theatre and society. His criticism of wealth, privilege, militarism and empire, and his Epic theatre theories open new paths to the reading and staging of such plays.

The quarrel over Brecht's reutilization of Farquhar is a small episode in a larger theatre history full of playwrights and philosophers who preceded Brecht and retroactively became part of his tradition with his prompting. In a book titled *Brecht's Tradition*, Max Spalter adeptly connected Brecht's theatre to the nineteenth-century German playwriting of Lenz, Grabbe, Büchner, and Wedekind; they too were Brecht's precursors. Spalter asserted that, like Brecht, these playwrights

demonstrate in vivid episodes that modern society is reducible to patterns of parasitism and victimization; they make us conscious of the degree to which human character implies the stereotyped expression of powerful

social, economic, and psychological forces. . . . Like Brecht, they are all
incongruous mixtures of moral outrage and cynical perception (Spalter xii).

An acknowledgement of debt to some of these writers (Büchner, Wedekind,
Lenz) can be found in Brecht's own statements, as well as Spalter's. Brecht's
spectre spreads backwards, from the twentieth century to the nineteenth to
the eighteenth, then further back and forward, if critics and artists care to
look; it is inseparable from the history of political theatre—a way of seeing
social struggle through theatre arts. Brecht knew he was a late arrival in a
'historic line' of Epic theatre writers and said so, although he neglected to
name a few of the authors discussed here as his predecessors (Brecht 1972:
xiii).

The German playwright's affinity with earlier authors—British as
well as German—also can be seen in their ability to intervene through
theatre in social and political discourse—to initiate dialogue onstage
that continues outside the theatre. This is part of another shared
artistic tendency that Spalter (referring to German authors) termed 'a
skeptical Brechtian sensibility', a trait that includes a 'pitiless debunking
attitude . . . hardheaded refusal to idealize or glorify . . . suspicion
of all sentimentalities'. Suspicion of sentiment is particularly acute in
some eighteenth-century satires such as Sheridan's *School for Scandal*,
where the 'man of sentiment' turns out to be a hypocrite as well as a
foiled rake.

Charlotte Charke the Cross-Dressing Rake

Rakes in some of the period's other plays—Macheath in *The Beggar's
Opera*, for example—tend to succeed more fully than Joseph Surface
(Sheridan's hypocrite) in their amorous adventures. As if to underscore
the transgressive nature of Macheath's character, the highwayman/rake's
role was performed not only by men in the Georgian era, but also by some
women, including the cross-dressing actress Charlotte Charke, another
precursor of Brecht's innovative and socially engaged theatre. Recent
studies of Charke have praised her pioneering exploration of gender
construction through her (and other actresses) taking on male roles, and
revealing their underside. Men are not what they seem to be, when women
portray them; they may be deceivers, aggressors, or benefactors, but they
are made rather than born that way. Man is alterable, Brecht would say,
'and all those explorations in some new direction which mankind has
embarked on in order to improve its lot . . . lead us to take pleasure in the
possibilities of change' (Brecht 1964: 202).

Besides performing male roles in the satires of Gay, Farquhar and
Fielding, Charke as author and director also brought the satirist Hogarth

onto the stage, as she turned his engravings of *A Rake's Progress* into a puppet play for her 1739 season at Punch's Theatre. While her father Colley Cibber was a supporter of Walpole and other men in power, Charke collaborated with the opposition, and her roles onstage no doubt had additional impact, as audiences saw the daughter rebelling against her father's generation, in satire mimicking rakes and men in high places.

Charke's cross-dressing impersonations of men in *The Beggar's Opera*, *The Recruiting Officer*, Fielding's *Pasquin*, *The Covent Garden Tragedy* and *The Historical Register for the Year 1736*, anticipated one of Brecht's observations about acting included in his *Short Organon*:

> If the part is played by somebody of the opposite sex the sex of the character will be more clearly brought out; if it is played by a comedian, whether comically or tragically, it will gain fresh aspects (Brecht 1964: 197).

When Charke performed the role of Silvia, the daughter who pretends to be a man 'fit for a soldier' in *The Recruiting Officer*, her impersonation would have caricatured aggressive male behaviour, particularly in the scene where the would-be soldier is charged with rape. The falsely accused woman mocks her accuser, the Constable: 'Is it your wife or your daughter? I ravished 'em both yesterday'. Recited by an actress dressed as a man, these lines might have sounded comic to spectators, although the judges hearing her in the play take Silvia seriously.

Farquhar's satire also could be a 'gay' play in the modern sense of that word. When Silvia Balance agrees to enlist, at a time women cannot join the ranks, she does so for love, and dresses as a man to follow Captain Plume wherever his service takes him. Plume's offer to share a bed with Wilful (Silvia in disguise) hints at same-sex attraction reiterated later in the play. Asked if Silvia is fit to be a soldier, Plume concedes the recruit is fit, because 'he's a very pretty fellow'. When it turns out that Silvia is a young woman who has a fortune to her name, Plume still finds her attractive, but in a more conventional manner, as he agrees to marry a rich daughter and give up his military career in the bargain. Perhaps this ending confirms the view of soldiers offered by Silvia's father, Justice Balance: 'The same heat that stirs them up to love spurs them on to battle', only here the heat of battle is surrendered for that of love.

Charlotte Charke also once created her own commentary on military aggression when asked to write a new prologue for Farquhar's play. The prologue was delivered not by her, but by an actor who had served as a sergeant in the British dragoons. To reflect his experience, Charke made the critique of war more explicit:

> From toils and dangers of a furious war
> Where groans and death successive wound the air,
> Where the fair ocean or the crystal flood,
> Are dyed with purple streams of flowing blood,
> I am once more, thank providence, restored
> Though narrowly escaped the bullet and the sword.
> Amid the sharpest terrors I have stood
> And smil'd at tumults for my country's good.

The speech reprinted in her 1755 memoir goes on to praise the King of England and his army; it was not an act of insurrection, but the first lines with their grim description of war's dangers are not what one expects in a comedy.

One other anti-militarist, early Brechtian role Charke never played, but should have, is that of the title character in Gay's 1732 play *Achilles*, a ballad opera with Trojan war heroes and male cross-dressing. *Achilles* opens with protector and Greek goddess Thetis instructing her son Achilles to disguise himself as a woman so he will not be sent to his death in combat. 'I know that odious siege of Troy would be the death of thee', Thetis tells the young man. Spectators who know their mythology will recognize that Thetis is prophetic here. For much of the play, Achilles keeps his dress on, except when sleeping with a female companion named Deidamia; but he cannot resist the attraction of military armour displayed later by the cunning warrior Ulysses. Enthralled by the fashion show of armour, the protected son lets his masculine identity be known, loses his woman's garb, and is taken off to war (although not before marrying Deidamia), where he will be slain. Sexual and military allegiances shift during the course of the play, and lose heroic stature, if they had any. It is surprising that Gay's *Achilles*, with its comic scenes of a would-be warrior wearing a dress to escape combat, has not yet been revised and staged as a modern anti-military companion to the play Brecht based on Gay's first ballad opera. The same might be said for stage plays by Charke, Fielding, Foote, Garrick and Phillips. These eighteenth-century artists not only offered satiric critiques of empire, militarism and patriarchy that would later be elaborated by Brecht; they also employed non-realistic stage conventions (such as direct address to the audience, gender disguise) in ways that anticipated Brecht's. Their plays attest to a continuing capacity of theatre arts for comic protest and entertaining social criticism, practices Brecht renewed by recasting eighteenth-century plays in his own language and forms.

Foote's Nabob: Ruling the Homeland as a Colony

Would Brecht also have reutilized Samuel Foote's 1772 satire, *The Nabob*, if Elisabeth Hauptmann called it to his attention? The satire originally featured Foote in the title role; but the spectre of Brecht can be found between the lines here too, as if the play awaits his adaptation. In the role of Sir Matthew Mite, Foote portrayed a cruel and self-serving businessman who expected London citizens to show him the deference and colonial subservience he won from natives in India. Foote's play was topical; when it opened England was suffering abuse from a number of returned nabobs, some of whom thought the wealth and power they acquired abroad could be used to corrupt Parliament with bribes. Foote, famous for his mimicry onstage of known citizens, probably copied traits of a living person at whom audiences wanted to laugh and wanted to see vilified when he portrayed Sir Mite. The character approaches marriage as a negotiable business agreement far removed from love, and his attitude is reinforced by a battery of legal practices that deprived women of property and independence in the eighteenth century. He regards his would-be father-in-law, Oldham, who owes him a financial debt, as part of a 'race of insolent beggars'. But it is the mortgage-holder, Mite, who turns Oldham into a beggar. Oldham incurs his debt in legal battles against Mite, who in Lady Oldham's words, 'profusely scattering the spoils of ruined province, corrupted the virtue and alienated the affections of all the old friends to the family'.

In one of Brecht's variations on the British India of Kipling, Mack the Knife fondly recalls his days in India with Tiger Brown, and together they sing about soldiers slaughtering natives. Foote's nabob might have depended on such soldiers for his own safety abroad. Back in England his retinue includes mainly a lawyer and black slaves brought from India. He expects servility from Englishmen as well as the Indians, but does not secure it. Around the time Foote wrote *The Nabob*, England's East India Company was on the verge of financial collapse. After years of corrosive and corrupt trade practices in India, the company's misdealing led to its own decline. Foote never refers to the East India Company's problems, only those of one particular nabob; but Mite represents a larger body of businessmen losing public esteem. The Mayor in the play admits he is 'not so over-fond of these Nabobs', and says: 'they do a mortal deal of harm in the country'. When the Mayor asks, 'where do these here people get all their wealth?' Touchit, a member of 'the Christian Club, of the borough of Bribe'em', answers, 'from our settlements and possessions abroad'. He further explains that such merchants grow too strong for the natives, 'turn them out of their lands and take possession of their money and jewels'. In other words he describes a process of colonial profiteering and conquest.

Touchit finds the nabobs 'but little better than Tartars or Turks', to which the Mayor responds: 'No, no . . . they have caught the Tartars in us', which is to say, the British empire builders have within them the makings of the so-called uncivilized. Later Marx would quote Montesquieu: 'If the Tartars were to flood into Europe today, it would be a difficult job to make them understand what a financier is with us' (Marx 1976: 920). The Brecht who went to school with Marx might have added that line to his adaptation of Foote, had he written one.

When the nabob threatens to take possession of the Oldham family house and evict its residents unless their attractive daughter Sophy marries him, Lady Oldham accuses him of 'voluptuously rioting in pleasures that derive their source from the ruin of others'.

> MITE: Ruin! What, you, I find, adopt the popular prejudice, and conclude that every man that is rich is a villain.
>
> LADY OLDHAM: I only echo the voice of the public. . . .
>
> MITE: I am sorry, madam, to see one of your fashion, concur in the common cry of the time; but such is the gratitude of this country to those who have given it dominion and wealth.

Foote's satire was enormously popular during its London premiere; the 'popular prejudice' of the time appears to have supported his satire of wealth and mortgage abuse. Lady Oldham and other characters who 'echo the voice of the public' on stage could be considered early, eighteenth-century practitioners of what the Occupy Wall Street movement terms a 'mike check'; she and Foote too repeat words—the 'voice of the public'—to amplify it, and make it widely heard.

One other indication of Foote's ability to locate sources of corruption abroad within his theatre at home can be found in Thomas Davies' biography of Garrick, which notes that Garrick's rival, Foote, led the audience to anticipate mockery of those among them:

> I am persuaded [writes Davies] many a man has entered the theatre of the Hay-market under the apprehension of seeing himself served up to the pub-lick . . . [the hearts of the public] told them, that they had no more claim to exception from ridicule than some whom he had unmercifully exposed (Davies 1780: 189).

Foote had engaged in this kind of mockery as early as 1747, with his satire on theatre titled *The Diversions of the Morning, or A Dish of Chocolate. The Nabob* was by no means his first 'publick' serving.

There is no reason renewal and repetition onstage of voices recorded by Foote, Farquhar and other eighteenth-century Brechtians might not continue today. In the past century, it should be noted, Gay's *Beggar's Opera* and its sequel, Brecht's *Threepenny Opera*, inspired additional satiric variants in new plays by Dario Fo, Wole Soyinka, Vaclav Havel, Carl Grose. A central tenet for Brecht's reutilization of past drama and history can be found in section 50 of his *Short Organon*, where he states that in Epic theatre:

> Just as the actor no longer has to persuade the audience that it is the author's character and not himself that is standing on the stage, so also he need not pretend that the events taking place on the stage have never been rehearsed, and are now happening for the first and only time (Brecht 1964: 194).

Theatre itself is an art of repetition; but as the same actors perform a rehearsed event, they renew and alter past drama by giving it a present tense, much as Brecht did in altering plays started by Gay and Farquhar.

It could and will be said that other forms of contemporary satire by Situationists, the Yes Men, Michael Moore, Stephen Colbert and the Daily Show have moved satire into new and post-Brechtian directions, and we have no need to return to eighteenth-century models. Yes, times have changed, media have taken new forms; but in our age of often impersonal electronic spectacle there is still something to be said for the early Brechtians and Brecht's own art, particularly in regard to their direct contact with a live audience, in which a modern nabob or his opponents may sit.

Unruly Actors, Unruly Audience

After Brecht opened the Berliner Ensemble, he wanted his post-war theatre to appeal to the working class, and entertain spectators with reflections of their own conditions and history. He may not have known that the 'afterpieces' featuring satire by Fielding, Gay, Foote and Garrick were popular among English working-class and lower-class spectators, but that was the case, particularly since these plays offered towards the end of a long evening could be seen for half price. Plans to rescind the half-price policy prompted riots. As Harry William Pedicord observes (without referring to the period's political satires in particular):

> despite his economic status, it appears the London workman attended some theatrical performance often enough to cause deep concern to moralists, and those in authority also professed to be alarmed at what was always termed the 'debauching' of the lower classes by the playhouse (Pedicord 1954: 28).

Prices were generally even lower at the 'minor', non-licensed theatres where Fielding's and Charke's most inventive work appeared. This too would have enabled the working class to see satire—as a Brechtian audience ahead of its time.

Allardyce Nicoll notes of eighteenth-century English audiences: 'In condemning a few plays, the spectators may sometimes have been motivated by political sentiments or by "moral" objections to the subject matter . . . but usually their hissing meant that they were bored' (Nicoll 95). These were not the early twentieth-century German spectators young playwright Brecht dismissed as drugged, spellbound auditors; they were, in their own way, an early Epic theatre audience, ready to judge the political and moral positions of a play, as well as its degree of vitality, and react accordingly.

Audiences also held the attention of actors, as performers would face spectators when speaking; realism, the illusion of performing in a separate room enclosed by four walls, came much later. Eighteenth-century actors conventionally stood front and centre, near the prompter's box, to have lines fed to them while they spoke directly to the audience. Brecht sought a similarly non-illusionistic situation for actors in which 'the theatre will stop pretending not to be theatre . . . The element of rehearsal in the acting . . . the whole machinery and the whole process of preparation: it all becomes plainly apparent' (Brecht 1964: 122). Comparable self-reflexive, transparent and presentational behaviour can be seen repeatedly in eighteenth-century 'rehearsal plays' about theatre, among them Edward Phillips's *The Stage Mutineers*, Charke's *The Art of Management*, Fielding's *Pasquin* and *The Historical Register for the Year 1736*, Garrick's *A Peep Behind the Curtain* and Sheridan's *The Critic*. Characters become social and theatre critics onstage as they evaluate their own work, question the achievements of their rivals and clear the way for the future by disavowing overrated plays and undemocratic management. Some of these figures become 'stage mutineers'; in the play with that title the character of Mrs Squeamish, an actress, announces:

> Lard, Mr. Prompter, was there ever such Managers, such a Part, and such a Poet. Well—play it that's [positive] I will not. . . . Such Enormities, such language, and such I don't know what—that I positively will not play it.

The Stage Mutineers (1733) and *The Art of Management* (1735) were comedies based on actual rebellions actors initiated against their tyrannical managers. The popular actor David Garrick joined one of these uprisings against management at Drury Lane in 1743. (The actors were seeking improved treatment and pay far in advance of the era when they could join unions.)

Such moments anticipate Brecht's efforts to impart a consciousness that social conditions, like scenes in rehearsal, are alterable, and that human action can be changed both within a theatrical space and outside it. Brecht also noted that events shown on stage were subject to larger, external influences in need of criticism. He redressed those musicians, writers and critics who:

by imagining that they have got hold of an [arts producing] apparatus [or means of production] which in fact has got hold of them . . . are supporting an apparatus which is out of their control . . . an obstacle to output, and specifically to their own output as it follows a new and original course which the apparatus finds awkward or opposed to its own aims (Brecht 1964: 34).

His objections are not entirely different from those of Mrs Squeamish, or Charke's character Mrs Tragic in the *Art of Management* who protests her mistreatment: 'Deprived Theatric Rights; confin'd to that of low Degree. . . . Farewell all, for Tragic's Occupation's gone!'

Discussing the English language authors read by Brecht, John Willett argued that 'without the English heritage there would have been no "epic theatre"' (Willett 1984: 24). This does not mean Brecht's theatre and earlier English stage practices are one and the same. Brecht opposed theatre that too readily equates past situations to present ones, and he might well have opposed the reverse, especially if it relocates him in the eighteenth century. It is not the equation of two historical periods or their conditions, but rather the act of their comparison that Brecht lauds in the appendix to his *Short Organon* when he praises the historical sensibility that takes 'a delight in comparisons, in distance, in dissimilarity—which is at the same time a delight in what is close and proper to ourselves'.

Henry Fielding's History of Corruption

To sustain this delight in dissimilarity, a new, current-day staging of Henry Fielding's portrayal of bribery need not be completely updated. In fact, Fielding made it clear when he wrote the play *Pasquin* in 1736 that he wanted it to stand as a record of malfeasance at that time. Presented in the form of a rehearsal play, with commentary onstage by the alleged author, Trapwit, one scene in *Pasquin* shows the author coaching his actors, encouraging them to render their enactment of bribery fully visible, so they will create a historical record of their corrupt age:

MAYOR: My lord, we are sensible of your great power to serve this corporation, and we do not doubt but we shall feel the effect on't.
LORD PLACE: Gentlemen, you may depend on me; I shall do all in my power. I shall do you some services which are not proper at present

to mention to you; in the meantime, Mr. Mayor, give me leave to squeeze you by the hand, in assurance of my sincerity.

TRAPWIT: You, Mr., that act my lord, bribe a little more openly, if you please, or the audience will lose that joke, and it is one of the strongest in my whole play.

LORD PLACE: Sir, I cannot possibly do it better at the table.

TRAPWIT: Then get all up, and come forward to the front of the stage. Now, you gentlemen that act the mayor and aldermen, range yourselves in a line; and you, my lord and the colonel, come to one end and bribe away with right and left. . . .

FUSTIAN: Is there nothing but bribery in this play of yours, Mr. Trapwit?

TRAPWIT: Sir, this play is an exact representation of nature; I hope the audience will date the time of action before the bill of bribery and corruption took place.

In the 1736 production of Fielding's *Pasquin*, the role of Lord Place was originated by Charlotte Charke, impersonating a man as influential as her father Colley Cibber's friends at court. The play stands as a comic record of the time, and if staged today it would recall past scandals, at the same time as its scenes might provoke thoughts of more recent corruption. A June 2012 Texas newsletter humorously edited by Jim Hightower and Phillip Frazer reports that 'in our Brave New SuperPAC Democracy . . . as little as $1 million can buy you some influence in your government' (Hightower 2012: 4). Brecht's Peachum offers a poor man's—or Beggar King's—comic variant on such bribery, by informing Sheriff Brown: 'Our judges are totally incorruptible; it's more than money can do to make them give a fair verdict.' The bribery, financial chicanery and injustice witnessed by Brechtian satirists lives on in their plays and pamphlets.

Brecht's Gulliver and Garrick's

In Brecht's essay on classical status as an inhibiting factor, he argues that modern staging of a classic

> must bring out the ideas originally contained in it; we must grasp its national and at the same time its international significance, and to this end we must study the historical situation prevailing when it was written, also the author's attitude and special peculiarities (Brecht 1964: 272).

This method of thinking historically provided him with a framework for approaching older texts, understanding their past and their current utility, and adapting them for a contemporary audience. Now it may be necessary to apply the same method to Brecht's own plays and his 'classical status'. Writing about Brecht in 1998, Fredric Jameson observed that:

> it seems to be customary today to complain of 'Brecht fatigue', and to wonder how to go about continuing to be a Brechtian today, as others wonder that one could continue to be a Marxist, or even a socialist, after 1989 (Jameson 18).

But times change, and as these words are written in 2015, it again may be easier to be a Brechtian, and appreciate the eighteenth-century Brechtians, in a period when abuse of wealth and privilege by 1 per cent of the population at the expense of the other 99 per cent inspired the Occupy Wall Street movement in United States, and comparable protests elsewhere.

Protests against 'great men' who wield wealth and privilege can also be found in a satire that inspired both Garrick and Brecht: namely, *Gulliver's Travels*. Garrick based his play *Lilliput* on chapters in Swift's narrative. Brecht in a journal entry for 19 March 1940 contemplated 'a short epic work *The Apprehensions of Mr. Keuner* modelled after Candide or Gulliver'. The resulting Herr Keuner anecdotes Brecht wrote about tyrants, bribes and great statesmen recall Augustan wit on the same topics at times. Brecht also composed dialogues for two new Gullivers named Ziffel and Kalle, who endure war, forced exile and military occupation in the 1930s. At one point in *Conversations in Exile*, the two refugees discuss a Utopia Swift never imagined: 'a country with a system which makes such terrible virtues as patriotism, thirst for freedom and unselfishness' unnecessary. Ziffel and Kalle call that that elusive system socialism (Brecht 1986: 18).

Virtues or lack of them were central to another, earlier conversation in exile featuring an anti-heroic protagonist. David Garrick's comic afterpiece *Lilliput* shares with Brecht's *Conversations in Exile* a wry view of virtue. While not otherwise heroic, Gulliver in exile displays one virtue in Garrick's stage adaptation of Swift: restraint. He exerts no special influence on courtiers or the law. The giant eventually chooses to flee the Lilliputians, rather than fight them in court, or simply crush them under his foot. Having served the nation by stealing its enemy's naval fleet in scenes Garrick never shows, Gulliver has here become a pacifist. Conquest of individuals and countries is anathema to him, particularly the diminutive versions of conquest practised in Lilliput. The great would-be conqueror in the play is Lady Flimnap; her desire for an affair with Gulliver, by turns comic and grotesque, constitutes an odd rebellion against patriarchy, as she plans to leave her husband the royal Treasurer for her new love. Unlike Gulliver, the Lady is quite willing to abandon virtue and conventional marriage (as is her husband) in this comedy. She finds Gulliver's fidelity to his wife 'monstrous' and unacceptable; in her world, betrayal is the norm.

The 1757 Drury Lane production of *Lilliput* featured an adult actor, Astley Bransby, as the giant Gulliver living among a large population of smaller folk, all portrayed by children. As in *The Beggar's Opera*, here too a 'great man' appears onstage, but he finds his stature a disadvantage. 'My greatness begins to be troublesome for me', Garrick's Gulliver confesses. (The line anticipates a lament of Brecht's Galileo: 'Unhappy is the land that needs a hero'.) In the play's epilogue the actress playing Lady Flimnap asks: 'Was it not Great?—A lady of my Span / To undertake this monstrous Mountain Man?' She answers her own question: 'The Prudes I know will censure, and cry, Fie on't! / Prepostrous sure!—A Pigmy love a Giant! / Yet soft—no Disproportion Love can know. / It finds us equal, or it makes us so.' The half-serious epilogue proved to be prophetic; a critic for London's *Examiner*, shocked that Garrick cast child actors in scenes involving seduction, censured the play as 'petite, trifling, indecent, immoral, stupid and scandalous'. Brecht might have enjoyed the play and its censure, as they recall his acerbic *Threepenny* lyrics about sexual urges: 'How fortunate the man with none'.

Swift's Most Ingenious Friend

The critic who condemned Garrick's *Lilliput* in 1757 was not Colley Cibber, but the criticism recalls Cibber's assertion that 'nothing is more liable to debase and corrupt the Minds of a People, than a licentious Theatre' (Dobrée 1959: 228). Perhaps his own fear of licentious theatre led Cibber, when he was manager of Drury Lane, to reject *The Beggar's Opera* after Gay submitted it to him. The new ballad opera form, and its sympathy for a highwayman who is reprieved at the end, departed too far from conventional and sentimental theatre for Cibber. Gay and other Brechtians of the day were not fond of Cibber, his vanity or his poetry. His daughter Charlotte Charke parodied the bigwig on stage in several Fielding plays. Pope (who co-authored a play with Gay) gave Cibber a lead dunce role in *The Dunciad*. Another lively jest at Cibber can be found in Jonathan Swift's theatrical dialogues, titled *A Complete Collection of Genteel and Ingenious Conversation, According to the Most Polite Mode and Method Now Used at Court, and in the Best Companies of England, in Three Dialogues by Simon Wagstaff, Esq*. Swift's pseudonymous anthology of conversations attributed to Wagstaff and printed in 1738 satirizes the language of 'genteel', refined ladies and gentlemen by treating clichés, commonplaces, innuendoes and quaint maxims as if they are precious and necessary expressions. It is not difficult to imagine Cibber as a habitué of the high society Swift mocked, for the poet laureate was, in Bonamy Dobrée's words, 'a clever and confessedly vain man' capable of rattling on in 'garrulous chatter about himself and his virtues' (Dobrée 1959: 349).

The practitioners of Swift's polite conversation trade jargon, fatuities and puns, fill their conversation with non-sequiturs and impolite, curt answers, at the same time as the inconsequentiality of their talk undermines assertions of self-importance. Herbert Davis argues that Swift's purpose in writing these dialogues was 'also political'—'to expose the banality of the tasteless, moneyed society of the Whig Hanoverian era' (Davis 1964: 264). While Swift never planned for his satiric dialogues to be staged in a conventional theatre, he estimated that six plays could be derived from the material. He was too modest to claim they would be farces, or equal those of Gay or Fielding; but he (or rather his stand-in, Simon Wagstaff) claimed that his

> most ingenious Friend . . . Mr. Colley Cibber, who doth so much Honour to the Laurel Crown he deservedly wears . . . was pleased to tell me, that if my Treatise were shaped into a Comedy, the Representation performed to the Advantage of our Theatre, might very much contribute to the spreading of Polite Conversation among all Persons of Distinction through the whole of the Kingdom.

Swift invented Cibber's offer to adapt his treatise for the stage just so he could reject it, although he is polite in his rejection:

> I own, the Thought was ingenious, and my Friend's intention good: But I cannot agree to his Proposal. For, Mr. Cibber himself, allowed, that the Subjects handled in my Work being so numerous and extensive, it would be absolutely impossible for one, two, or even six Comedies to contain them.

Would that we had one of Swift's plays, for every six that Cibber wrote.

Swift's compendium of 'genteel and ingenious conversation' was presented on stage for one night as a play titled *Polite Conversation*. Performed at Drury Lane on 23 April 1740 in an adaptation by James Miller, it featured leading actors of the period, including comedian Henry Woodward and character actress Kitty Clive, who portrayed the feuding, flirting couple Mr Neverout and Miss Notable. (Cibber no longer managed Drury Lane at this time.) Miller's shortened version of Swift's text may have confused spectators, because its parts were mixed with acts from Shakespeare's *Merry Wives of Windsor*. Part one of *Polite Conversation* appeared after Act Two of Shakespeare's play, and part two followed the conclusion of *Merry Wives* (Genest III: 610). Some Shakespeare lines, such as Falstaff's 'Methinks you prescribe to yourself very preposterously', might have applied to Swift's characters too; but despite the supporting roles played by Shakespeare's characters, one night of Miller's adaptation was evidently enough for the London audience in 1740.

The trading of once popular phrases and non-sequiturs by Swift's genteel characters at times resembles an eighteenth-century version of Ionesco's *The Bald Soprano*, which was based in part on an English language primer. In his introduction to the dialogues, Swift's Wagstaff urges readers to avoid 'Absurdities' in society by memorizing his prescribed lines and gestures ahead of time in order to make themselves 'witty, smart, humorous, and polite'. But those who follow Wagstaff's directions, and recite Swift's mocking dialogues, perform in a theatre of fatuities where the well-to-do would fare well only if they have the comic gifts of a Henry Woodward or Kitty Clive.

Could this high society be the one to which Brecht's Macheath aspired two centuries later (taking changes of fashion and language into account) wearing white kid gloves and holding a walking stick with an ivory handle? One can imagine some lines in Swift's treatise recited by the would-be banker. Macheath could say, as Neverout does: 'If ever I hang, it shall be about a fair Lady's Neck'. Swift's Neverout recites these words in response to a more familiar remark that 'he that is born to be hang'd, will never be drown'd'. When Brecht parodied an instruction manual, and offered his readers mock lessons for conduct in the *Manual of Piety*, he wrote poems far more personal and original than the idioms repeated in Swift's treatise. Despite their different locations and languages, however, both Brecht and Swift were responding with iconoclasm to what was (in Eric Bentley's description of Brecht's 1927 Germany) a 'country of pedantry and prissiness, propriety and punctilium' (Brecht 1996: xii), and responding to language that sustained such propriety. Through their inventive guidebooks they recuperated some of language's bite and humour, and rejected 'proper' speech and action.

If *Polite Conversation* were staged today, its exchanges of once modish phrases, its upper-class word games, and the seemingly endless banquet in the second half might be seen as a comedy of entropy; language, fashion and large appetites are exhausted, as glib pleasantries, gibes, flirting, eating and drinking go on far too long. Perhaps every known adage, and some forgotten ones, must be recited before the guests can leave. Or could this be Swift's version of a last supper for the Augustan upper class and its table manners?

Swift's comedy now can be read, along with other satiric eighteenth-century critiques of wealth, polite society and power, as precursor to Brecht's theatre. The qualities of drama that attracted Brecht to the writing of Gay, Swift and Farquhar surfaced in other satires of British militarism and patriarchy—Fielding's *Pasquin* and *The Historical Register for 1736*, Hogarth and Charke's *A Rake's Progress*, Foote's *The Nabob*, Garrick's *Lilliput* and Sheridan's *School for Scandal*. As to what gave rise to this pre-Brechtian consciousness of illegitimate authority, abusive wealth, comic concupiscence and class-biased injustice, here again one might turn to Brecht's teacher in satire, Marx: 'The writings of the time', he noted in a passage on the Bank of England's early years, 'show the emergence of this brood of bankocrats, financiers, rentiers, broken stock-jobbers, etc.' (Marx 1976: 920). The language and gestures of these emerging characters were recirculated in satire, placed on stage where the public could see otherwise guarded, privileged moments in the lives of the bankocrats and their associates, including the nabobs, the slave traders, bribe takers, recruiting officers, Lilliputian lovers and tea-table fatuitists. Unfortunately, we have not yet seen the last of these characters off-stage; and they are seen all too rarely where the eighteenth-century Brechtians placed them, in satire, ready for a close-up and then a close-down.

Brecht's Spectre Departs

Brechtian theatre has been acknowledged as a major development in modern drama; but it is time to acknowledge that such theatre, like the various crises to which it responds, was never exclusively Brecht's, any more than political theatre or the Epic theatre tradition are his alone. Instead of a spectre, Brecht can be seen as part of a corps of accomplished political theatre and satire creators, an international collective whose members collaborated and learned from one another over centuries. The past has a claim on these artists and their radical theatre; the future should claim them too.

CHAPTER TWO

Cross-Dressing Soldiers and Anti-Militarist Rakes

So you've been pulling the wool over my eyes. Hiding a criminal love affair under the king's uniform.

> Balance to his daughter in
> *Trumpets and Drums* (Brecht 1972: 318).

The daughter who pretends to be a rake in the uniform of the king fails to deceive her father in Brecht's *Trumpets and Drums* (1955). But she misleads the recruiting officer, Captain Plume, in other scenes of the play based on Farquhar's *The Recruiting Officer* (1706). The victory of crossing-dressing over militarism is acknowledged by Plume when he admits to Victoria that it is 'more glorious to be defeated by your charms than to conquer all America' (Brecht 1972: 324). His surrender could even be the beginning of the end for British colonial rule. 'The sun is setting on the British empire', contends Victoria's father, Balance, after he reads a report of rebel victory in America.

Since male actors first portrayed women on stage in ancient Athens, it might be said that cross-dressing and anti-militarism have been linked ever since Aristophanes had Lysistrata lead a women's strike for peace. Eighteenth-century drama continued to question militarism and gender conventions with cross-dressing in a number of plays.

Before Brecht adapted Farquhar's *The Recruiting Officer*, however, he encountered episodes of cross-dressing and anti-militarism in Karl Valentin's and Lisl Karlstadt's Munich cabaret comedy. Brecht links these practices in *The Messingkauf Dialogues* (1939–42), imaginary dialogues among a dramaturg, a philosopher, actress, actor and electrician, where the Dramaturg recalls the impact Valentin and Karlstadt had on the playwright (called the Augsburger in honour of Brecht's birthplace). Cross-dressing comedian Lisl Karlstadt is not named, but a reference to her and to Valentin's suggestion of a new way to portray soldiers are both introduced in one of the Dramaturg's speeches:

The man he [Brecht, the Augsburger] learnt most from was the clown Valentin, who performed in a beer-hall. He did short sketches in which he played refractory employees, orchestral musicians or photographers, who hated their employer and made him look ridiculous. The employer was played by his partner, a popular woman comedian who used to pad herself out and speak in a deep bass voice. When the Augsburger was producing his first play, which included a thirty minutes' battle, he asked Valentin what he ought to do with the soldiers. 'What are soldiers like in battle?' Valentin promptly answered: 'White. Scared' (Brecht 1965: 69–70).

It is no accident that a recollection about scared soldiers follows one about cross-dressing; both ideas influenced Brecht's direction of *Edward II* in 1924. His scared soldiers wore whiteface, as Valentin himself did at times on stage. In one *Edward II* scene the soldiers' make-up suggested that 'worn by clowns in the circus' (Fuegi 33). Karlstadt's cross-dressing may have inspired Brecht to cast his female assistant Asja Lacis as young Edward in the same production.

Karlstadt and Valentin specialized in clowning full of grotesque, eccentric humour, and its application to any battle scene would have made the combatants look unheroic. With his tall, lanky, comic body that towered above Lisl Karlstadt, Karl Valentin could make militarism look ridiculous simply by wearing an old spiked helmet—increasing his height, not his readiness for battle. The 'deep bass voice' and padded costume mentioned by the Dramaturg were integral to Karlstadt's portrayals of men in her cabaret acts. Her male garb and voice abetted the mockery of bosses, their wealth and privilege. 'In her gross fat suits and beards', wrote Sue-Ellen Case of the actress, 'she utilizes a style close to the agit-prop portrayal of Mr. Capitalist' (Case 1981: 9).

Karlstadt's acts mocking higher authorities and well-heeled men were not quite the same as those Charlotte Charke created two centuries earlier in England; but Charke too portrayed privileged men, notably Lord Place in Fielding's *Pasquin* and Hen the auctioneer who takes bids for 'interest at court' in Fielding's *Historical Register for the Year 1736*. Charke also performed the 'breeches' role of the cross-dresser Silvia in *The Recruiting Officer* (as noted in Chapter One).

The practices of cross-dressing artfully developed in eighteenth-century British theatre by Charlotte Charke, Peg Woffington, and their contemporaries, were probably first introduced to Brecht in 1919 when he joined Valentin and Karlstadt to play clarinet with their Oktoberfest band. In a photograph from the period, the young clarinettist Brecht stands next to Valentin, who holds a tuba; and bell ringer Karlstadt wears a man's coat and top hat. Brecht's developing theory of Epic Theatre also may have fostered his openness to cross-dressing. As Double and Wilson have noted:

The idea of cross-casting appealed to Brecht because he saw it as a kind of alienation device, arguing that if a woman plays a man, we realize 'that a lot of details which we usually think of as general human characteristics are typically masculine' (Double and Wilson 2006: 41).

When Brecht revised Farquhar's *The Recruiting Officer* as *Trumpets and Drums* in 1955, he would have found aspects of his own Epic Theatre practices, including the distanciation or V-effect, accomplished through cross-dressing in the English play. He would have found the mockery of military recruitment and training shown in his plays *A Man's a Man* and *Mother Courage* also present in Farquhar's eighteenth-century comedy. The German playwright's steps from Munich cabaret to Farquhar at the Berliner Ensemble moved back as well as forward in time, from Lisa Karlstadt's antics to Marlowe's battle scene to his own plays about war to the 1706 play in which Charlotte Charke (among other actresses) impersonated a British army recruit. It might be said he returned to Augustan theatre late in his life, and thereby became a late Augustan.

Woman in an Army Uniform, Man in a Dress

Eighteenth-century resistance to the army of the British empire began before the American Revolution, in the stage plays of George Farquhar and John Gay. Both these authors display sceptical attitudes toward recruitment of new soldiers. Newcomers are unfit for battle, and veteran soldiers in the plays tend to be comic characters or opportunists, certainly not heroes. Brecht moved *Trumpets and Drums* forward in time from early in the eighteenth century, where Farquhar set his version, to a period when Britain had begun to lose its war against the rebels in North America; but Farquhar's play had already portrayed some resistance to military activity and questioned why a man (or woman) would join the British army.

Asked in *The Recruiting Officer* what led him to become a soldier, Sergeant Kite answers: 'Hunger and ambition. The fears of starving and hopes of a truncheon led me along to a gentleman with a fair tongue and fair periwig who loaded me with promises. . . .' Patriotism, the wish to defend England and its burgeoning empire, played no role in Kite's entering the army, and the same can be said about other recruits portrayed in the 1706 play. When Silvia Balance agrees to enlist, at a time women cannot join the ranks, she does so for love, and dresses as a man to follow Captain Plume wherever his service takes him.

Plume appears not to know that he is asking a woman to join his unit as a soldier, although he has earlier proven himself to be a womanizer in military uniform, when he asked Sergeant Kite to take care of another woman whose child he fathered. Plume and Kite have no scruples about fathering a future generation of soldiers; perhaps they see it as a patriotic duty. But they seduce men as well as women into the ranks. (Brecht in *A Man's a Man* briefly parodies military recruitment when Galy Gay the innocent porter is asked to join a machine-gun unit. The 1926 play's vision of militarism is more about turning men into killing machines than mistaking a woman for a man; but characters in Brecht's play too have their manhood questioned.)

Whether Farquhar's recruiters seek only men fit to serve, or seek to fill their quota by any means necessary (as do Galy Gay's recruiters), is another question. Early in the eighteenth century, laws enabling British conscription of the unemployed turned the army into a compulsory labour force, and the law itself may have abetted conscription of men unsuited for service, or at least unwilling to serve. The grim and coercive aspects of militarism are hardly conducive to humour; yet both Farquhar and Gay set on stage comic situations where the authority of military officers seeking new recruits becomes a topic for witty jokes and criticism of policy. (The military recruiters who seek Mother Courage's two sons resort to unscrupulous methods that are less humorous than those used by Plume and Kite.)

None of these recruiters would think of enlisting a woman in the army. When a woman manages to infiltrate, the ranks are invaded and disordered. It could be taken as one more sign that the British army was not inviolable during the Augustan period. Discussing the woman who dresses as an army officer in Charles Shadwell's 1713 comedy, *The Humours of the Army*, Beth Friedman-Romell finds a historical basis for such cross-dressing:

> Far from a disciplined, 'masculine' sphere, the army world [in the play] functions as a carnivalesque world-upside-down, in which inversions of status and gender continually threaten to disrupt the established order. The text capitalizes on topical circumstances surrounding Britain's wretched campaign on the Iberian Peninsula during the War of the Spanish Succession. . . . By 1713, a few months before the Treaty of Utrecht was signed, . . . Britons . . . were heartily sick of nearly a quarter century of foreign wars (Friedman-Romell 1995: 471–72).

Similar disillusionment with the military, based on Farquhar's own experiences as a recruiter, may have led the author of *The Recruiting Officer* to create his anti-militaristic cross-dressing drama a few years before Shadwell. When Farquhar's play opened, England was still at war.

But the battle in his play is sexual as well as martial. Before Silvia is signed on by Plume, she disguises herself as a young gentleman named Wilful and competes with the Captain for the affections of another young woman named Rose. Silvia claims 'I have as good a right as you have' to

Rose. After Plume denies he has slept with Rose, he offers her to Wilful (Silvia) as compensation for Silvia's willingness to enlist in the army. 'I'll change a woman for a man any time', vows Plume. Of course Silvia herself already has changed a woman—herself—for a man. Here again, as in the later Shadwell play, 'the proliferation of unregulated sexuality' is part of the 'critique of army life' (Friedman-Romell 1995: 472).

Silvia spurns Plume's offer of payment to enlist, but admits she wants to live under his command. The new recruit so charms Plume that he kisses her; presumably he does so under the impression he is kissing a man (Act IV, scene i). When Plume next invites her to lodge at his quarters and 'have part of [his] bed', theatre spectators might wonder whether he secretly knows he has enlisted a woman, or whether he simply wants the new male recruit close by him at night, to insure the fellow doesn't escape.

Plume at one point denies his reputation as a rake: 'I have got an air of freedom that people mistake for lewdness', and perhaps he is telling the truth. But one of Sergeant Kite's jobs seems to be taking care of the women who claimed that the Captain fathered their children. When it turns out that Silvia is a young woman who has a fortune to her name, Plume trades life as a rake and a military man for marriage. Silvia becomes a triumphant recruiter in the end, although she offers a wife, not a war, to her recruit.

The choice between marriage and warfare abroad is also offered in John Gay's farce featuring military conscripts. In *The What d'ye Call It*, a young man named Filbert, sentenced to wartime service for denying that he fathered a child, would rather die in war than marry when given the choice: either 'wed [Dorcas] straight, or else you're sent afar, / To serve his gracious Majesty in war'. An attendant sergeant sees only one choice possible in this matter:

> Zooks! Never wed, 'tis safer much to roam;
> For what is war abroad to war at home?
> Who wou'd not sooner bravely risque his life;
> For what's a cannon to a scolding wife?

The suggestion that marriage itself can be a war zone, with serious casualties for its combatants, can be found in other plays of the period, although they rarely offer the fighting men an alternative battlefield away from home, in France or at sea, as does Gay's play. Filbert admits that he hates the wench he has been asked to marry, and he would rather 'bear a musquet then against the French'. The Spanish War of Succession, going on a few years before Gay's play was staged in 1715, would have provided Filbert just such an opportunity to choose war over marriage. In the same play another army man, Peascod, is slated to be shot for desertion, unless he can raise a five pound bribe; he receives a reprieve, however. A Sergeant who seemed more loyal than Peascod is arrested for stealing a mare and sentenced to hang. Gay's soldiers are not particularly admirable figures in this play, nor in his later portrait of warriors, *Achilles*, a ballad opera with Trojan war heroes and a cross-dresser.

The play opens with protector and Greek goddess Thetis instructing her son Achilles to disguise himself as a woman, so he will not be sent off to his death in combat. 'I know that odious siege of Troy would be the death of thee', Thetis advises the young man. As noted in Chapter One, Achilles keeps his gender secret, except when sleeping with a female companion named Deidamia; but he cannot resist the attraction of military armour displayed by Ulysses. Enthralled by the fashion show of armour, the protected son gives himself away, and he is taken off to war.

The attempted rape scene Achilles endures during his career as a young woman at court adds a disturbing moment to his peacetime life. Achilles' own choice of death by warfare goes unacknowledged, as his demise is not shown. Sexual attraction and related combat over it take stage centre in this play; other, more lethal warfare, remains in the background. But cross-dressing lets the legendary young man survive for a while.

Perhaps John Gay's own attitude toward militarism is most cogently summed up by Periphas, toward the play's end, when he admits that he was foolish to fight Ajax for the favours of a young woman who turned out to be Achilles in a dress. Unlike the Trojan War allegedly fought over Helen of Troy, the duel between Periphas and Ajax had no such cause.

> PERIPHAS: Our Duel, Ajax, had made a much better figure if there had been a Woman in the Case. But you know, like Men of violent Honour, we were so very valiant that we did not know what we were fighting over.

Curiously, Farquhar in his prologue to *The Recruiting Officer* also discussed the Trojan war over Helen, and did so to introduce Ulysses's 'recruitment' of Ajax. His prologue begins:

> In ancient times when Helen's fatal charms
> Roused the contending universe to arms,
> The Grecian council happily deputes
> The sly Ulysses forth—to raise recruits.
> The artful captain found, without delay,
> Where great Achilles, a deserter, lay . . .

Could Gay's *Achilles* have been inspired by Farquhar's prologue, as well as Homeric legend? For both Farquhar and Gay, the legend of Achilles, 'deserter' and 'recruit' of Ulysses, provided a starting point for new anti-militaristic, cross-dressing stage comedy.

As English women began to portray men on stage after the Restoration, and comedies of gender identity were written for them, the qualities that make a man, including readiness for war, were thrown into question. In John Gay's *Polly*, the title character acquires military prowess along with her manly disguise, as she captures an enemy leader in battle. The man she captures turns out to be her husband, although she doesn't know it at the time, and she unwittingly delivers Macheath to an executioner. Polly's war victory reconfirms the complaint made by Periphas in Gay's *Achilles*; she too is so valiant she does not know what she is fighting for. She subsequently laments her conquest.

In the twenty-first century, the legend of Achilles might be revived again, for an age in which an American soldier named Bradley Manning changed his name to Chelsea, and vowed to live as a woman after he was sentenced to a long prison term for revealing war crimes committed by others. (Only after the sentence did he reveal his own gender preference.) John Gay's *Achilles*, staged as written or adapted, might take on new resonance in the age of Chelsea Manning. Not a deserter but a whistleblower in the view of his supporters, Manning, with his public exposure of war crimes, his gender switch and his rejection of army regulation, might qualify as the model for a new Achilles.

Brecht Against War After War

When Brecht adapted Farquhar's *The Recruiting Officer* with other artists at the Berliner Ensemble, Germany was divided in half, and both states were recruiting new troops. Carl Weber, who was there with Brecht in Berlin recalls that '[Elisabeth] Hauptmann found the play [Farquhar's] . . . at a time when both German armies started to train armies and were recruiting'. In the Berliner Ensemble, Weber continues:

> at the end of the first reading [of *Trumpets and Drums*] one of the actors said this was 'a little bit awkward' because the DDR was recruiting an army at the time. And Brecht said, 'So much the better' (Weber 2013).

Brecht's personal anti-militaristic position, which included doubts about the wisdom of recruitment, was more fully articulated on 4 July 1956, when he published a letter to the West German Bundestag opposing 'compulsory military service' in both parts of Germany, 'since I am against war' (Volker 189). *Trumpets and Drums* opened at the Berliner Ensemble on 19 September 1955, and constituted an earlier, more theatrical critique of compulsory military service than Brecht's 1956 letter. His choice of

4th July for publication of an antiwar statement coincided with celebrations of the American Declaration of Independence, which Brecht must have known, since he had an excerpt from the Declaration read aloud in scene eight of *Trumpets and Drums*. ("'That all men are created equal, that they are endowed by their . . .' I can't make out that word, 'with certain rights . . .'" says Lucy in scene eight, as a reference to 'that word' 'Creator' cleverly omitted by Brecht allows him to expel God and secularize human rights. Brecht 1972: 293) . He made his own declaration of independence against war and recruitment, first with the Farquhar adaptation, then through his 4th July announcement.

Brecht the anti-militarist joined forces with Farquhar to question rearmament in his own time, much as he had earlier questioned the brutality of war by writing lyrics for the 'Cannon Song' in his adaptation of *The Beggar's Opera*. That song about slaughtering people of colour abroad had little precedent in Gay's original ballad opera; but Gay had depicted intense battles between British colonists, pirates and indigenous people in *Polly*. If Brecht did not know the play devised as a sequel to *The Beggar's Opera*, he seems intuitively to have shared with the early Brechtian John Gay a satiric attitude toward colonial war and empire.

A closer look at Polly Peachum and the play Gay titled in her honour suggests that Miss Peachum's life as a Brechtian character began not in 1928, but 1728.

CHAPTER THREE

Polly Peachum and the New Naiveté

In one of his notes on *The Threepenny Opera*, Brecht advises, 'It is absolutely essential that the spectator should see Miss Polly Peachum as a virtuous and agreeable girl' (Brecht 1979: 94). The advice seems out of character for Brecht. The man who seeks to protect and honour Miss Peachum's virtue, if only in an author's note, elsewhere admits to women that he is 'someone on whom you can't rely' (Brecht 1976: 107). In any case, the playwright must have been well aware of Polly Peachum's original attractions—her virtue and innocence first shown on stage in 1728—when he insisted on their preservation in his reutilization of John Gay's play.

In adapting Gay's first ballad opera, Brecht kept Polly's naiveté largely intact—but not completely. When Macheath instructs her in business practices, his new wife's naiveté surfaces like that of a new student not comprehending the lesson, as she questions her husband's plans. Macheath announces he will switch from burgling to banking, and asks Polly to help the police arrest gang members. She in turn asks how he can 'look them in the eye when you've written them off and they're as good as hanged? How can you shake hands with them?' (Brecht 1979: 37). Polly's innocence and newly married state allow her to ask Macheath questions others would not dare speak. She inquires about practices that place profit above employee welfare, almost expressing a Marxian view without the vocabulary for it. Perhaps her attitude can be explained by Hans Mayer's definition of the 'new naiveté' that Brecht valued at the end of his career. According to Mayer, the playwright discovered 'the naïve as an aesthetic category . . . the naïve was the most natural part of theatre'. Brecht saw this naiveté

> linked to the dialectical process of cognition. Naiveté as synthesis, as negation of negation. For the theater, this must mean understanding the events on stage in their contradiction . . . The result is an intelligible, bright and cheerful theater, not a theater determined by grim, heavy doctrine (Mayer 1971: 157–58).

At her wedding, in a subtle loss of innocence, Brecht's Polly Peachum begins to see her husband's subordinates as the soon-to-be-hanged. In a 'negation of a negation', she pretends to be innocent of this knowledge when Mackie's gang enters, and she cheerfully greets the 'boys'. Her new naiveté, compounded of knowledge and disposable innocence, can be seen in the fearlessness she displays toward one of her husband's employees. 'You shit, that's a fine way to start in. . . . Of course you're not saying anything against me', she screams after Matt the Mint doubts that a woman could give orders to the gang (Brecht 1979: 38). Her angry words are nothing like the lines Polly recited in 1728; but Brecht makes such fearless speech part of her 'new naiveté' in 1928. He may not have used that term at the time; but Polly embodies it.

The first appreciation of Polly Peachum's innocence took the form of undialectical public adulation on 29 January 1728, when *The Beggar's Opera* opened at Lincoln's Inn Fields. The idolatry did not begin immediately. Not until the tenth scene of Act One did London spectators at the opening of *The Beggar's Opera* express their enthusiasm, after Lavinia Fenton, the actress portraying Polly, began to sing:

> O ponder well! Be not severe;
> So save a wretched Wife!
> For on the Rope that hangs my Dear
> Depends poor Polly's Life.

Polly's crowd-pleasing air is a plea to her parents for understanding after she confesses that she married the highwayman Macheath. The fact that she has married the Captain does not impress Mr and Mrs Peachum, who would prefer to see their new son-in-law hanged so their daughter becomes a wealthy widow. Their resolution to turn in the criminal (that is, to peach Macheath, which would be appropriate coming from the Peachums) makes Polly 'a wretched Wife', as her song lyrics confirm. Her musical plea for those before her to 'be not severe' won approval from her larger audience, the ones paying for tickets, as they relented, broke their silence, applauded and sided with her for the rest of the evening. For months afterwards, they adored Polly and the actress portraying her.

Displaying naïve but ardent love for a man whose criminal record she hardly knows, Polly Peachum, her songs and her subsequent faithfulness to Macheath, became the talk of the town. Her picture was displayed on playing cards, fire screens, ladies' fans. Her pleas for parental approval were especially winning. When Hogarth painted a scene from *The Beggar's Opera*, he chose another tableau of Polly pleading—in Act III where she kneels before her father and asks him to secure Macheath's release from a death sentence. She more or less repeats her first appeal for parental mercy. Hogarth, and later Blake, transforming Hogarth's painting into an engraving in 1790, preserved an image of Polly at her most abject, a beautifully dressed beggar—the opera's most beloved beggar, perhaps— pleading for her husband's life, The portrait captured one of her attractions: innocence enhanced by the purity of her ample white gown shining in the centre of a dark prison cell. The contrast is especially visible in Blake's black and white engraving based on Hogarth's multi-coloured canvas. In both print and painting, Macheath and the Duke of Bolton (the latter in the audience that was seated on stage) have their eyes on Polly, as if to confirm her begging attracted men in the play and out of it.

Fig. 1.   Detail from William Blake's engraving of *The Beggar's Opera* based
on a painting by Hogarth. Polly Peachum, the beautiful beggar in the
centre, pleads for her husband's freedom, with Macheath on her left and
her father Jeremiah Peachum on her right. The Duke of Bolton at far right
holds a copy of the play, but looks at the actress rather than the text. John
Gay stands immediately to the right of Mr Peachum.

The beauty of Lavinia Fenton probably had something to do with the Duke's attraction, too. But even without Fenton in the lead role (as Brecht's defence of her virtue attests), Polly's devotion to Macheath, her readiness to beg on her husband's behalf, the marshalling of her beauty and her songs for a man's freedom, won her a devoted following. That first night in 1728, and for centuries of performances that followed, Polly's virtue was heightened by the contrasting vice shown by the criminal element around her in the dark cell and other London haunts.

A poem published 'To Miss Polly Peachum' soon after the play's premiere summed up the character's popularity, and her capacity to allay adversity (including 'increasing taxes and declining trade') for an admirer announcing:

> Farewell! Ye Nymphs, who range the humble Plains;
> Henceforth a nobler Subject swells my Strains,
> And all ye Muses, all your strength combine;
> For in dear Polly all the Muses shine.
>
> When on the Stage you act the moving Part,
> My ears and eyes conspire to rack my Heart;
> I gaze; I listen; and in Doubt am lost
> Which happy Faculty is ravished most . . .
>
> Through every Scene thy rigid Fate I moan,
> And in thy soft Distress forget my own;
> Domestick charges, courtly bills unpaid,
> Increasing taxes and declining trade.

While Lavinia Fenton's performance was central to the play's initial success and the public's love of Polly, some of the character's popularity may be attributed to the novelty of *The Beggar's Opera*, its English lyrics in a nation that previously expected opera to be delivered in Italian. The new opera also offered novel preservation (through Polly) of virtue in a Newgate prison 'pastoral', where many inhabitants rest not on a country estate but inside a locked cell if they cannot afford to bribe judges and gaolers. It was hardly a setting where one would expect her innocence to last; but Miss Peachum remained faithful to her husband, in a thrall much like that her admirer described in his farewell to nymphs.

Neither her parents' disapproval, her husband's imprisonment, nor his dalliance and marriages with other women deter Polly's steadfast devotion. Her faithfulness could be seen as comic self-deception; but judging from reports of audience response to her first song, and the subsequent idolatry, spectators took Polly's behaviour seriously. The most sentimental character in the play, she lived on stage in an age when sentimental comedy had a following—despite the genre's undermining by John Gay's satire elsewhere in his ballad opera. As Bateson notes, 'the Polly of *The Beggar's Opera* is equally a real character of sentiment and a caricature of sentimentalism', although the 1728 audience admired the sentiment and steadfast love more than the caricature (Bateson 102).

Gay's mockery of sentimental drama through Polly's excessive devotion to Macheath surfaces when Mrs Peachum condemns 'those cursed

Fig. 2.   Lavinia Fenton, engraving by John Faber, 1728.

play-books' for having led to her daughter's ruin. Was Polly reading Steele's *The Conscious Lovers* or a play by Colley Cibber? We can only speculate, but her mother is probably attributing the young woman's downfall to sentimental plays rather than satiric ones. Besides play reading having shaped Miss Peachum's emotional state, the stage proved to be her source of fame. Sometime after opening night in 1728, the playwright recognized that Polly's sentimental love was winning crowds nightly. In writing the sequel, *Polly*, and naming the new play after his enormously popular character, Gay kept her sentimental love alive in a new setting. The author knew what the audience wanted (more of innocent Polly), and gave it to them in the title and the text itself.

In *Polly* Macheath takes a secondary role, and he is reportedly hanged, while at the end of her West Indian adventure his wife still lives, ready for Part Three if only Gay had lived to write it, and Walpole had permitted Part Two to open. Perhaps the ministry of Walpole also knew, when it denied Gay permission to have *Polly* staged, that Miss Peachum was one of the author's greatest attractions. Could it be that a play with her name in the title, not simply its satire of the government, made it too appealing for the ministry to let this ballad opera premiere after Gay completed the text in December of 1728?

To some extent Miss Peachum cannot be regarded as wholly honest or innocent in Gay's second instalment of her adventures; she deceives others by pretending to be a young man after disguising herself to escape slavery. Nor is she the most virtuous character in the play. That honour goes to Cawwawkee, the Indian Prince who falls in love with her. Almost as if to replace Polly's innocence with one less tainted, Gay introduces a number of West Indies natives—noble savages fit for the tribes Rousseau praised. The Prince and his cohorts display an honesty that also recalls the learned horses whose virtues Lemuel Gulliver admired. Could Swift who once suggested a 'Newgate pastoral' to Gay also have suggested a 'colonial empire pastoral', with noble Indians instead of horses as the models of virtue?

Knowing Brecht's interest in Swift and Gay, he might have enjoyed *Polly*, its anti-colonial satire and the title character's life among pirates if he ever read the play. (The next chapter suggests he might have been aware of the text.) The Brechtian qualities in *Polly*'s plot are astutely described by Robert Dryden (without his mentioning Brecht) when he writes:

> Gay is one of the first eighteenth-century writers to represent the English colonial merchant, not as a hero, but as a kind of pirate . . . Gay condemns the British planters, the British soldier, the British slave trade, the transportation of British criminals, and the pirate . . . [in a] thoroughly Swiftian style (Dryden 540).

As a young poet Brecht wrote a 'Ballad of the Pirates' in 1918, and it is not difficult to imagine him adapting Gay's story about Miss Peachum and Macheath the pirate, if anyone had commissioned the work.

In Gay's play, Polly Peachum survives enslavement, warfare and treachery. In the face of British colonial corruption and piracy, her friends the indigenous natives look exceedingly noble. They are not pacifists; but their virtue appears to give the Indians superior military strength, as they triumph in battle. One of the men captured in the war, the pirate Macheath is condemned to be hanged, much to Polly's distress. She tries and fails to save her husband's life. But it is no accident that the play ends with her in the company of the Indians; they share qualities of naiveté, earnestness and fidelity that first won Polly so many admirers.

Punch as the New Macheath

The full history of Polly Peachum's life on stage and her long lasting naiveté could take up volumes. One book, *Polly Peachum: The Story of Lavinia Fenton and The Beggar's Opera*, traces her history on stage through 1886. Far more could be added to that now outdated study by Charles Pearce, which ended before *The Beggar's Opera* led to Brecht's *The Threepenny Opera* in 1928. Brecht's two-hundredth year anniversary tribute to Gay's play has a long history of its own by now.

Another rendering of Polly's story linked her to popular theatre tradition and the naiveté of the folk play a century before Brecht's *Threepenny Opera*. *Punch and Judy* introduces the innocent young woman to another famous criminal, namely Punch. In 1828, when John Payne Collier published the first transcribed text of the puppet play's dialogue in English, his edition included Polly Peachum as a supporting character.

Punch replaces Macheath as the criminal who attracts her, in a scene that takes place after Punch has beaten his wife to death and thrown his child away. (This being a puppet play, Punch's violence usually evokes laughter and disbelief rather than disapproval, when properly performed.) Act I, scene iv begins with the entrance of 'Pretty Polly', whose appearance leads Punch to sing an air from *The Beggar's Opera*: 'When the heart of a man is oppress'd with cares, / The clouds are dispelled when a woman appears.'

In Gay's first ballad opera, Macheath performs this song after declaring Polly is 'a fond Wench' who 'is most confoundedly bit'. He admits that he cannot be content with one woman, since he loves 'the Sex' as a whole and 'must have women'. After Punch's rendition of Macheath's song lyrics, the famous puppet confides in an aside to the audience: 'What a beauty! What a pretty creature!' Soon he is kissing Polly, dancing with her, and singing about how he would kill all his wives 'for my Pretty Poll'. That is the last we see of the couple. Punch falls in love with no one else in the play, and in that regard you could say he remains faithful to Polly. In Act II of the 1828 version, Punch resolves to mount his horse and 'take a ride to visit my Pretty Poll'. Thrown by his horse, the rider never reaches his lady friend; but before he falls he sings about Polly, 'the darling of [his] heart', she who is 'so plump and jolly'.

In a long footnote to the Punch and Polly courtship scene, Collier reprints another version in which Polly asks who killed her father. Punch claims he did, because the father would not let him have the daughter. Polly then sees Punch weeping or pretending to weep in regret, and decides she must love him if he killed for love of her. 'The whole scene', notes Collier, 'seems modelled upon the interview between Richard III and Lady Anne'. So Shakespearean tragedy as well as ballad opera can be found in this variation on Gay's original scene.

By 1828, at the age of 100, Polly embraces a homicidal lover, and she is no longer devoted only to Macheath. She still finds criminals attractive, as they find her, judging by her relationship to Punch. She moved from one popular theatre form—ballad opera—into another, with humour, songs and dance, but perhaps with less innocence than she had in 1728.

Kneehigh's Punch and Polly

Polly and Punch were reunited, or at least appeared again in the same play, in a 2014 adaptation of *The Beggar's Opera* written by Carl Grose and staged by the Kneehigh company in England. In the new play titled *Dead Dog in a Suitcase (and other love songs)* Macheath is a hired killer who confers with the puppet Punch. Macheath knows he is wrong for Polly and may do her harm. Punch reaffirms this view and functions as the hit man's conscience (while he hits Macheath) in one scene:

MACHEATH
Do I deserve her?

PUNCH
You deserve this world and this world deserves you, ya shit!
WHACK!

MACHEATH
Ow! Answer the question.

PUNCH
You're a damned bloody bastard, and she's a good girl.
WHACK!

PUNCH
No, you don't deserve her.

MACHEATH
It's true. She is a good girl.

PUNCH
She'll pay the price, knowing you . . .

Polly's father is possibly more reprehensible than Macheath in Grose's version of the story. Mr Peachum secretly hires Macheath to murder their mayor, then takes over the mayoral office himself through a rigged election. Polly remains relatively innocent, unaware that she has married a contract killer—although she inquires about her husband's crimes once married to him. With new songs and new situations, the Kneehigh variation on John Gay's play brings its characters into the twenty-first century, with outrages fit for an age of environment despolation, decadent nightclubs, and million dollar rewards for capture of a criminal. A dead dog in a suitcase is all the mayor's wife has left after her husband and her dog are assassinated. An accidental switch of suitcases later leaves the assassin holding the dead dog, the widow holding a suitcase full of money. Macheath's future here is bleak, but perhaps no more so than in John Gay's vision of Newgate prison life and death by hanging. Grose's Macheath at one point escapes his executioner with a trick more indebted to Punch and Judy than John Gay; the wiles of Punch and Macheath fuse in cruel and grotesque comedy. The old rivalry between Peachum and Macheath continues, with Polly's marriage still the source of their contention. 'The world may be tearing itself apart but at least the myth of Macheath lives on'; that's the only consolation one character (Filch) can offer in Grose's play.

By comparison, the lives of Punch and Polly in earlier centuries seem simpler, less mercenary than the society Kneehigh and Grose depict. Not that Punch was without his own violent and cruel streaks earlier. Henry Fielding made Punch a nasty husband in his 1730 play, *The Author's Farce*. Joan, not Judy, was Punch's wife that year. Polly Peachum had just barely entered the theatre world through *The Beggar's Opera*, but Punch was ready for her, or at least ready to leave his wife Joan, as he indicated in a song Fielding wrote:

> Joan, Joan, Joan has a thundering tongue,
> And Joan, Joan, Joan, is a bold one.
> How happy is he
> Who from wedlock is free,
> For who'd have a wife to scold one?

Sometime later (date unknown) Punch murdered his wife Judy (no longer Joan) and began courting Polly. Philip John Stead notes that before

Polly 'metamorphosed into [Punch's] paramour', her name was that of Punch's and Joan's Daughter (Stead 62). Daughter Polly appears in the anonymously published 1741 puppet play, *Politicks in Miniature, or The Humours of Punch's Resignation: A Tragi-Comi-Farcical-Operatical Puppet-Show*, where Punch resigns as a stage character and becomes a prompter behind the scenes, ready to give cues to all those he previously bribed or was bribed by, including a bishop, a military officer, and legislative officials. The play ends with the 'resigned' figure of Punch controlling church and state behind the scenes. Stead sees Punch 'identified with the unpopular Walpole' in this play, and it is likely the satire was penned by an anti-Walpole satirist. Daughter Polly is told by her father that she will become a 'Lady of Qual[ity]', a transitional stage in her loss of innocence and rise to the level of first Minister's daughter. She sings:

> As a Lady of Quall
> I'll flaunt in the Mall,
> While 'tis said as I trip it along:
> With no Title Miss
> A new Lady is,
> Our Lords and their Ladies among.

While Polly sang about her rising social status in 1741, Collier's 1828 version of *Punch and Judy* featured a mute Polly whose silence would have appealed to Fielding's Punch of 1730, tormented as he was by wife Joan's thundering tongue. Polly's silence and her attractive looks captivate the man who becomes her paramour (no longer her father) by 1828.

Punch captivated others besides Polly, too. He had an enthusiastic following in 1728, judging from Jonathan Swift's poem, 'Mad Mullinix and Timothy'. The same year that Miss Peachum (in the company of Macheath, not Punch) first stepped onto the stage, Swift wrote:

> Observe, the audience is in pain,
> While Punch is hid behind the scene;
> But when they hear his rusty voice,
> With what impatience they rejoice! . . .
> You every moment think an age
> Til he appears upon the stage.

Polly's entry into Punch's world, and the extension of her life and Gay's musical play in puppetry long after the lady was first seen on stage, confirm that this popular female character remained well known in 1828. The only character in *Punch and Judy* not beaten or killed by the male lead, a frequenter of theatre houses and puppet booths, Polly Peachum still had

Fig. 3   Polly Peachum meets Punch in 1828, illustrated by George Cruikshank.

seeming innocence, charms to disarm a wife-killer, and the vitality to live on stage for another century or two. She continued to live as John Gay's creation until 1928, after which she became one of Brecht's most famous characters, no longer quite so innocent despite her 'new naiveté'. As she sings 'Pirate Jenny' Polly imagines being asked who should be killed, and she answers: 'the lot!' (Brecht 1979: 20). She sounds more like Punch or Macheath than Polly Peachum. No wonder her husband disapproves of the song; the innocent woman he married has turned into a pirate. 'I don't like you play-acting; let's not have any more of it', he tells Polly. (Brecht 1979: 22)

CHAPTER FOUR

Pirates and *Polly*: A Lost *Messingkauf Dialogue*

Brecht's Messingkauf Dialogues, *imaginary conversations about theatre introduced earlier (Chapter Two), at times recall some of the playwright's own experiences with the German stage. In the dialogues Brecht refers to himself as the Augsburger, an homage to the region where he was born. He never published the selection that follows, possibly because it hints that he wrote only part of* The Threepenny Opera. *English version by Joel Schechter.*

DRAMATURG: No respectable playwright would write an entirely original text. Even Shakespeare and Molière (far too respectable) stole plots from other writers. The Augsburger turned to Shakespeare, Molière, Farquhar, Gay for play ideas; he considered it collective authorship.

PHILOSOPHER: One of his assistants in Berlin [Ed note: Elisabeth Hauptmann] provided him with the translation of a play by John Gay, and it subsequently became a popular entertainment [Ed. note: *The Threepenny Opera*] attributed to the Augsburger himself. He did write some of its scenes and song lyrics; but he can hardly be said to have invented the ballad opera form, or the characters of Macheath and Polly Peachum.

DRAMATURG: While your information is accurate, it is not complete. His assistant gave the Augsburger two plays by John Gay. The second one had been banned [Ed. note: *Polly*, 1728], and was not too well known even in England.

If you know the banned play, you will appreciate that the Augsburger particularly enjoyed its depiction of pirates. The pirate fantasies of international looting [Ed. note: *Polly*, Act II, Scene ii, where the West Indian pirates led by Macheath plan to take over Mexico, Cuba and Peru] amused him so much as a comment on empire that he included an acknowledgment of them in *The Threepenny Opera*. Polly Peachum has developed a little ritual there: she has to be called Jenny the pirate's bride before she can deliver the 'Pirate Jenny' song. To help her get in character, she needs to be asked: 'Waschst du immer noch die Gläser auf, du Jenny, die

Seerauberbraut?' 'Are you still washing the glasses, Jenny the Pirate's bride?' a clear reference to Jenny, the pirate's bride in Gay's banned play. [Ed note: Jenny Diver lives with the pirate Macheath in *Polly*.] Polly assumes the role of pirate Jenny, sings about a ship with fifty guns, then her new husband objects to his bride's play-acting.

PHILOSOPHER: It's one of the few occasions, perhaps the only one, when the bourgeois husband sides with the parents of his bride by objecting to her theatrical interests.

ACTOR: Regrettably, the Augsburger never adapted another one of Gay's plays. I gladly would have played the pirate Macheath.

PHILOSOPHER: The critics would see you as a stand-in for the author and his redistribution of John Gay's intellectual property.

CHAPTER FIVE

The Duchess of Queensberry
Becomes Polly Peachum

But you know, Mackie, I could talk to somebody . . . I might even ask the
Queen in person.

> Polly Peachum in *The Threepenny Opera* (Brecht 1979: 73)

The Queen of England reprieves Macheath from hanging in Brecht's play
after Polly Peachum says she'll have a word with her Highness. We never
see the Queen or hear her conversation with Miss Peachum, but it seems
that the daughter of an underworld criminal had friends in high places in
Brecht's play as well as John Gay's. Polly's earliest appeal to nobility began
when Lavinia Fenton performed the role to great acclaim at Lincoln's Inn
Fields from January to June of 1728. After that six-month period, inspired
perhaps by Macheath's liaisons with Polly and his other wives in the play,
the Duke of Bolton took the leading lady away from the stage and kept her
as his mistress for twenty-three years. When Bolton finally married Miss
Fenton she became a duchess. Less than a month after her retirement from
acting, in July of 1728 Gay wrote in a letter to Swift that Bolton had 'run
away with Polly Peachum', as if the Duke was enamoured of the play's lead
female character, not the actress Fenton.

Over the same decades Lavinia Fenton spent becoming a duchess,
another English woman, already a respected duchess, slowly transformed
herself into Polly Peachum, and did so in the company of royalty. This
performer's name will not be found among the cast lists for *The Beggar's
Opera*. The Duchess of Queensberry never performed on stage in the role,
but her activities as John Gay's friend and defender turned her into a new
Polly Peachum devoted to rescuing Macheath and his associates from the
law when they were banned by the Lord Chamberlain. 'In this way', to
cite Brecht on Epic theatre, her 'performance becomes a discussion (about
social conditions) with the audience [s]he is addressing' (Brecht 1964:
139). And the duchess did have an audience, as she spoke to friends of the
court and the court itself in favour of the banned playwright.

Queensberry's campaign on behalf of *Polly* and John Gay included acts of kindness towards her favourite writer, for which she won high praise from Gay in his letters to Swift. Within the correspondence one can read another drama, a series of events that might be called *The Duchess's Opera*. This story, lived in English drawing rooms and royal chambers which were stages in their own way, features as its lead character a virtuous young woman who seeks to rescue a man (in this case Gay himself, not Macheath) from adversity. She performed her role in front of the nation's ruler, and without knowing it anticipated a dream voiced by an actor in Brecht's *Messingkauf Dialogues*: '. . . in this new theatre I shall transform my audience into kings. Not only into the semblance of kings, but the real thing' (Brecht 1965: 100). Brecht's actor revises his goal a few sentences later, and describes his theatre as 'a laboratory for this great mass of working people', a view more in line with Brecht's own proletarian theatre interests than the goal of performing for royalty. The *Messingkauf* actor's point was to 'alter the world' through theatre. His spectators would become 'kings' and all of them would share the position. In the case of the Duchess of Queensberry, her 'opera' was performed for men already in power, including the King of England. Brecht's later hope (expressed in the poem 'To Posterity') that without him, the 'rulers would have been more secure', might have been realized by the Duchess in her life as Polly.

After *Polly* was banned from the stage in December 1728, the Duchess sought to win the play's release in different venues. She tried to read the play to King George II, who declined to hear it; instead he said he would be pleased to spend time with the Duchess in his closet on more amusing entertainment. His licentious remark almost sounds like a line from Gay's play. In one scene the patriarchal Mr Ducat purchases Polly Peachum for household service, bolts the door of a room and informs the newly acquired young woman: 'I have in mind to have a little conversation with you, and I would not be interrupted'. His use of the word 'conversation' is questionable, since Ducat next kisses his new 'property' and she sings 'You're monstrous rude'. Without knowing it, the King had asked the Duchess to play Polly's role to his Ducat in a royal closet. Or perhaps he had read the play and it inspired his scene with the Duchess.

The Duchess of Queensberry did not secure a royal reprieve for Macheath or Gay. But with determination comparable to Polly's, she displayed qualities of spirit, honour and goodness that Gay noted in a letter to Swift. While staying at the Queensberry residence in Burlington Gardens, the playwright wrote to Swift on 18 March 1729:

> While I am writing this, I am [in] the room next to our dining room with sheets all-round it, and two people from the Binder folding sheets. I print the Book [*Polly*] at my own expence in Quarto, which is to be sold for six

shillings with the Musick. You see I don't want industry, and I hope you will allow that I have not the worst Oeconomy. Mrs. Howard hath declar'd herself strongly both to the King and Queen as my advocate. The Duchess of Queensberry is allow'd to have shown, more Spirit, more honour, and more goodness than was thought possible in our times; I should have added too more understanding and good sense. You see my fortune (as I hope my Virtue will) increases by oppression.

Gay's fortune did greatly increase with oppression. The printed version of *Polly*, assembled in the Queensberry residence, brought him £1,200, much more than conventional stage productions earned for their authors at the time. This new play with pirates in it also was pirated by printers—a back-handed tribute to its popularity. Gay and his lawyers had to fight pirates in court, rather than in the West Indies where Polly's friends battle in the banned play; but in both cases, a Pollyannish woman was at the centre of the battle.

John Gay reiterated praise for his off-stage Polly, the Duchess of Queensberry, in another letter to Swift sent 9 November 1729. Writing from Queensberry's hunting lodge in Oxfordshire, Gay noted in passing that 'the Lady I live with [to whom I owe my Life & fortune] . . . Hath so much goodness, virtue & generosity that if you knew her you would have a pleasure in obeying her as I do'. Gay remained a bachelor, but he was more or less living with the Duchess and happily so, in 1729. In this particular letter, his expression of debt to his patroness sounds remarkably like the Indian Prince Cawwawkee after Polly rescues him. The Prince on his West Indian island admits owing life and liberty to his saviour (Act III, scene iii). At the time he is rescued, the Prince thinks that Polly is a young man, since she has disguised herself, and for this reason the Indian says of her: 'To him are owing my life and liberty. And the love of virtue alone gain'd me his friendship.' The parallels between Polly and the Duchess falter here; the latter was not known for cross-dressing, although she seems to have liked its portrayal in *Polly*, insofar as she liked the play.

If the dating of Gay's letters is correct, his admiration for the Duchess began before *The Beggar's Opera* was performed in 1728. A letter from Gay to Pope (originally thought to have been written in March 1729, then re-dated October 1727) refers to the 'divine Looks, the kind Favours and Expressions of the divine Duchess, who hereafter shall be in Place of a Queen to me, (nay, she shall be my Queen)'. Such words suggest that the Duchess of Queensberry could have been a source of inspiration for Polly's character; and that in turn could explain why the Duchess was so favourably inclined toward both instalments of Gay's plays about Miss Peachum—assuming she knew the role was inspired by her own virtues.

Virtues are a central topic in Gay's banned play. In the West Indies to search for Macheath after he has been transported there, the natives Miss Peachum befriends embody the virtues and dedication to good deeds Polly herself inspires. It is only fitting that she should end up admiring, and be invited to live with them, at the end of the play. The Duchess also sought their company, insofar as she wanted to see them on a stage in London.

After the success of *The Beggar's Opera*, Gay again wrote about his patroness in a letter to Swift. On 15 February 1728, noting that 'the Playhouse hath been crouded every night; to night is the fifteenth time of Acting, and 'tis thought it will run a fortnight longer [it ran for sixty-two nights, a record for the era]', Gay adds that: 'The Duchess of Queensberry hath signaliz'd her friendship to me upon this occasion . . .' He doesn't indicate how she 'signaliz'd' her friendship, but by March of 1729 he was able to tell Swift that:

> the Duchess took up my defence with the King and Queen in the cause of my Play [the banned *Polly*], and . . . She hath been forbid the Court for interesting herself to increase my fortune for the publication of it without being acted.

In the same letter he notes that the Duchess of Marlborough gave him a £100 for a copy of the play; but that price, while quite high, was not as high as the one the Duchess of Queensberry paid (loss of audiences at court) for championing the author.

A comically exaggerated rumour of incendiary playwriting was sent by Gay's friend, John Arbuthnot, in a 19 March 1729 letter to Swift: 'The inoffensive John Gay is now become one of the obstructions to the peace of Europe, the terror of the ministers, the chief author of the Craftsman, and all the seditious pamphlets.' While Arbuthnot was only joking here, jovially aggrandizing Gay's influence, the same letter more accurately notes that Gay's partisan, the Duchess of Queensberry, was turned out of Court for favouring his first ballad opera, and predicted another 'seven or eight Duchesses' might 'suffer martyrdom on his account'. Only one duchess suffered such martyrdom, as it turned out; but was it martyrdom, or a royally bestowed honour, to be out of favour, banned almost like *Polly*, for defence of the play?

The Duchess of Queensberry might well have spoken some of Polly Peachum's lines aloud, or read them aloud, during her crusade on behalf of Gay's persecuted play. When Polly meets the Indian Prince Cawwawkee in the West Indies, and wins his freedom from the pirates who capture him, she admits that 'The pleasure of having serv'd an honourable man is sufficient return' for her troubles (Act III, scene xii). Her virtue is almost cloying, and she is not ashamed to praise it herself: 'my behaviour shall justify the good opinion you have of me; and my friendship is beyond professions' (Act III, scene iii).

Miss Peachum has her faults, as she admits in *Polly* when explaining her unending attraction to the highwayman Macheath: 'What had not the love of virtue directed my heart? But, alas, 'tis outward appearance alone that generally engages a woman's affections! And my heart is in the possession of the most profligate of mankind' (Act III, scene xii). Held prisoner by her heart, even after she has escaped captivity from the man who bought her (Ducat) and the pirates who encounter her, Polly declines the advances of her seeming equal in virtue, Prince Cawwawkee, as long as she dreams of finding Macheath alive. Near the very end of the play, when it is revealed that Macheath had disguised himself as Moreno and is about to be hanged, Polly melodramatically pleads for his life: 'Macheath! Is it possible? Spare him, save him, I ask no other reward' (Act III, scene xiii). Her appeal comes too late, apparently. With macabre humour, Gay has the Indians silently return from their attempt to rescue the condemned pirate (Macheath). They do not say he was executed, but Polly sees them and declares: 'He's dead, he's dead! Their looks confess it. Your tongues have no need to give it utterance to confirm my misfortunes!' The rumours of Macheath's death are exaggerated by Polly; for all we know, he lives on. Why else did the author silence his messengers, the Indians? The third instalment, a sequel to *Polly*, could have been titled: *Macheath and Polly*. When Henry Fielding set out to premiere Gay's *Polly* in an 'improv'd' version in 1737, he made sure both their names appeared in the advertised title: *Macheath turn'd pyrate; or Polly in India*. He too might have given audiences more than instalments one and two, if only the government had let him. (This episode is discussed in Chapter Fourteen.)

Instead of writing a third instalment, with Polly and Macheath again onstage, John Gay lived out his remaining years in illness, comforted with the good friendship and support of the Duke and Duchess of Queensberry. It could be argued that the Duchess herself created the third part of Polly's life, by embodying her virtue and keeping her words alive in the drawing rooms of her friends (though not in the royal chambers) as she read lines aloud and called for a reprieve of the stage ban imposed on *Polly*. As Polly Peachum awaits the news of Macheath's rescue, so too the Duchess might have awaited the first staging of the banned play: 'What, no news yet? Not yet return'd!'

John Fuller thought the Duchess of Queensberry might have helped Gay rhyme some of the song lyrics in *Polly* while he was composing that play at the Queensberry residence. Could she have written these lyrics, sung by Polly, about her own devotion to John Gay:

> Farewell, farewell, all Hope of Bliss,
> For Polly always must be thine:
> Shall then my Hart be never his,
> Which never can again be mine?
> O Love, you play a cruel Part,
> Thy Shaft still festers in the Wound,
> You should reward a constant Heart,
> Since 'tis alas so seldom found.

There is a final act to the story involving the new Polly, the Duchess of Queensberry. When Gay's banned play was finally allowed onstage in June, 1777, the Duchess (aged considerably) was there in the audience to hear it. Legend has it she sang along with all the songs—finally triumphant, at one with Polly Peachum and her lyrical voice. 'She attended this production more than once, and died very shortly afterwards', according to Fuller (Fuller 55). It is tempting to say that she lived only to see Gay's *Polly* and her own lyrics onstage. But there is another, less happy ending to the same story. While the play performed in 1777 was titled *Polly*, the text had been adapted and cut by playwright George Colman the Elder, with new music supplied by composer Samuel Arnold. A look at the Colman libretto shows some of Gay's pointed satiric lyrics are missing—perhaps cut to appease the Lord Chamberlain.★ So while the Duchess was able to sing a number of her favourite songs, Gay's own voice remained muted. The Duchess would have been unable to sing along to such lines as:

> What can Wealth
> When we're old?
> Youth and Health
> Are not sold.

★Peter Reed writing on *Polly*'s 1777 reception notes in *Theatre Journal*, page 247 (2007): 'Responses to the play's 1777 performances . . . avoid openly acknowledging political issues. "Mr. Colman has expunged every thing introduced by Mr. Gay that could give offence", one newspaper review claims. Colman had indeed cut some expressions of underclass insolence, lines that, as the review implies, could give cause for offence. Reviews largely ignore [the black pirate] Morano's presence, focusing instead on the performance's aesthetic propriety. Comments on "happily chosen" music, "well adapted to please the taste of an English audience" replace social criticism; any controversy seems to have receded by 1777. Implying that Colman and his cast have tamed Morano's rebellious qualities, the reviews imagine the play as the epitome of good theatrical taste.' Colman's version of *Polly* seems to have secured a lift of the ban by cutting or downplaying the original text's more provocative passages.

Nor would she have heard lyrics asserting:

> I hate those coward Tribes
> Who by mean sneaking Bribes,
> By Tricks and disguise,
> By Flattery and Lies,
> To Power and Grandeur rise.

Fortunately, the Duchess performed her finest scenes before 1777, and the censors never stopped those. The transformation of an actress (Lavinia Fenton) into a duchess and a duchess (Queensberry) into an actress doubly confirms a tendency Gay portrayed in *The Beggar's Opera* for one social class to mimic the behaviour of another, and take on another group's vices (or occasional virtues) as its own. This is not to say that classes or people are interchangeable; but theatrical activity (or withdrawal from it, taking a bow and exit as Lavinia Fention did) allows for the mimicry to be shown in public. In Gay's Introduction to *Polly*, the Poet 'venture[s] to own that [he wishes] every Man of Power or Riches were really and apparently virtuous, which would soon amend and reform the common People, who act by Imitation'. At least one woman of riches was really and apparently virtuous in Gay's era when the Duchess of Queensberry performed the role Polly Peachum.

CHAPTER SIX

Macheath Our Contemporary

Ageless, John Gay's Macheath has turned up in a number of new situations since he first appeared on stage in 1728. Gay portrayed him as a highwayman in The Beggar's Opera *and then as a pirate in* Polly. *More recently, over the past century he has been given new roles by notable authors including Wole Soyinka, Dario Fo, and Vaclav Havel. Macheath alias Mack the Knife continues to be seen at times in Brecht's* Threepenny Opera, *and on those occasions the former pirate speaks of entering a more socially acceptable profession. He has found it, if these recently written confessions can be trusted.*

It was only a matter of time before I left my gang of highwaymen behind and became a legitimate banker. I asked my wife Polly to send all our profits to Jack Poole's banking house in Manchester, while I took a brief vacation in the Newgate district. (My stay in the prison there ended with a reprieve from the Queen of England, who honoured my entrepreneurial talents with knighthood.) Some of my early career was reported with wild inaccuracy by the German writer Bertolt Brecht, in his musical titled *The Threepenny Opera*. Before that John Gay maligned my name in *The Beggar's Opera* and *Polly*. But the most recent developments in my life have yet to be told. My enchanting wife Polly and I are now older, and we have changed with the times. Ever since I decided owning a bank is preferable to burgling one, and more profitable, I have thrived through modern financial transactions. Rather than let Brecht or that other satirist Dario Fo or another one of their followers again misrepresent my admittedly exciting adventures in capitalism, I decided to pen this modest memoir myself and send it to the United States Senate's banking committee.

The honest and rewarding life I lead as an international banker might not win approval from everyone. We businessmen of the twenty-first century live in a time when some of the public would rather hear about stock market scandals and wrenching crashes than read dull financial page accounts of billion dollar loans, rising, usurious interest rates, and other regular banking news.

Once I transferred my Manchester holdings to the United States, bought a skyscraper in New York, and installed a steel vault in the building, my life as a banker led me to friendships with prominent corporate executives and high government officials. I cannot name my friends here; they would lose public trust if linked to my infamous history of highway robbery and extortion. But I am now an honourable man, with partners in high places (not just my skyscraper, either). I adhere to the finest laws that lobbyists can secure, all of which exempt me from prosecution. Once I understood the newly deregulated banking laws, I could see that I was born to occupy Wall Street as a seller of derivatives, mortgage packages and hedge funds.

A firm like mine is now too big to fail; therefore when the firm falters it receives generous government bailouts. In a December 2010 speech, Senator Bernie Sanders must have had me in mind when he mentioned a secret bailout by Federal Reserve officials who loaned $780 billion to Goldman Sachs, $2 trillion to Morgan Stanley, and $2.4 trillion to Citigroup, all without public disclosure. America is indeed a land of opportunity. Where else could a man like me borrow trillions? Little did Brecht know when he wrote *The Threepenny Opera* that this new era of bank bailouts would warrant a sequel: *The Three Trillion Dollar Opera*.

Knowing that wealth remains unevenly distributed, and some populations need help, I recently appointed Polly director of a new disaster relief firm called 'The Widow's Friend'. The company designed for an age of climate change provides emergency loans to nations that suffer floods, hurricanes, drought, oil spills and other environmental catastrophes. Polly's father, Jeremiah Peachum, pioneered the practice of profitable disaster relief. (Although known as 'The Beggar King', the man became inordinately wealthy from fundraising on behalf of war veterans and the unemployed.) While Polly will give away millions to widows and orphans, she also will collect billions from new oil, gas, uranium and electronic media rights we secure from governments in their time of trouble. Her firm also will find great demand for its services in areas that need rebuilding after wars. (Although not a pacifist, Polly has no plan to fund war weaponry in those regions; prominent arms manufacturers already control the market.)

My old comrade in arms, Tiger Brown, who fought by my side in India, and served as London's police chief, now advises Scotland Yard on counter-terrorism strategy, and oversees security for famous singers with unruly admirers. Brown's daughter Lucy often hires her father's guards, as she performs Brecht and Weill songs with a very popular band. Occasionally I accept her complimentary tickets, and listen fondly to the old refrains: 'The world is poor and men are bad / And we have nothing more to add.'

Nothing like an evening of art to prepare one for re-entry into the fray. The competition never rests, and I buy out as much of it as I can afford. While I have no interest in taking a seat in the government's cabinet (why buy what you already own?), I expect to be appointed to the Federal Reserve Board; for the present I am content to slowly repay its loans.

No longer an outlaw, but a friend of judges, I now marvel at the benefits law confers on those who can afford to abide by it. Not long ago a firm of mine was fined $550 million by the Securities and Exchange Commission because we held one-hundred per cent of the short side on collateralized debt obligations before the American housing market collapsed, at the same time as our firm was advising investors that their obligations would be paid in full. I never admit to such conduct in public, my subordinates are well paid to endure the discredit; but if fined for it, we immediately pay the millions asked, and write it off as part of the firm's operating costs. Such fines cut into the profits, but I can handle a few cuts; that is why friends still call me Mack the Knife.

I have outlived my critics (Brecht among them) by decades; for which survival I acknowledge wonderful government support in the form of banking deregulation, undersight (certainly not oversight) of stock market trading, tax cuts for the wealthy, and the occasional rewriting of my alibis.

Polly wept as she read Senator Carl Levin's description of American mortgage firms and Wall Street banks as 'a financial snake pit rife with greed, conflicts of interest and wrongdoing'. 'He didn't mention your firm once', she lamented. I told her not to worry, we will survive the Senator's neglect; in fact benign inaction by him and other officials has helped us acquire great financial wealth and respectability.

In case you didn't see it, when Senator Levin reprimanded the Goldman Sachs Group Incorporated (13 April, 2011), he announced that 'Goldman clearly misled their clients, and they misled the Congress'. What is the world coming to, when a Senator so openly praises the achievements of my colleagues? It almost makes me want to become a Senator myself.

CHAPTER SEVEN

Swift in Hollywood:
Another *Messingkauf Dialogue*

In 1942 Brecht wrote his sequence of poems, 'Hollywood Elegies', and lamented the difficulties of adjusting to life in the world's film capitol without capital. This Messingkauf Dialogue *fragment seems to have been scribbled and forgotten that same year. English version by Joel Schechter.*

DRAMATURG: The Augsburger occasionally visited his friend Fritz Lang to discuss one of their film projects [ed. note: *Hangmen Also Die*, directed by Lang]. In the studio canteen he encountered other exiles and misfits who spoke for hours about their countries of origin and their untranslated manuscripts.

ACTRESS: We also wondered if all of Europe would succumb to the Austrian housepainter's art.

DRAMATURG: One day in the canteen the Augsburger drank too much coffee with brandy . . .

ACTOR: He also ate a deluxe soyburger drenched in avocado dressing, sweet potato pie, and then fell into a daydream. He thought he saw Cervantes and Swift seated nearby drinking schnaps in the canteen.

PHILOSOPHER: Swift bemoaned Max Fleischer's technicolour animation of *Gulliver's Travels* [ed. note: film released in 1939] which led millions to see the satire as a children's cartoon.

DRAMATURG: Cervantes said it was better to be a children's author in America; it was a young country. 'But they roast, fricassee and devour their young here,' Swift insisted. 'Fleischer won't animate that story, will he?' asked Cervantes.

PHILOSOPHER: Still in a daydream the Augsburger offered to collaborate with the two writers on an epic satire of the film industry. They regretfully declined, saying their studio contracts prohibited independent thought.

CHAPTER EIGHT

Swift's *Polite Conversation* with Falstaff

The 1740 stage production of Polite Conversation *based on Swift's text was briefly discussed in Chapter One. Here more details are provided about the actors, spectators, and Drury Lane performance of a text written before 'studio contracts prohibited independent thought'. Dialogue by Swift and Shakespeare is spoken in some passages.*

Henry Woodward glanced at the audience from behind the curtain. The spectators in the front rows looked very much like the actors backstage—all wearing Georgian finery. He glanced behind him, then out front again; it was hard to tell the groups apart. Was he standing on the right side of the curtain? The actress Kitty Clive joined him and whispered: 'Is the Countess of Puddledock where she should be?'

'In a most ornate white gown; it fills the entire box, and leaves no space for the Count. I assume that is why he had to sit elsewhere with another woman,' replied Woodward.

'So the drama already started out there, let ours begin, too,' said Clive, 'it is past six.'

'Curtain rising,' whispered the prompter.

One of Drury Lane's leading comedians, Henry Woodward never hesitated to accept his new role in *Polite Conversation*, although he had doubts about it. He had played fools before, but to portray Mr Neverout after acts Two and Five of *The Merry Wives of Windsor* made him feel doubly foolish. He was Slender in the Shakespeare play. First he wooed Mistress Anne Page, then courted Miss Notable in Swift's scenes. Falstaff, Pistol and Mistress Quickly would converse with him in one act, and he would dine with Georgian lords and ladies in the next. Mrs Clive insisted that one role that evening was enough for her singular talent.

When Reverend James Miller asked Woodward to perform in his adaptation of Swift's *Collection of Genteel and Ingenious Conversation*, the actor was flattered to be cast opposite the excellent Kitty Clive, and play bachelor suitor to her eligible Miss Notable. Miller described it as the greatest courtship since Falstaff chased Mistress Page and Mistress Ford at the same time. But Miller was no Shakespeare. He hardly changed Swift's demanding text, only shortened it, and combined it with Shakespeare's comedy, as if the two authors were interchangeable. (They were not.) Neverout and Notable still flirted wittily, after Falstaff in a laundry basket was thrown into the Thames. Like Shakespeare's characters, Swift's repeatedly fended off one another's advances. Only Swift's men and women assembled in a drawing room for tea, rather than a tavern for beer.

The Dean's compendium of speeches had originally been designed as an ironic text, allegedly created to instruct its readers in proper conduct and witty conversation; it was never intended for the stage. As Brecht would later write, 'Swift feigned innocence. He defended a way of thinking which he hated intensely with a great deal of ardor and thoroughness'. Brecht was referring to *A Modest Proposal* when he wrote these words about Swift in 1935; the same statement might apply to the polite conversations of Notable and Neverout, except that any hatred of the society depicted is leavened with the humour of wordplay and flirtation.

During the first reading in April of 1740, while Miller listened to the dialogue he wondered if the audience would be as polite as the Georgians portrayed on stage. The dialogue proceeded through puns, non sequiturs and jests at eighteenth-century English language, with only a few confrontations. Miller had not set out to disturb the audience, although satirists like Swift were not known to please the public with their black humour. Without seeking trouble, Miller had met enough of it already. Audiences rioted when his play *The Coffee House* opened in 1738. Templegate lawyers thought he was maligning their favourite coffee house hostess; he never meant to do so, but the lawyers in the front rows would not relent. *The Coffee House* spectators also disapproved of the role Theophilus Cibber took that night; his character was named Theophilus Cibber. The playwright allowed the notorious actor to portray himself with sympathy. Young Cibber had been hostilely portrayed on stage before— by others; audiences enjoyed disapproving of him. He was not cast in *Polite Conversation*. Nor was Miller's own association with the play widely advertised. A later record would list the afterpiece's dialogues 'written by D____ Swift,' assisted by 'Compiler unknown' and the text 'Apparently not published' (Scouten Part 3: 834). The text survived only because a handwritten copy was submitted to the Lord Chamberlain, and found its way to the Huntington Library in California.

Swift declined to attend the first performance. 'I read the polite dialogues already, sir', he wrote Miller, 'and they would not amuse me further, even in your august company'. Swift neglected to cite ill health as an excuse for staying away; he had been ailing, but kept that to himself. The Dean was interested enough to ask Woodward (rather than Miller) for a report on the London premiere of the play. He sought no further correspondence with Miller after the adaptor informed Swift his dialogues would be featured on a double bill with a Shakespeare comedy. But in a letter to Woodward from Dublin the satirist reportedly approved of the pairing, and remarked: 'The other author won't be there to object, why should I? Better Shakespeare than Colley Cibber.'

When Swift conceived the dialogues for a pamphlet on the art of conversation, he joked in the preface (attributed to Samuel Wagstaff) that he wrote enough to fill six plays by Colley Cibber. And Cibber's plays were not short. 'I make Miss Notable my heroine, and Mr. Thomas Neverout my hero', wrote Wagstaff in the preface, 'into their mouths I have put the liveliest questions, answers, repartees, and rejoinders; because my design was to propose them both as patterns for all young bachelors and single ladies to copy after'. The satirist was not entirely serious here; he exaggerated to say the least, and as an indication of his distance from Colley Cibber and the proposed models of speech, signed the preface with his Wagstaff pseudonym. (Later another satirist, one Groucho Marx, would also claim the name Wagstaff—Quincy Adams Wagstaff—when performing the role of college president in the film *Horse Feathers*, where he sang: 'Whatever it is, I'm against it'.)

Whatever Swift was against appeared in scenes of 'polite conversation' among well-educated, highborn lords and ladies who met for tea and for dinner. Their assembly in between acts of a Shakespeare comedy might have led some of the audience at Drury Lane on 23 April to question the surprising order of events. It was Shakespeare's birthday, however, and Swift's tea party added new wit to a celebration of the old. If only someone had said so aloud.

Miller briefly introduced the show with a prologue (his own), but that hardly prepared spectators for the polite pandemonium to follow.

> Clad in the armour of an hundred years
> Our author stands without an author's fears.
> For sure the hardest critick will not dare
> With snarling sounds to cry down ancient ware.

And so on. Miller introduced Swift's play as if its language was as aged, and therefore as venerable as Shakespeare's. In fact Swift wanted his dialogues to constitute a compendium of the past century's clichés, tired witticisms and maxims. The conversations were hardly ancient, however, completed just two years earlier, although Wagstaff in his preface claimed he spent decades collecting the quaint and charming lines.

In preparation for the evening, Henry Woodward and Kitty Clive privately read through some of their scenes, and tried to give their characters actions that suited their curious verbal exchanges. In one scene, wholly Swift's and not a jot of Shakespeare, they flirted with these lines:

NEVEROUT: Miss, your tongue runs before your wit; nothing can tame you but a husband.

MISS NOTABLE: Peace! I think I hear the church clock.

NEVEROUT: Why you know, as the fool thinks, miss, I'll think on this.

MISS: That's rhime, if you take it in time.

NEVEROUT: What! I see you are a poet.

MISS: Yes; if I had but the wit to shew it.

NEVEROUT: Miss, will you be so kind as to fill me a dish of tea.

MISS: Pray let your betters be served before you; I'm just going to fill one for myself; and, you know, the parson always christens his own child first.

NEVEROUT: But I saw you fill one just now for the colonel; well, I find kissing goes by favour.

MISS: But pray, Mr Neverout, what lady was that you were talking with in the side-Box last Tuesday?

NEVEROUT: Miss, can you keep a secret?

MISS: Yes, I can.

NEVEROUT: Well, miss, and so can I.

[As Miss rises, the chair falls behind her]

MISS: Well; I shan't be lady-mayoress this year.

NEVEROUT: No, miss, 'tis worse than that; you won't be married this year.

MISS: Lord! You make me laugh, though I ain't well.

[Neverout, as Miss is standing, pulls her suddenly on his lap.]

NEVEROUT: Now, colonel, come, sit down on my lap; more sacks upon the mill.

MISS: Let me go. Aren't you sorry for my heaviness?

NEVEROUT: No, miss; you are very light; but I don't say you are a light hussy. Pray take up the chair for your pains.

MISS: 'Tis but one body's labour, you may do it yourself; I wish you would be quiet, you have more tricks than a dancing bear.

[Neverout rises to take up the chair, and Miss sits in his]

NEVEROUT: You wouldn't be so soon in my grave, madam.

MISS: Lord! I have torn my petticoat with your odious romping; my rents are coming in; I'm afraid I shall fall into the ragman's hands.

NEVEROUT: I shall mend it, miss.

MISS: You mend it! Go, teach your grannam to suck eggs.

NEVEROUT: Why, miss, you are so cross, I could find in my heart to hate you.

MISS: With all my heart; there will be no love lost between us.

NEVEROUT: But pray, my lady Smart, does not miss look as if she could
   eat me without salt?
MISS: I'll make you one day sup sorrow for this.
NEVEROUT: Well, follow your own way, you'll live the longer.

The dialogue was not spectacular; but the physical comedy devised by
Woodward and Clive added an element of surprise. Clive walked over to a
side box near the apron as she asked about the lady formerly seated there.
Woodward joined her, climbed into the box, looked around, asked a lady
in the box if she could keep a secret, then climbed back on stage to say,
'And well miss, so can I'. At which point, as Clive rose and her chair fell,
Woodward pulled her to his lap, raised her up like a toy while he remained
seated, then stood up with her held high until he lowered the actress and
she seated herself humbly. Woodward indeed had 'more tricks than a
dancing bear', and Clive appeared to be his cub.
   Her torn petticoat was instantly, magically removed and handed to the
lady when Neverout said he would mend it. After suggesting Miss Notable
could eat him, Woodward gave her knife and fork and placed his head atop
a china plate on the table. For a moment it looked as if he had served his
head on a platter, with his body concealed behind the tablecloth.
   Spectators were not quiet during these scenes. The woman in the box
visited by Woodward proclaimed: 'This is a private box, sir, and I'll ask you
to leave as you have a fine view of the stage already.' When the comedian
lifted Clive into the air, cries of 'It's a ballet' and 'Next she'll be flying'
were heard.
   In an earlier production Woodward had been called Lun Junior, after
the great pantomime artist Lun, alias John Rich, and deservedly so; the
actor knew all Rich's pantomime artist's manoeuvres, and could move
as deftly as an acrobat. Clive for her part knew enough to go along with
Woodward's act. She pretended to be humbled and manhandled when in
fact she was quite proud of her self-restraint; she could have followed his
example, and thrown him off balance, or placed her head on an adjacent
plate to match his move. When she told him this, Woodward insisted she
follow through; it would add to the flirtatious rivalry of the couple. 'Miss
Notable's character requires notable acts', he said. Clive not only put her
head on a platter next to his, she then put an apple in his mouth, another
notable act, before Neverout could say: 'Well, follow your own way, you'll
live longer.' 'We both would have the world served us on a plate', quipped
Woodward, as the apple rolled across the table.
   The two talking heads on plates then covered themselves with napkins,
a kind of curtain closing the scene. Georgians rarely dined with such
antic manners, but the unruly behaviour suited Swift's anarchistic conversations.

Centuries later, Orwell would praise Swift 'as a rebel and iconoclast . . .
A Tory anarchist despising authority while disbelieving in liberty'. Breton
in the preface to his surrealist anthology of black humour credited Swift
as the 'inventor of savage and gallows humor . . . Remarkably modern in
spirit . . . Possessed by a frantic need for justice'. Had either of them seen
the 1740 performance at Drury Lane, it might have confirmed their views,
as the play brought pantomime arts and Georgian wit together, in between
acts of Elizabethan comedy. It had all the promise of a Tory anarchist's
feast of unreason with aristocratic Londoners trading well-worn maxims,
folk sayings, and witticisms, an exhausted language consciously chosen by
Swift to demonstrate the decline and fall of fashion in his own (or rather
England's) high society. The conversations would have been all the more
exhausted and past Swift's time had Orwell or Breton heard them spoken
in the 1930s.

At Drury Lane in 1740 another kind of disorder was added through
the non sequitur of Shakespeare's *Merry Wives of Windsor* commanding
the stage before and between Swift's conversations. Language here
too was out of date. With their comic colloquial phrases, Shakespeare's
comedians could have been the grandparents of Notable and Neverout.
The bawdy dialogue was admittedly from an earlier age, and not the finest
of Shakespeare's wit, but masterful nonetheless. After his unexpected
submersion in the Thames, wet but not drowned Falstaff (portrayed with
bellows by James Quin) said:

> FALSTAFF: Come, let me pour in some sack to the Thames water; for
> my belly's as cold as if I had swallowed snowballs for pills to cool the
> reins. Call her in!
> BARDOLF: Come in, woman!
> QUICKLY: By your leave; I cry you mercy: give your worship good
> morrow.
> FALSTAFF: Take away these chalices. Go brew me a pottle of sack finely.
> BARDOLF: With eggs, sir?
> FALSTAFF: Simple of itself; I'll no pellet-sperm in my brewage. How now!
> QUICKLY: Marry, sir, I come to your worship from Mistress Ford.
> FALSTAFF: Mistress Ford! I have had ford enough; I was thrown into the
> ford; I have my belly full of ford.
> QUICKLY: Alas the day! good heart, that was not her fault; she does so
> take on with her men; they mistook their erection.
> FALSTAFF: So did I mine, to build upon a foolish woman's promise.
> QUICKLY: Well, she laments, sir, for it, that it would yearn your heart to
> see it . . . She desires you once more to come to her between eight
> and nine: I must carry her word quickly: she'll make you amends, I
> warrant you.

FALSTAFF: Between nine and ten, sayest thou?
QUICKLY: Eight and nine, sir.
FALSTAFF: Well, be gone: I will not miss her.

Falstaff's assignations failed to bring him the money and adoration he anticipated, and Mistress Ford was far less available to him than Miss Notable to Mr Neverout; but the couples, or would-be couples, in their separate stories complemented each other in odd, unpredictable manners.

Woodward as George Slender in the Shakespeare play competed for Miss Anne Page's hand, which he lost to a gentleman named Fenton. His character was not as witty a wooer as Neverout, but he had his comic lines, particularly after the night he mistook a boy dressed in white for Anne, and brought the lad to church.

SLENDER: I came yonder at Eton to marry Mistress Anne Page, and she's a great lubberly boy. If it had not been i' the church, I would have swinged him, or he should have swinged me. If I did not think it had been Anne Page, would I might never stir!—and 'tis a postmaster's boy . . . For all that he was in woman's apparel, I would not have had him . . .

MRS PAGE [Anne's Mother]: Good George, be not angry: I knew of your purpose; turned my daughter into green, and, indeed, she is now with the doctor at the deanery, and there married.

Shakespeare's cast originally featured boys in all the women's parts, so it was more understandable that Slender might mistake a postmaster's boy for Miss Page. In Woodward's time, such errors were less excusable, but funnier, perhaps, particularly as the scene was only retold by the comedian, and not shown on stage. At the conclusion of this act (Five in *Merry Wives*), Woodward returned as Neverout, to lose (or at least not marry) another young woman. Their last exchange before parting went this way:

NEVEROUT: Miss, I hope you'll dream of your sweetheart.
MISS NOTABLE: Oh, no doubt of it: I believe I shan't be able to sleep for dreaming of him.

But before that parting, a few moments of romance had been charted by Swift, and these deserve inclusion in the summary, too. Swift's concession to love is fleeting:

MISS NOTABLE: I own, I love Mr. Neverout, as the devil loves holy water: I love him like pye, I'd rather the devil had him than I.
NEVEROUT: Miss, I'll tell you one thing.

NOTABLE: Come, here's t'ye, to stop your mouth.

NEVEROUT: I'd rather you would stop it with a kiss.

NOTABLE: A kiss! Marry come up, my dirty cousin; are you no sicker? Lord! I wonder what fool it was that first invented kissing!

NEVEROUT: Well, I'm very dry.

NOTABLE: Then you're the better to burn, the worse to fry.

When staged at Drury Lane, Miss Notable stopped Neverout's mouth by holding a glass of wine up to Woodward's lips. He drank before saying he would prefer a kiss, and drank again after explaining he was 'very dry'. Then the comedian lowered her glass and took the kiss before she could recommend his burning. Her face turned quite red at the same time. (How Clive turned her face red on cue was a mystery of her art.)

Lady Puddledock applauded the romantic interlude, and confided to her husband the Count (still seated in another box with another woman): 'That's how it is done, my dear.' 'He knows that already, my lady, I'll swear he does', replied the Count's lovely companion, Miss Celia Kelly. The audience applauded that exchange as if it was part of the play— and perhaps it was, since Swift referred to Lady Puddledock in his own dialogues, too.

Henry Woodward sent Swift a personal letter after the first (and only) night of the play. 'Reverend Dean', he began,

I never sought to confine my theatrical superiority to harlequin entertainments, and gladly took the part of Neverout that you ingeniously conceived for a comedian such as myself. The first night of the play was in fact its only night at Drury Lane, and I fear we shall not see its like again on a London stage. A few friends in the audience found the humour appealing, a few enemies were appalled. But most of the spectators and critics wondered why Mistress Quickly never spoke to Neverout, and why Miss Notable was never wooed by Falstaff. The conjoining of your play with Shakespeare's was a marriage of two authors that gave Drury Lane an attractive double bill, and gave some actors (myself included) a new doubling of parts. But divorce may be the order of the day. Regrettably, the playbill did not indicate where one play stopped and the next began; some of the audience thought your scenes written (oddly) by Shakespeare. Perhaps that is a great disguised compliment to your Deanship. You have enlarged the lore of Falstaff and his companions so it now includes Neverout, Notable, and Swift.

During the Second World War, George Orwell recorded another polite conversation in which Swift was involved. In a 1942 radio broadcast, during which neither speaker could be seen, only heard outside the studio, Orwell asked Swift to 'admit that we have made a certain amount of progress' over two hundred years. Listeners heard Swift answer:

> Progress in quantity, yes. The buildings are taller and the vehicles move faster. Human beings are more numerous and commit greater follies. A battle kills a million where it used to kill a thousand. And in the matter of great men, as you still call them, I must admit that your age outdoes mine. Whereas previously some petty tyrant was considered to have reached the highest point of human fame if he laid waste a single province and pillaged half a dozen towns, your great men nowadays can devastate whole continents and reduce entire races of men to the status of slaves (Orwell 1985: 113).

It was nothing like the exchange between Miss Notable and Mr Neverout; times had changed, the language had changed. Falstaff was silent, probably due to his wartime preference for discretion. But even in wartime, in a new century, Swift still showed himself a master of the art of polite conversation. A later reader would describe his tea table dialogues as a satire of wealthy, corrupt Georgians; but Swift (or Wagstaff) disclaimed such an aim in his preface to the volume: 'although there seems to be a close resemblance between the two words *politeness* and *politicks*, yet no ideas are more inconsistent in their natures'. And to this day politics rarely benefits from polite conversations like Swift's. When Orwell sensed a 'special connection between politics and the debasement of language', he added 'where [this] is not true, it will generally be found that the writer is some kind of rebel'.

CHAPTER NINE

Henry Fielding, Brechtian Before Brecht

When Walter Benjamin praised Brecht as an artist who did 'not supply the [theatre] production apparatus without, at the same time, within the limits of the possible, changing that apparatus', he might have been writing about Fielding's politicizing of the stage—promoting through innovative art and his own theatre company 'publick Resentment' toward a government minister and other officials, as the *Daily Gazeteer* accused the Georgian author on 7 May 1737 (Benjamin 93). To do this, Fielding further developed ballad opera and rehearsal play forms with his alternative theatre company—the Great Mogul's Company of English Comedians. The company was announced as 'Newly Imported' when Fielding's satire *Pasquin* opened at the Haymarket on 5 March 1736. His mock-pantomime *Tumble-Down Dick* was added to the repertoire on April 29th. Lewis notes the irony in Fielding's use of the term 'Great Mogul', which previously had been 'used to describe theatre managers, notably Theophilus Cibber, because of dictatorial powers they wielded' at Drury Lane and Covent Garden (Lewis 150). Those moguls limited actor opportunities through cartel agreements. 'Great Mogul' Fielding had no such power over actors in his unlicensed theatre; but he became a rival of the other managers through his comic writing and season planning, and the popularity of the works staged. Like Brecht, he created his own theatre company capable of innovative and politically engaged artistry.

Also like Brecht, Fielding early in his career found a playhouse to which he returned later, and made his own through direction of its company. In Fielding's case the house was the Little Theatre in the Haymarket, where his farce *Tom Thumb* opened to acclaim in 1730, and where his later satires also thrived. In Brecht's case, the Theater am Schiffbauerdamm, where *The Threepenny Opera* opened in 1928, became the site of his Berliner Ensemble two decades later. Brecht in his *Messingkauf Dialogues* erroneously reports that in 1928–29, around the time his collaboration with director Erwin Piscator began, 'each of them had his theatre, Piscator one of his own am Nollendorfplatz and the Augsburger [Brecht] one am Schiffbauerdamnn, where he trained his actors'. The English translator of this passage, John Willett, questions Brecht's statement in a footnote: 'At the time in question (*c.*1928–9) the Theater am Schiffbauerdamm was actually directed by Ernst-Josef Aufricht' (Brecht 1965: 68–69). Was Brecht mistaken here, or was he convinced that, even if Aufricht was nominally running the theatre, the Augsburger was the one responsible for its artistic innovations? When Brecht returned to the site late in his career, he made it more distinctively his own space, with actors trained for Epic theatre, and his wife, Helene Weigel, performing lead roles.

Unlike Brecht, Fielding late in his career had to disband his company despite popular support for it. The Licensing Act of 1737 and the closure of the Haymarket did not completely silence Fielding, or end his writing about theatre. Following the example of the Ghost of Common Sense who enters his play *Pasquin* after the Queen of Ignorance triumphs, the author continued to haunt England's theatres, only his new satire appeared in journals, novels and pseudonymous pamphlets instead of theatre houses. After 1737, his dissenting satirist's voice could be heard, and still can be heard, in journalistic publications attributed to Hercules Vinegar, Sir Alexander Drawcansir, John Trott-Plaid, and Mr. T . . . . C . . . . ., as well as some signed under his own name. (One play later attributed to him opened at Drury Lane in 1742; but critics still debate the authorship of the unsigned play, *Miss Lucy in Town*, which was not a political satire.)

If there is any doubt that Fielding regarded theatre as a politically engaged art, it might be allayed by one essay he composed late in life. Although he was joking to some extent, in 1752 he announced plans for a new book in which theatre would be seen as inseparable from politics:

> . . . The Government I mean is that of the Stage; a Government founded on a Set of Politics peculiar to itself, and practised by no other Nation in the Known Parts of the World. . . . No State, of which we have any Record in History, hath ever suffered a greater Variety of Revolutions, been engaged in more continued Wars, or torn to Pieces with more intestine Divisions. . . . The Subject deserves to be treated more at large, and I am now preparing a Book for the Press in which these several Matters will be more copiously explained. (Fielding 1964: 224)

Fielding never completed his book about the State of the Theatre, its Revolutions and its Government. But he issued its equivalent in instalments: a series of journal columns about actors and managers, and a number of stage plays that comically discuss their own innovations as well as playhouse rivalries. Fielding's writing on these subjects describes a theatrical empire demarcated by the larger stages of Drury Lane and Covent Garden, and unlicensed smaller ones such as the Little Theatre in the Haymarket and a booth at Bartholomew Fair—precincts where he thrived until the government of England took over the government of his stage.

Henry Fielding's theatre history book might have concluded with the censorship law introduced in 1737; by June of that year he was deprived of the right to produce plays in the Haymarket. Legislated censorship, closure of his playhouse, and objections to his satire in the press could be cited as evidence of his playwriting's popularity before it was repressed. The satirist won the enmity of England's first Minister, Robert Walpole, and leading theatre managers, because he threatened their empires theatrical and political. His achievements led George Bernard Shaw to call Fielding England's 'greatest dramatist, with the single exception of Shakespeare . . . between the Middle Ages and the nineteenth century [the period before Shaw arrived]'. Facing government censorship himself in the 1890s, under the same Licensing Act that Fielding suffered, Shaw praised the Georgian playwright as a man who 'devoted his genius to the task of exposing and destroying parliamentary corruption, then at its height' before he was 'gagged' (Shaw xiii–xiv). The reference to Fielding's adversarial playwriting recalls praise given to Shaw himself by Brecht, who called the author of *Major Barbara* and *Saint Joan* a 'terrorist' whose 'brand of terror is . . . that of humour' (Brecht 1964: 10). Fielding deserved both sets of compliments. His finest satires alarmed government censors much as Shaw and Brecht did through dramatic incursions into political and social discourse. It could be argued that Brecht faced book-burnings and government-sponsored interrogations far more severe than Fielding's persecution; but that does not make Fielding's satires any less disturbing, historically speaking, to the government officials who objected to his plays.

After his own 'wars' and 'revolutions' within London theatres, after his finest stage satires were written and incurred government censure, Fielding's extratheatrical performances in journal columns and a memoir followed the tendencies shown earlier within the plays written up to 1737, where many odd characters can be heard joking, debating, even rioting over the empires ruled by government ministers and theatre managers. Act II, Scene I of *Pasquin* (1736) includes instructions for a riot: stage directions place a 'Mob on each side of the Stage, crying out promiscuously' as they 'fall together by the Ears, and cudgel one another off the stage'. Part of a play-within-a-play mocking both political parties before an election, as well as Walpole's plan for an excise tax, the riot was meant to be comic; it hurt no one, at least not physically. At that point Fielding was not asking his audience to speak out or campaign against the Prime Minister and his allies; the spectators already had done so in many cases. Stage satires such as *Pasquin* and *Eurydice Hissed*, and Fielding's journal columns enlarged and celebrated existing opposition to Walpole that was far more vocal in the street than inside playhouses.

John O'Brien adeptly observes that Walpole's

concern and his ability to marshal support against such plays [as Fielding's], and ultimately to pass the Licensing Act, were also prompted by the widespread public agitation and occasional rioting over the effect of the Gin Act in 1736 . . . discontent that had been observable since at least the time of Walpole's attempt to pass the Excise Act in 1733–34 . . . [and exacerbated] by weakening economic conditions owing in part to overproduction in the colonies (O'Brien 2004: 192).

Walpole could not control some of the extratheatrical sources of discontent (including pseudonymous journal entries); but he was able to quell theatre audience laughter at his government, and end Fielding's reign by instituting the Licensing Act. If a 1780 account by Thomas Davies is to be believed, Walpole

had received such provocations from Mr. Fielding, in his plays and farces, just before that time [June 1737], acted at the little theatre in the Haymarket, that he [Walpole] was not displeased to have it in his power to stop the current of stage abuse against him, which then ran very high.

Davies gives special credit to Fielding's provocative portrayal of a ministerial levee in *Eurydice Hissed*, and to a scene in *The Historical Register for the Year 1736* where a Walpole-like leader fiddled while members of parliament danced to his tune at the Haymarket playhouse. (Davies Volume II, 1780: 151).

Fielding's reign at the Haymarket unceremoniously ceased before the Licensing Act took effect, when the building's owner John Potter obstructed rehearsals of *Macheath turn'd pyrate* (based on John Gay's *Polly*) and another new production in the final weeks of the 1737 season. Potter wanted to keep his theatre free of government interference, too, and did so by filling the popular performance space with timber and bricks instead of people. Landlord Potter evidently created this obstruction with Walpole regime encouragement, since he billed the government for his expenses after closing the playhouse. The cost of 'taking down the scenes & decorations so the theatre was Rendered Incapable of having any Play', and filling the space 'with deale & timber Bricks and Lime' came to twelve pounds and twelve shillings, less than the weekly salary of some actors (Hume 245–46).

Until he lost the space, Fielding as lessee and manager oversaw his company's play selection and rehearsals at the Haymarket. He never had greater liberty, or lost greater liberty in the theatre, than that he enjoyed there in the spring of 1737. As his own producer, Fielding also could earn more money than playwrights usually received. Normally they were paid if their play reached a third performance, then a sixth, then a ninth. This gave Fielding another motive for independence from the Patent houses, since his plays were quite popular and remunerative. The fact that his oppositional satire sold well must have incensed political and theatrical adversaries, and added to the 'severe' tension that Raymond Williams says existed 'between the monopoly patent theatres [that sought to 'restrict serious drama to minority audiences'], and the so-called 'minor theatres' [such as the Haymarket] pushing up everywhere. . . .' (Williams 1980: 132).

One, Two, Many Fieldings

During the period Fielding enjoyed his liberty as a playwright, numerous pseudonymous satires could be found in journals and on stage. Unacknowledged authors (not all of them poets like Shelley's 'unacknowledged legislators') thrived, from the early eighteenth-century writings of Swift, Pope, Gay and Arbuthnot, who collectively used the pseudonym Scriblerus, to Fielding as Scriblerus Secundus, and quite possibly as Mr T . . . . C . . . . ., author of *An Apology for the Life of Mr. T . . . . C . . . . .* in 1740. (The 1733 play *The Stage-Mutineers* discussed later, and Fielding's *Historical Register for the Year 1736* also were originally printed without an author's name on the title page.) Fielding produced other satires by unknown authors at the Little Theatre in the Haymarket, and appears to have inspired satire at other theatre houses, too. Cross observes that by 1737 the Haymarket author's stage satires 'were so successful that the managers of the patent theatres took the alarm; and to compete with him they were forced to provide plays of a decided political cast'. A February 1737 Drury Lane play contained 'in the songs and dialogue remarks on the bribe as the courtier's instrument for obtaining what he wants' (Cross 225). In light of these pseudonymous practices, it might be said that Fielding's satire had many authors, or there were one, two, many Fieldings. While corruption was widespread, satire of corruption was spreading, too. This development might have led Walpole's supporters to institute new censorship even without the introduction of *The Golden Rump* (discussed soon) and its scandalous jests at royalty.

Satire may be what first drew Fielding himself to the theatre. He entered the scene in 1728–29, around the time John Gay's *Polly* was banned from stage production, after Gay had become rich (and producer Rich gay) from the success of *The Beggar's Opera*. Fielding's own first play, *Love in Several Masques* (1728), was hardly political satire; but later the same year, Martin and Ruthe Battestin speculate, the playwright anonymously published a satiric ballad sung by Walpole's opponents (Battestin with Battestin 1989:

68). Fielding subsequently aligned himself with the satirical practices of Swift and Gay (although he did not necessarily share their Tory party affiliation) by signing the preface to his 1731 mock-heroic tragedy, *The Tragedy of Tragedies*, 'H. Scriblerus Secundus' ('H' for 'Henry'). That pseudonym linked him to the men who had co-authored mock-scholarly memoirs and essays using the name Martinus Scriblerus. Fielding planned to have Scriblerus Secundus make a stage appearance in *The Grub-Street Opera* (1731), a ballad opera that followed the example of Gay's *Beggar's Opera* in more than its title, as it employed the musical form of social and political satire Gay first popularized. Scriblerus Secundus never made his stage debut in 1731, because the play was withdrawn from production before opening, probably to avoid government censure. Cross cites mockery of Walpole within *The Grub Street Opera* as the reason that 'Government had in some way intervened [prior to its 1731 opening], presumably in a quiet manner through the Lord Chamberlain, as the newspapers speak of no arrests' (Cross 110). The manner was so quiet that the circumstances behind the withdrawal remain unknown.

More is known about *The Fall of Mortimer*, another anti-Walpole play staged in 1731 at the Haymarket. Fielding was not the author, but an arrest warrant issued for the *Mortimer* cast ended the play's run, and made it clear that artistic freedom was at risk years before 1737. So did the ban placed on Gay's *Polly* in December of 1728, and a 1730 government agent raid on the offices of the journal, *The Craftsman*, which had been critical of Walpole (Goldgar 68). In 1731 Fielding may not yet have been a writer prepared to risk reprisal. Later in his career, while pseudonyms and satiric impersonations could have protected him from arrest, he was undeniably, visibly in charge of the Haymarket and its satire. Given his 1737 commitment to the staging of *Macheath turn'd pyrate*, it is tempting to say that Fielding in that year assumed Gay's mantle, much as Marx said revolution of a later period employed earlier costumes and battle cries. He was pirating Gay's pirate play to defy Walpole again. And with fitting symmetry, the play first banned in the season Fielding entered London's theatre scene was unable to open once again at the termination of his stage satire efforts. While it has been said (even in these pages, below) that the Licensing Act was passed to keep a play titled *The Golden Rump* out of production, someone behind the scenes in government chambers also must have wanted to insure that *Polly* did not return from banishment.

A few critics, Hume for one, have asked why Fielding did not vocally protest against the Licensing Act after its passage. In fact he continued to ridicule Walpole and the Cibbers, and the censors; but not through stage satire. The proliferation of satires by unacknowledged authors at the Haymarket in the spring of 1737 previewed a practice that would continue for years. If he could not write for the stage without licence, he would write (or his friends would write) unsigned and pseudonymous journal columns, and later the counterfeit autobiography of Mr T . . . . C . . . . ., often quite critical of those in high places. The author became an actor, and gave himself disguises and new locations in which to perform. He rarely left behind a handwritten manuscript. His contemporary, Arthur Murphy, said Fielding wrote some scenes on tobacco wrappers. Identity hid in the anonymity of unsigned columns or (before the ban) unsigned dialogues. Besides protecting an individual's identity, the anonymity also gave Fielding's collaborators a more prominent group identity at the Haymarket: the Great Mogul's Company of English Comedians received top billing in advertisements. The source of attraction was not any one performer or writer, although Fielding always stood behind the scenes. His name was humorously deleted or downplayed in listings that simply attributed *The Historical Register for the Year 1736* and *Eurydice Hissed* to 'the Author of Pasquin'. *Pasquin* itself had within its cast of characters two authors, Trapwit and Fustian. Yet another playwright, Spatter, introduced the tragedy inside *Eurydice Hissed*, and Medley claimed to have written much of *The Historical Register*. Fielding in playbills and listings acknowledged a sizable group of playwrights (Trapwit, Fustian, Spatter, etc.) involved in his Haymarket productions; some were fictitious, some not. Colley Cibber tried to blot out Fielding's own name by referring to him only as 'a broken wit' in his 1740 *Apology*; but historians have had no trouble deciphering the reference. Too much about Fielding's life in the theatre remains known for him to be blotted out by a rival playwright or a censorship act.

Much as actors and colleagues supported Fielding at the Haymarket in 1736–37, Brecht benefited from the support of artistic collaborators known as the Brecht Collective when he wrote *A Man's a Man* (1926) and other plays. Later at the Berliner Ensemble he worked so closely with his assistant directors and dramaturgs that at least one guest (Carl Weber, who became a director there, too) could not tell who was in charge when he first arrived. The rehearsal looked like a series of casual conversations going on during a break. During this period, Brecht and his assistants adapted plays by Molière, Lenz, Shakespeare, and Farquhar, playwrights who became, as it were, his collaborators too.

Fielding's Ensemble, Brecht's and Piscator's

Among the actors participating in the Great Mogul's productions at the Haymarket were Roberts, Jones, Machen, Boothby, Pullen, Lacy, Yates, Miss Jones, Mrs Haywood, Mrs Lacy, Mrs Charke, 'Madame la Charmante, piping-hot from Paris', 'Mons De la Soupe Maigre'. They constituted a company of satiric actors, while Fielding served as company manager and resident playwright from spring 1736 through to May 1737.

'Exactly how Fielding went about assembling actors we will probably never know', according to Hume (Hume 1988: 206); but the playwright knew many of them from earlier collaborations, and they must have known him from the continuing popularity of plays such as his Molière adaptation, *The Mock Doctor*, in the Patent theatres.

Hume argues that Fielding's formation of his own company was a last resort, and he 'became manager of his own company because that was the only way he could get his work performed' (Hume 200). From another perspective (call it the 'early Brechtian' view), the creation of his independent company can be seen as a culmination of earlier one-play productions rather than seasons of his work at the Haymarket, which had given him liberty to write, cast and direct as he pleased, practices he sought to continue. McCrea distinguishes the 'farces in the tradition of the Scriblerus Club, satirizing human weakness and representing a scene of corruption and folly' staged at the Haymarket from Fielding's Drury Lane plays, 'mostly five-act comedies in the tradition of Sir Richard Steele and Colley Cibber' (McCrea 58). Fielding's satiric afterpieces rejected Cibber as well as his five-act structure. The success of *Pasquin* at the Haymarket in spring 1736 must have encouraged the satirist to create new work for the same space the following season. In spring 1737 his grateful 'Dedication to the Public' accompanying the publication of *The Historical Register* and *Eurydice Hissed* informed Fielding's supporters:

> The very great indulgence you have shown in my performance at the little theatre, these two last years, have encouraged me to the proposal of a subscription for carrying on that theatre, for beautifying and enlarging it and procuring a better company of actors.

With that encouragement, Fielding's Great Mogul's Company continued to move against the current. Its manager was 'intent on being a trouble maker' according to Scouten; but the audience welcomed such 'trouble' and the apparatus that supported it (Scouten Part 3, Volume I: lxxxvi). Walter Benjamin later saw Brecht's theatre 'apparatus' change to serve socialism. Fielding's theatre served an earlier political cause, the opposition to Walpole sometimes called the 'Broad-Bottom' movement. While that opposition had its own parliamentary spokesmen, its heterogeneous supporters included landed property owners, excise-tax-resisting merchants, and Tories as well as satiric playwrights. Members of the same diverse group probably supported the Great Mogul's company. Fielding wrote in his 21 May 1737 letter to *Common Sense*:

> I shall not be industrious to deny . . . that I am buoy'd up by the greatest Wits, and finest Gentlemen of the Age; and Patroniz'd by the Great, the

Sensible, and the Witty in the Opposition. Of such Patrons I shall be always proud.

The increasing number of patrons awaiting his plays, and the 'Great, Sensible and Witty in the Opposition' standing among his friends, including the Prince of Wales, disturbed Walpole's ministry at the same time as it cheered the playwright on.

The Philosopher in Brecht's *Messingkauf Dialogues* might have been speaking of Fielding's Haymarket when he contended: 'The theatre was acting in the public interest, so it must have aroused the interest of the public' (Brecht 1965: 24). Brecht knew a comparable theatre experience before he started the Berliner Ensemble. Piscator's experimental company in Berlin, with which the German playwright collaborated, was later described by the Dramaturg in the *Messingkauf Dialogues*:

> It was an up-to-date theatre, not only when dealing with topical questions but also when its problems were hundreds of years old. A team of playwrights used to conduct more or less non-stop discussion on the stage, and this discussion continued right through the whole immense city in newspapers, drawing-rooms, pubs and cafes (Brecht 1965: 65).

Was this a later version of the Little Theatre in the Haymarket? Fielding needed an unlicensed theatre, the Haymarket, to house plays and a team of playwrights dealing with topical questions that probably would not have been accepted at the Patent theatre houses.

Fielding and Garrick Take Charon's Ferry

Fielding's versions of *The Mock Doctor* (1732) and *The Miser* (1733) became standards in London's Patent theatre repertoires, and continued to be shown after he left the playwriting profession. His jests at wealth and upper-class life derived from Molière's in these adaptations were not aggressively 'political' insofar as they did not refer in detail to British government officials or prominent artists, like Fielding's later satires; but in retrospect, they can be seen as part of a progression in the author's career. As an English Molière he mocks doctors and miserly men of wealth. He also writes satires about tragic bombast and luckless playwrights early in his career, variants on Molière's rehearsal play, *The Impromptu of Versailles*. Of course Fielding never writes at the invitation of the court, although he seeks Walpole's approval at least once. Later (in his *Tartuffe* phase?) he moves into 'a libel against the ministry'—or alleged libel—in 1736–37. The later oppositional drama turns out to sell as well as his English versions of Molière's farces, once Fielding has his own company of actors, his own 'forms and instruments of production' at the Haymarket, and he need not submit to the whims of Patent theatre managers like the Cibbers, Rich or Fleetwood.

Before Brecht adapted Gay and Molière for his *Umfunktionierung* of drama, Fielding turned to them, as well as ancient Greek drama. Brecht also shared Fielding's interest in Aristophanes. In two 1946 letters the Germań author recorded plans to write a 'revue' based on *Plutus*, the Aristophanic farce about the god of wealth (Brecht 1990: 321, 421). The same play was translated into English by Fielding—with a co-translator— who wrote an introduction to the work in 1742. Perhaps both playwrights saw in ancient satire of wealth anticipation of their own concerns. Fielding the classicist knew the work of Aristophanes, and consciously reutilized ancient Greek practices of stage satire as early as 1730 in *The Author's Farce*, where, as in *The Frogs*, Charon ferries a variety of characters across the River Styx. David Garrick was to employ Charon a few years later in his first afterpiece, *Lethe* (1740), and may have been inspired in this by Fielding's earlier depiction of the boatman, although he too would have known classical literature.

State of Emergency, False Alarm

The spate of satires at the Haymarket in Fielding's last months there suggests another parallel between this early Brechtian's stage career and Brecht's: both artists responded with creativity and defiance to 'a state of emergency', as Benjamin termed the crisis his countrymen faced during the rise of fascism. The state of emergency that threatened to extinguish oppositional culture, and forced Brecht to flee Hitler's Germany also led him to write plays directed against Nazi tyranny and war, notably the cycle *Fear and Misery of the Third Reich*, *The Resistible Rise of Arturo Ui* and the screenplay for *Hangmen Also Die*, as well as drafts of *Mother Courage* and *The Caucasian Chalk Circle*. For Fielding the 'state of emergency' that ultimately closed his theatre led to the aforementioned frenzy of new satires and farces, and a period of pseudonymous journalism. You can hear the situation reflected in lines like those spoken by the playwright Pillage to a Poet in *Eurydice Hissed*: 'You know my farce comes on today and I have many enemies. I hope you will stand by me.' The Poet bravely replies: 'Depend on me, never fear your enemies. I'll warrant we make more noise than they.' This vow was first spoken at the Haymarket on 13 April 1737, less than two months before the theatre closed. Pillage can be seen as a stand-in for Walpole as well as Fielding; both faced trouble at the theatre in this period, and farceur Pillage's manoeuvring resembles that of a first Minister.

While Fielding himself may be only half-serious here, he has the Muse in *Eurydice Hissed* articulate a fervent defence of liberty and rejection of oppression, a call for social conscience that would qualify his Muse as an eighteenth-century Brechtian:

> Sooner will I whet
> The Ordinary of Newgate's leaden Quill;
> Sooner will I indite the annual Verse,
> Which City Bellmen, or Court Laureates sing;
> Sooner with thee in humble Garret dwell,
> And thou, or else thy Muse disclaims thy Pen,
> Would'st sooner starve, ay, even in Prison starve,
> Than vindicate Oppression for thy Bread,
> Or write down Liberty to gain thy own.

In the months before June of 1737, theatre itself became Fielding's alternative to existing government: his liberty, a law unto itself, his shadow government, where supportive spectators were constituents and actors were the mock-legislators. In his defiance of would-be censors, he opened satire after satire, while legislators debated bills to declare actors vagabonds and censor playwrights. Fielding practised a form of the 'political disobedience' Bernard Harcourt attributed to the Occupy Wall Street movement in 2013: not the same as civil disobedience, 'political disobedience' 'resists the very way in which we are governed . . . challenges the conventional way in which political governance takes place and laws are enforced . . . turns its back on the political institutions and actors who govern us . . .,' and, I would add, finds new roles for its own actors as it mocks the theatrical poses of those in power (Harcourt 47).

For all his references to the theatre empire where actors become kings and ministers, Fielding only once wrote a play critical of George II; as the author of *The Welsh Opera*, revised as *The Grub Street Opera* (1731) he appears to have altered and moderated its references to the King's feud with his son the Prince of Wales, to avoid trouble. During the crisis Fielding faced at the Haymarket in spring 1737 he was accused of far greater disrespect. Walpole and his allies circulated a play titled *The Golden Rump* (or alleged excerpts from a probably non-existent play) to increase support for censorship; this satiric play, never staged or published, reportedly ridiculed the King and his golden posterior. The satire was considered seditious, and cited as evidence that theatre had to be more fully controlled by the government, to prevent horrid insults to the throne. The exact source of the controversial play has been debated, with some details provided in *An Apology for the Life of Mr. T . . . . C . . . . ., Comedian* (discussed more fully in Chapter Fourteen), and by Thomas Davies in his 1780 biography of David Garrick. Davies reports that a theatre manager gave the script to Walpole and said a dire financial situation had 'reduced' him (the manager) 'to the necessity of acting a dramatick piece, which would certainly fill his house . . . ; but, though he wished to mend his fortune . . . he abhorred the principles and the slander [in the play]'. To assist the troubled theatre manager, Walpole reportedly paid Giffard of Goodman's Fields one thousand pounds for *The Golden Rump*, and alarmed legislators by letting them read it. They then voted in favour of the Licensing Act. 'Thus,' concludes Davies, 'at a very cheap rate, the ministry gained the power of hindering the stage from speaking any language that was displeasing to them: and it has been said, that the whole matter was a contrivance of Sir Robert Walpole' (Davies 1780 Vol. II: 151–52).

Davies's account of the scandal suggests that Walpole himself created the 'state of emergency'; without his involvement, the 'dangerous' play might never have been circulated. Perhaps it would have been staged by Giffard; but it was more profitable for the manager not to do so. Walpole did not write *The Golden Rump*, but for his promotion of its dangers and arrangement of its private reading, he might be regarded as the Other Fielding, the unknown satirist whose play in the end stopped Fielding's stage satire—the anti-theatrical playwright to end all anti-theatrical playwrights. (John Gay also met with objections to dialogue he never wrote; in the preface to *Polly* he protested that before the play's ban 'particular passages which were not in the Play were quoted and propagated' to support false accusations of 'slander and calumny against particular great persons'. Was this too Walpole's handiwork, or that of Walpole's friends?)

Unstaged, unpublished, of unknown authorship, *The Golden Rump* was a threat seen only by legislators who read the text, or said they read it. The state of emergency here anticipated recent ones discussed by Slavoj Zizek:

> the state we are approaching in developed countries around the globe, where this or that form of emergency state (deployed against the terrorist threat, against immigrants, and so on) is simply accepted as a measure necessary to guarantee the normal run of things (Zizek 47).

In a way, *The Golden Rump*'s rumoured threat was the ultimate tribute to Fielding—Walpole's creation of a satirist so dangerous his work could not be shown to the public in any form. It was also a fictive creation; such danger existed only in the imagination of legislators, who then normalized their control over dramatic literature through the Licensing Act.

Late in his career, after Fielding had stopped writing plays and entered the legal profession, he created his own parody of censorship laws.

Writing columns pseudonymously for London journals, inspired by earlier columns of Richard Steele in *The Tatler*, he wrote scenarios for a 'Court of Censorial Inquiry,' and then a 'Court of Criticism' wherein testimony was given, and various edicts and verdicts were issued. Often comic and ironic, his judgments constituted an alternative to the existing judicial system in which he took part as a lawyer and justice of the peace after 1740. Through his columns, he returned to the theatre in the sense that he took on the role of a comic judge, and held a journalistic version of the 'Pie Powder Court' Ben Jonson created in his satire, *Bartholomew Fair*. Fielding decreed, for example:

> That the Business of an Actor, as well as of a Writer, is to copy Nature, and not to imitate the Excellencies of their Predecessors. That Mr. Garrick, Mr. Quin, Mrs. Cibber, Mrs. Clive, and Mrs. Woffington, are all, in their several Capacities, Examples of this Merit (Fielding, *Jacobite's Journal* No. 10, 6 February 1748).

What he could no longer do on stage—comment on plays, playwrights, and legislative policy—as he had in rehearsal plays such as *Pasquin* and *The Historical Register*—he did in journals. The impulse he followed here to create his own court of law was shared later by Brecht, who contemplated creating a theatre in which famous persons would go on trial in stage plays. Trials also can be found in Brecht's learning plays (*Lehrstücke*), as well as *Galileo* and the radio play *The Trial of Lucullus*. (Brecht, like Fielding, also became a novelist after facing a repressive government. He wrote *The Threepenny Novel* in 1934 and *Business Affairs of Mr. Julius Caesar* in 1938 when it was difficult to find a producer for his plays.)

Of course Fielding was not entirely a Brechtian before Brecht. As suggested earlier, he could be called a Shavian before Shaw, too. He learned from examples set by Aristophanes, Jonson and Gay, as he introduced the 'Politicks' of Georgian England to the stage in new ways. After Walpole lost his hold on the ministry, and other politicians replaced him, Fielding supported Whig policies and the new ministry. He was no longer the subversive, oppositional playwright so active in 1736–37. Still, if Fielding was in fact the author behind Mr T . . . . C . . . . .'s 1740 *Apology*, he may well have completed his book on theatre wars and empire after all—under a pseudonym. In that volume, a writer whose identity has been secret for centuries boasts: 'No one is better vers'd in Rebellions, Revolts, Revolutions, Factions, Oppositions etc. than myself' (Mr. T . . . . C . . . . . 1740: 127). The claim could be an exaggeration; but Fielding witnessed some riots inside the theatre and out during his career as a playwright. In the last months of his residence at the Haymarket, leading up to the government-imposed state of emergency, he was one of the most outspoken and inventive dissenters of his age, a theatre artist and practitioner of 'political disobedience' who gave voice to the discontented on stage and off.

Cibber's Dynasty Endangered

> Was it not high Time to take this dangerous Weapon of mimical Insolence and Defamation out of the Hands of a mad Poet, as to wrest the Knife from the lifted Hand of a Murderer?
>
> Colley Cibber's *Apology*, 1740

In a number of his plays, Fielding mocked the poet laureate, actor and playwright Colley Cibber, who knew the danger of theatrical satire: unchecked 'this dangerous Weapon' (called such in Cibber's autobiographical *Apology*) could destroy an empire, or at least dethrone a ruler, particularly if his name was Colley Cibber, and his 'empire' was the theatre he managed at Drury Lane. The Cibber family's theatre dynasty, with its extensive influence over play production in London, fell low in a theatre full of audience laughter when mimicked in scenes by Fielding. Complaints, censorship and police actions followed, as Fielding's opponents sought to end such 'mimical insolence and Defamation'.

In our own times, if an actor or stand-up comedian refers to a public figure, the act is usually brief and far less of a popular cultural intervention than the sustained comic references to state leaders and prominent artists repeated nightly on Fielding's stage. Theatrical satire as effective as his has become an endangered species, to the extent that it would be appropriate to speak about the genre in the past tense, and ask what political stage satire once was. Not stand-up comedy or bedroom farce, or televised one-liners, or brief comic sketches, but sustained comic performance directed against persons of wealth and power enabled playwrights, actors and directors to offer entertaining resistance to injustice, corruption, Walpole, and the Cibbers. The objections voiced on stage often echoed public opposition already taking place outside the theatre; as noted earlier, Fielding's plays did not necessarily initiate dissent, but echoed and celebrated it. Such performances would last much longer than the seconds or minutes of comedy delivered in our age of punch lines, instant messaging, Twitters and sound-bite quotation. If well-received, they were repeated night after night, week after week, to a live audience. The staged commentaries constituted an early and well-attended form of the theatre practice Brecht sought later, in which a performance refers to events that have taken place, but 'does not pretend to be the actual event', at the same time that it 'has a practical purpose, intervenes socially' (Brecht 1964: 122). The world of 'great men' ruled by Walpole found itself repeatedly mocked on stage, as its programmes and character were cheerfully questioned.

Brecht's creation of theatre that serves a 'practical purpose' and 'intervenes socially' shared with Fielding's at least one source; both writers were inspired by John Gay's *The Beggar's Opera*, and its satiric depiction of wealth, poverty, crime and injustice. Brecht also shared with Gay and Fielding the experience of state censorship directed against playwriting. From exile in 1934 he wrote an essay on 'Writing the Truth: Five Difficulties', and cited Swift's *Modest Proposal* as an example of cunning authorship responding to oppression. Brecht's own exemplary political theatre practices, particularly his adaptation of *The Beggar's Opera*, in turn inspired satiric creations (often in times of turbulence) by Marc Blitzstein, Dario Fo, Wole Soyinka, Vaclav Havel, Joan Littlewood's Theatre Workshop, Yuri Lubimov's Taganka, the San Francisco Mime Troupe of the 1960s and 1970s. The list could be expanded with names of other writers, directors, actors and ensembles. But most of such practices would be past history, with a doubtful chance of continuation in the future.

Theatrical satire at its best has attracted a group of spectators who laughed together as they watched comic actors portray contemporaries. In ancient Athens as many as fifteen thousand citizens sat outdoors in a festival amphitheatre to see actors impersonate and mock state leaders, generals, philosophers, and artists. Socrates was asked to rise from his seat so spectators could compare him to the masked actor imitating him in Aristophanes's *The Clouds*. Plato suggested that stage satire led to the trial and courtroom condemnation of his teacher. The size of audiences attending satiric theatre in Henry Fielding's day was smaller than those in Athens—his Haymarket space seated around 800; but in close confinement, with some spectators seated on stage, they still were able to laugh in a special, holiday-like gathering, while actors portrayed the less noble side of well-known citizens. The Berlin theatre where Weill and Brecht's *Threepenny Opera* premiered in 1928 seated somewhat less than eight-hundred spectators; here too the impact of the play was not limited by the small size of the house. In fact, the small seating capacity made it more likely the space would be full, and tickets eagerly sought.

Not all of Fielding's popular plays were full-length works. *Tom Thumb*, a short comedy about a short man, was an 'afterpiece', a second play that followed the main, longer comedy, *The Author's Farce*, also by Fielding, at the Haymarket in 1730. Plays of either length were capable of attracting a large crowd, as were ballad operas, although few of those musical satires ran as many nights as the model for them all, Gay's *The Beggar's Opera*. The multiple-billing allowed new, untested plays to be placed on a programme with an already popular work, serious or farcical. A rotating repertoire with new additions gave the audience reasons to return, and gave an author like Fielding a chance to write and stage short topical plays (such as *Eurydice Hissed*) quickly when so inspired. According to his younger contemporary Arthur Murphy, Fielding was 'obliged for immediate supply to produce almost extempore a play, a farce, a pamphlet, or a news-paper' (Battestin 1989: xv). New songs and scenes could be inserted in the changing repertoire, which allowed for timely, updated satire. In Fielding's last season at the Haymarket the advantages of this production system became quite apparent, when one political satire after another (by different authors) opened. A few of them were extremely popular. Others now forgotten went unpublished and unreviewed; but they too may well have drawn in curious spectators who wanted to see the next *Pasquin*.

The loss of such stage events means that a special kind of opposition that satiric playwrights posed to those in power has largely disappeared. Film, television and internet media may reach a wider audience than plays, and do so speedily at times; but they lack the capacity of theatre to capture alive, in the flesh, the physical and verbal likeness of the persons mocked—to proceed as if influential, well-known men and women are present on stage, or at least as if their spokespersons are there, and recognized as such, while spectators in the same space laugh at the faces of wealth, deception and abusive authority. Here artists and audience experience something like the carnivalesque celebration Mikhail Bakhtin described: a world turned upside down, but shared by all, with rulers temporarily uncrowned in an alternative, freer and more joyous society. A crowd empowered through its celebratory assembly collectively takes over the space it fills. Those present in person (on stage and in the audience) collaborate, conspire as it were, in the public disapproval of power. Dissent is both sanctioned and enjoyed under these conditions. Comedians are kings, or at least they uncrown other rulers for a night, with spectators complicit in the mock-rebellion as they applaud the usurpers. Perhaps this is one reason television comedians (the cast of 'Saturday Night Live', Stephen Colbert, Jon Stewart's 'Daily Show' which lasted years in the United States) have welcomed a live, vocal audience in their studio. Usually the crowd cheers its approval, possibly with off-camera coaching. The capacity of theatre houses to display unruly attitudes in public, to thrive on public support and the democracy of freely chosen laughter, also could explain why Robert Walpole wanted to prevent the opening of new stage satires by John Gay and Henry Fielding between 1728 and 1737, a period when *The Beggar's Opera* and then *Pasquin* and other Fielding satires played to full theatres month after month. Fielding joked in 1752 that theatre managers 'have many Kings among the Number of their Subjects . . . many of their Subjects [actors] arrogate to themselves the splendid Appellations of Bassas, Doges, Princes, Emperors and the like' (Fielding 1964: 222). Today Prime Ministers and Presidents need not worry about theatre managers ruling over them, or their impersonators becoming a laughingstock in the theatre; such comic stage empires hardly exist anymore, or if they do, a corporate executive rather than a satirist usually rules.

Fielding's species of satire in Georgian England made some money, but it also led to censorship and at least one accusation of treason. He defended himself in print against the charge of bringing 'Secrets of Government' onto the stage after *The Daily Gazeteer* published an attack on Fielding's political plays. The charge published on 7 May 1737 came from an anonymous *Gazeteer* contributor who signed himself 'An Adventurer in Politics'. This pro-Walpole spokesperson accused Fielding of 'bringing POLITICKS on the STAGE', as if no one had ever done so before *Pasquin* and *The Historical Register for the Year 1736*, both named as offending texts. The *Gazeteer* found that Fielding's writing 'with Wit and Humour' in *Pasquin* on 'the Practices of Elections, without coming so near, as to point any Person out', was tolerable; but when the playwright began to find fault with specific political leaders such as Walpole in *The Historical Register for the Year 1736*, he was viewed as a trespasser of unwritten theatre rules, and revealer of secrets.

Fielding, the article said, showed

> how much it is in the Power of such Exhibitions [his plays], to make a Minister appear ridiculous to a People, and if the Humour spreads, as possibly it may, and should take in Home-Affairs, how much and how unjustly he [the Minister] might be exposed to publick Resentment, from such humorous and poetical Colouring of Things.

Although written as a complaint, the lines now should be read as a tribute. No praise can be read into the *Gazeteer*'s conclusion, however: 'To encourage then Politicks on the Stage, is not only unjust in itself, and improper, but of a most pernicious Tendency to the Stage itself. . . .' (*Daily Gazeteer*, 7 May 1737). Fielding's crime, it would seem, was popular innovation—placing effective political satire on the stage in Walpole's London. The offending playwright published a reply to these criticisms in a 21 May 1737 letter to the journal *Common Sense*. Signed by 'Pasquin', the letter denied Fielding was the first to bring 'Politicks on the Stage', and mentioned precedents from Aristophanes and Gay. But he did not deny the value of 'the bringing of Politicks on the Stage', quite the contrary: 'if by your Politicks, you mean a general Corruption. . . . I cannot think our Politicks too sacred to be exposed'. Pasquin also joked he 'cannot expose to others, what I have not found out myself', and explained that he was looking at 'a general Corruption', not state secrets when he wrote for London's theatre public. He also doubted that 'all the Ambassadors of Europe [would assemble in his theatre] at the Hay Market Playhouse to learn the Character of our Ministry'. The May 1737 accusations of disloyalty through 'Politicks on the Stage' were quickly followed in June by government passage of the Licensing Act, dispersal of his acting company at the Haymarket and the end of Henry Fielding's ability to bring 'Politicks on Stage' through satire. Today he remains best known as the author of *Joseph Andrews, Tom Jones, Amelia,* and *Jonathan Wild*; many readers of his novels never hear about his plays. His 'Politicks on Stage' has been effectively silenced.

Cognitive Capital, Moneyocracy, and Mischief

'Economically as well as politically the early eighteenth century was a period of prosperity for the great landowners, the great merchants, and the great financiers, a period in which the rich became richer and more powerful', notes Paul Langford (Langford 5). Not entirely different from our own century in terms of its increased concentrations of wealth, the eighteenth century also was a period that experienced usurpations of public space and liberty that continue today in different ways, as Slavoj Zizek suggests when he refers to twenty-first century enclosure of the 'cultural commons', a zone that includes 'cognitive capital, primarily language, our means of communication and education' (Zizek 91). Fielding fought an earlier battle over the 'cultural commons' of language and its use in public. Some of these commons materials were newly available through the increased printing of books, pamphlets, and newspapers accessible to new readers, and production of new plays that attracted a new audience, middle-class citizens whose income permitted purchase of printed matter and theatre tickets.

Initially uncensored, the liberty of the 'cultural commons' was curtailed, as government officials sought more control over print and theatre, particularly when plays like Gay's and Fielding's prompted laughter at the behaviour of influential men. (Satiric journal writing also was prosecuted, as will be noted later.) Meanwhile the two licensed theatres in London competed for control of the theatregoing public, and their cartel practices which, through regulated hiring, made actors servants to the masters known as theatre managers of Drury Lane and Covent Garden.

England was in the throes of the larger changes which Marx saw in the House of Commons' exclusion of 'the common people' from parliamentary representation, in an era of monopolies where 'the bourgeoisie [was not] able to take its place except under the banner of moneyocracy . . .' (Marx 1971: 174). 'Moneyocracy' in this case meant the sway of monopolistic finance and its government supporters, who benefited from Walpole's corrupt regime and patronage. The first Minister's plan for an excise tax, defeated by vehement opposition from merchants and others, provides a measure of the reigning statesman's determination to impose his order, and of his opposition's increasing power in 1733.

Fielding's own familiarity with the moneyocracy was comically acknowledged a few years later. Walpole was still in office, and still among the satirist's targets in a 16 February 1740 *Champion* column advocating redistribution of wealth:

> But perhaps it will be asked me, whether I would raise a fund large enough to pay off the debt of the nation, or whether I would impoverish all the rich to enrich the poor? . . . I have in view a fund for that purpose, and could heartily wish to see a law, by which all ill-gotten estates should be applied to so good an end . . . To make these estates repair, in their dissolution, the mischiefs they had occasioned in their creation; and to convert a fund which hath been amassed by preying on the miseries of mankind to the relief of those miseries. In short, all estates which have been gotten by plunder, cheating, or extortion, which would include prime ministers, scriveners, pawnbrokers, stockjobbers and petty attorneys should be applied to this use.

The same column admitted the improbability such a law would 'pass this sessions, or perhaps the next', 'however desirable such a law would be'. While no longer able to mock the law or Walpole through stage satire, Fielding in such columns humorously called attention to the 'mischiefs' of the rich, and the economic hardship of the poor.

Bertrand Goldgar finds that by the time Fielding's *Pasquin* (1736) and *The Historical Register* (1737) premiered and became the writer's 'most open and unmistakable satire of Walpole', 'the literary hue and cry after Walpole had reached a level that no self-respecting wit could afford to ignore if he hoped to amuse the town' (Goldgar 151). Even if he was not the first writer to oppose Walpole and his schemes, Fielding for a few years was one of the most popular playwrights to do so. (The other was John Gay.)

The 99%

Any wit who sided with the excise-tax protesters joined a sizable majority, one that anticipated the recent, twenty-first century Occupy movement's claim to represent 99% of the public. An amusing 1733 summary of the Georgian anti-tax constituency invoked precisely that number:

> To sum up the whole, there are no Persons who oppose an Excise, except Jacobites and Tories, and Whigs, and Dissenters, and Revolutioners, and Murmurers, and Grumblers . . . and the Deluded and disaffected, . . . And the Rash and the Heady, and the Clamorous, and the Noisy (especially

noisy Sheep), and Factious Writers, . . . and Men of Sense, and Men of Honour, and the Fair Traders and Retailers, and the unfair Traders, and the Deceivers and Deceived, and the *Craftsman*, and *Fog*; who, if you take them altogether, will not amount to many more than 99 in 100. (*Fog's Weekly Journal*, 17 February 1733, quoted by Paul Langford in *The Excise Crisis* 1975: 61)

By the time Fielding joined the opponents of the excise tax and mocked it on stage, the tax plan had already been defeated; but even if the satirist was following the crowd, the crowd then followed him when it came to see his plays, and applauded views that corresponded to its own.

When the Mayor in *Pasquin* invites his drinking companions to 'fill the air with our repeated cries of liberty, and property, and no excise' in Act I, the words spoken in 1736 are more an echo of earlier rallies, and a recollection of past triumphs, than a new cry. But those words and others of the same oppositional tenor pleased audiences, and kept the Haymarket theatre full. Fielding was no longer a marginal artist by 1736, if he ever had been. Those in the rising middle class ('Fair Traders and Retailers, and the unfair Traders') who saw their interests threatened constituted part of the new theatre audience. Their sentiments were notably voiced by actors in Lillo's 1731 domestic tragedy, *The London Merchant*. Fielding parodied this play, as will be seen in the next chapter; but after that false start in *The Covent-Garden Tragedy*, which lasted one night, he managed to write plays that spoke to spectators through topical satire rather than a parody of domestic tragedy.

Writing in a period when, as Arnold Hauser has observed, 'for the first time, the literary product becomes a commodity, the value of which conforms to its saleableness in the free market', Fielding's political satire became a saleable commodity. Its 1736–37 mockery of Walpole's ministry became so popular that the ministry decided to make the market less free and intervene (Hauser Volume III: 53). One indication of this popularity surfaced in a 30 March 1736 report by London's *Daily Advertiser* that

his Royal Highness the Prince of Wales honour'd Pasquin last night with his Presence when it was acted the twentieth Time to a crowded Audience . . . and many thousands of People turn'd away for want of room' (Scouten Part 3: 566).

Whether people came to see the Prince or the play, whether thousands were turned away from a theatre that seated eight-hundred, or (discounting the newspaper's likely exaggeration) merely hundreds, the size of the crowd, the Prince's support, and the play's long run which went well beyond twenty nights would have shown Walpole's ministry that Fielding had quite a following. His audience kept coming back, too. Lord Egmont's diary recorded in April, 1737 that he attended Fielding's new play, *Eurydice Hissed*:

> an allegory on the loss of the Excise Bill. The whole was a satire on Sir Robert Walpole, and I observed that when any strong passages fell, the Prince, who was there, clapped, especially when in favour of liberty (Scouten Part 3: 660).

Goldgar adds that

> the image of the Prince of Wales attending Fielding's farce at the Haymarket and clapping vigorously at strong passages in favour of liberty is a crucial one to keep in mind if we wish to understand the violent attacks on Fielding in the [pro-Walpole] *Daily Gazeteer* (Goldgar 155).

The success of *Eurydice Hissed* and other plays at the Haymarket cut into the profits of the Patent houses at the same time as its success cheered Walpole's opposition. The era of monopolies to which Marx referred included a near monopoly through cartel arrangements by the licensed managements at Drury Lane and Covent Garden. Their ability to underpay and fire actors with impunity was threatened by an actor rebellion in 1733 (discussed in Chapter Sixteen). Not eager to share control of the market with one another, let alone third theatres and unruly actors, the patent house managers welcomed the elimination of competition in smaller, unlicensed spaces. For this reason they supported the Licensing Act, which deprived free choice of plays and free expression to Fielding's theatre company among others.

As an equal-opportunity satirist, Fielding ridiculed both Drury Lane and Covent Garden in his mock-pantomime, *Tumble-Down Dick*, which opened at the Haymarket toward the end of April 1736. In the play managers from both licensed houses bid 'for a Dog in a Harlequin's dress', playing out Fielding's anxiety that animal acts and pantomime clowning would be favoured more than dialogues like his at the two sanctioned houses. (The Little Harlequin dog previously appeared at Drury Lane in Theo Cibber's pantomime, *The Harlot's Progress*, incidentally, and the bid for the dog seems to be a reference to Cibber's canine collaborator.) This satire of theatre houses was part of Fielding's 'anti-theatrical' writing directed throughout his career at select playwrights and managers.

He never claimed to be writing 'anti-theatre', but London readers would have known the term from another source. In 1720 a periodical titled *The Anti-Theatre* began publication in response to Richard Steele's journal, *The Theatre*. Steele started his journal after he encountered difficulties with the Lord Chamberlain, who briefly withdrew Steele's licence to supervise plays at Drury Lane. *The Anti-Theatre*'s bi-weekly columns, pseudonymously signed in the name of John Falstaffe, supported the Lord Chamberlain's position, and spoke favourably of theatre conditions in ancient Athens where 'the same persons who governed the Commonwealth, supervised the Stage'. Fielding humorously reiterated that line of thought about stages and government in *The Historical Register for the Year 1736*, where one of his characters argued that 'there was a strict resemblance between the states theatrical and political' in England. If he was an 'anti-theatre' writer in this regard, Fielding by no means was a supporter of state censorship or a contributor to the journal *The Anti-Theatre*. His 'anti-theatre' writing began in 1730 with *The Author's Farce* and *Tom Thumb*, plays that turned theatre against theatre, as they mocked bombastic tragedy and the imperious management of Drury Lane, where some of his first plays were staged, and some rejected. Fielding's anti-theatrical writing finds the world too much like a stage at times, with its leading players in overbearing roles, as they try to govern the Commonwealth and supervise London's theatre.

Besides writing satire about theatre managers whose government disturbed him, particularly Colley Cibber and his son at Drury Lane, and John Rich at Covent Garden, Fielding was not fully aligned with either of the ruling political parties in his day (Whigs and Tories). Though at times he served one or the other, and remained in opposition to Walpole for years, his stage satires maligned both parties, as well as their 'actors'. The fact that Walpole and his friends were offended does not mean their opponents were always praised by the satirist. Thomas Cleary observes in *Henry Fielding, Political Writer*, that from 1728 to 1735 the satirist 'behaved most inconsistently for seven years, alternating abuse and eulogy of Walpole and opposition leaders'. After 1735, 'Fielding's task as new partisan was clear and he performed brilliantly . . . The anti-ministerial satire in his plays of 1736–37 is regularly balanced by equally severe satire on opposition hypocrites and Tory boobies' (Cleary 6). 'Lord Both-Sides' wins the bid for 'a most curious remnant of political honesty' during the mock-auction held in *The Historical Register for the Year 1736*; the fact that he will pay no more than five pounds suggests neither side or party places much value on truth-telling. At the same auction, no one will pay for patriotism or for modesty. By contrast, everyone at the auction bids high for 'interest at court', a place where the playwright had few friends. (Incidentally, a satiric ballad opera titled *Politicks on Both Sides* opened on 30 July 1735 at Lincoln's Inn Fields; its authorship is unknown and it was not published. Perhaps it inspired *Pasquin* and the character of 'Lord Both-Sides' or could have been an early draft of *Pasquin* or another play written by Fielding.)

A Hiss from the Voice of the People

Fielding ably fuses 'political with theatrical criticism', Cleary observes, when he 'slyly insults Walpole' by having Pistol, Theophilus Cibber's stand-in, call himself 'Prime Minister theatrical' in Act Two of *The Historical Register for the Year 1736*. In the same play Cleary sees another stand-in for Theo Cibber become Walpole when—as Apollo—he says of 'the voice of the people': 'Let them hiss. Let them hiss and grumble as much as they please, as long as we get their money.' Medley, the playwright within the play, adds to this declaration: 'There, sir, is the sentiment of a Great Man', as clear a reference to the Prime Minister as any used in earlier satires by Gay or Fielding (Cleary 99–100). In such jokes theatre and ministerial politics are as inseparable as the Cibbers and Walpole in their mutual support and their imperious behaviour.

For Fielding's patrons, who went to plays critical of the government at a time when (in Marx's words already cited) the House of Commons began excluding 'the common people' from parliamentary representation, theatre became their assembly hall, their house of representatives, and their commons, where voices critical of corrupt officials and Walpole's policies were applauded nightly. Marx's praise for the bourgeoisie in *The Communist Manifesto*, although written a century after Fielding's satires, may apply to the new middle-class audience watching Haymarket actors mock Walpole's ministry:

> The bourgeoisie, historically, has played a most revolutionary part. . . . It has pitilessly torn asunder the motley feudal ties that bound man to his 'natural superiors', and has left remaining no other nexus between man and man than naked self-interest, than callous 'cash payment'. . . . It has resolved personal worth into exchange value.

The mock-auction scene in Fielding's *Historical Register for the Year 1736* graphically illustrates a reduction of all values to cash-payment, as morality, honesty, and interest at court are sold to the highest bidder. Fielding's society was not as 'modern' as Marx's; but the commodification of morality and literature, and by extension the commercial dependence of artists on 'free trade' and paying customers, had begun early in the eighteenth century, and Fielding's satires acknowledge the transition.

A comic effort to resist the rise of the merchant class and its influence is launched by Fielding's Lord Place, who sides with Walpole and the excise taxers in *Pasquin* by calling for an end to Tradesmen. Evidently Tradesmen only get in the way of those who would regulate commerce. 'I'll bring in a Bill to extirpate all Trade out of the Nation', says his Lordship, and the Mayor's wife in the play agrees that that would benefit 'People of Quality who don't want [i.e. lack] Money'. In a 1752 column in *The Covent-Garden Journal*, a half-serious Fielding asked: 'what is the true Fountain of that Complication of political Diseases which infests this Nation, but Money? Money!' Claiming he alone had 'penetrated to the very Bottom of all the Evil', Fielding's not quite Biblical revelation also described money as 'the certain Cause of all that national Corruption, Luxury, and Immorality, which have polluted our Morals' (Fielding 1964: 337). The reference was not strictly Biblical because he also cited a Greek Poet who found in money the source of 'Wars and every Kind of Bloodshed'.

Another citing of 'the icy water of egotistical calculation' such as Marx descries in bourgeois behaviour surfaces in Fielding's *Historical Register*. Quidam, the 'fiddler' and stand-in for Walpole, gives patriots gold, invites them to say they are rich, then retrieves all the coins as the patriots dance to his tune without noticing the money falls through holes in their pockets: 'the poor people, alas! Out of their own pockets pay the whole reckoning', observes Medley. This scene and others (such as bribery in *Pasquin* mentioned earlier) show the 'moneyocracy' engaging in callous and cunning cash payment schemes. Most of those who paid to watch the spectacle were quite pleased by such capers, presumably because they saw others—not themselves—as the centre of attention and the source of folly.

As he continued to express the age's sensibility through satire, Fielding must have noticed the diversity of his audience, including less wealthy patrons. He wrote a paean to gallery spectators in 1752. His approval of spectators in the low-priced gallery seats might have begun during February 1737 at the Drury Lane premiere of his *Eurydice, or the Devil Henpeck'd*, when pit occupants protested against the behaviour of footmen mostly in the gallery. Theophilus Cibber, performing *Cato* that night, stood onstage and promised the protesters that footmen would be banned from the gallery. The footmen then protested, and broke a door to return to the gallery they had been forced to leave, although they 'kept some order while the play was in progress', and objected only between the acts of *Cato*, which preceded Fielding's afterpiece (Battestin 1989: 213). Their considerate behaviour during the performance, as well as their opposition to Cibber's promise, may partially explain why Fielding later praised 'the Mob' and its 'immediate Correction and Admonishment' to 'any Persons of Fashion' who display 'indecent Particularities of Behaviour' during a performance. Comparing gallery spectators with obnoxious patrons in boxes in a 4 April 1752 issue of *The Covent-Garden Journal*, Fielding praised 'the Mob' for its displays of 'Decency'.

> If our People of Fashion will examine the Matter fairly and without Prejudice, they cannot have the least Decency left, if they refuse to allow, that, in this instance, the Mob are most manifestly their Betters.

> Who is it that prevents the Stage being crowded with grotesque Figures, a Mixture of the Human with the Baboon Species? Who (I say) but the Mob? . . . no sooner doth one of these Apparitions [a Gentleman seated on stage and disrupting the show with his commentary] present its frightful Figure before the Scenes, than the Mob from their profound Regard to Decency, are sure to command him off.

Commenting on the closure of *Eurydice*, O'Brien notes,

> from the point of view of middle-class theatergoers, what had become intolerable was that the footmen's rowdiness was now understood to be usurping their betters' claim to have a monopoly on critical judgment. From the point of view of the footmen, however, the gallery and the ability to launch judgments from it had attained the status of a 'customary' right . . . (O'Brien 203).

The new middle-class audience asserted its right not against Walpole but against theatre management and the underclass in this situation. With great resourcefulness, Fielding turned that debacle into a new success at the Haymarket by writing a sequel, *Eurydice Hissed*, in which a hissed playwright named Pillage can be seen as first minister Walpole, a man 'once adored by a crowd of dependents' who finds himself 'deserted and abandoned by all those who courted his favor'.

The misbehaviour by 'People of Fashion' in Fielding's later stage satires (as opposed to misbehaviour of the people watching those satires) involved not the usual comedy of marital infidelity, nor the disapproval of footmen, but rather infidelity to countrymen through bribery and corruption; such activity shown in jest constituted a new Georgian theatre practice, if the 1737 *Gazeteer*'s assessment of the playwright's 'power to make a Minister ridiculous' is any indication. The innovative political farces, sometimes described as 'irregular' drama, were neither conventional comedy or tragedy. Fielding's debunking of wealth and privilege in these plays may have appealed to spectators with low or middling income ('the Mob') because they could enter a theatre for half price after act three of the evening's main play.

His satires presented in afterpieces also would have drawn audiences seeking novel entertainment at a time when newly developed pantomimes at Rich's Covent Garden were outdrawing older forms of drama. Martin and Ruthe Battestin note in their Fielding biography that the playwright

> had a talent for a kind of pointed, inventive foolery that audiences had not seen on stage before—a talent for ridicule and brisk dialogue, for deft and emblematic characterization, and for devising absurd yet expressionistic

plots that have scarcely been matched in the experimental theatre of our own century (Battestin and Battestin 83).

Beginning with *Tom Thumb* and *The Author's Farce* in 1730, Fielding's 'inventive foolery', and the audience's willingness to pay for it renewed and extended the kind of enthusiasm that John Gay generated with *The Beggar's Opera*. Gay himself had mocked conventional theatre genres in his early 'Tragi-Comic-Pastoral' farce called *The What D'Ye Call It* (1715) and in *Three Hours After Marriage* (1717, co-authored with Pope and Arbuthnot). Then he parodied Italian opera and used English lyrics that everyone in the audience could understand. The success of his first ballad opera may be one reason Walpole thought censorship of Gay's sequel, *Polly*, was in order; the form was too popular, and threatened to become more so. When Fielding tried to stage a revised version of Gay's *Polly* in 1737, as noted previously, he was challenging the 1728 ban and Walpole's authority. Hume supports this view, contending that 'To advertise Polly was to issue a direct challenge to Walpole; could he again block production?' (Hume 243). In asking the question, Hume neglects to note that the play's title was changed, and it is possible Fielding and Charke—probably taking a lead role, possibly suggesting new lines— were revising or adding to the original text. Since Fielding's version went unpublished, we will never know how or if he was improving Gay's insinuations that Walpole was a highwayman like Macheath. Whether he relocated the play in India, or simply kept it in the West Indies, Fielding probably would have looked sceptically at colonial exploitation and corruption, as Gay had, with 'Indians' of India or a new world island more virtuous than any British colonist except for Polly Peachum. And, to give Fielding credit as an entrepreneur, the once banned play might have been enormously well-attended, and profitable to its producer because it had been banned. Applause was likely to follow the outlawed play's first lyrics for a song written by Gay:

> The Manners of the Great affect,
> Stint not your Pleasure:
> If Conscience had their Genius chekt,
> How got they Treasure?
> The more in Debt, run in Debt the more,
> Careless who is undone;
> Morals and Honesty leave to the Poor,
> As they do at London.

These lines still would have sounded new and timely in 1737, even though they were written in 1728. Audiences who had not read Gay's libretto might wonder whether he or Fielding wrote such biting references to Walpole's England.

Sons of Dullness

During his playwriting career, Fielding rarely left 'morals and honesty' to the poor; but he did not want to become one of the poor, either. When the author's Muse in *Eurydice Hissed* claims she would rather starve, 'ay, even in prison starve, / Than vindicate oppression for thy bread,' bread remains an issue, even if conscience accompanies the breadwinning. In the same play, worry about work being condemned on opening night surfaces again, as it had seven years earlier in *The Author's Farce*, where the playwright self-reflexively addressed the prospects for profit to be made from new comic entertainments.

Playwright Luckless hopes to pay his landlady by earning income from a benefit theatre night. This impoverished writer's innovative play within the play, performed by human actors cast as Punch, Joan and other puppets, mocks contemporary opera, tragedy, even puppetry — and the market on which they depend. Goldgar's assessment of later Fielding satire applies to this 1730 farce as well; compared to themes of other satirists of the period, Fielding's themes 'are political motifs which have the maximum literary significance; that is, he is acutely sensitive to the triumph of the "sons of dullness" over men of wit and merit and to efforts to limit the freedom of the stage' (Goldgar 151). The market for new plays is diminished by the 'dullness' of Colley and Theophilus Cibber (both featured as paragons of dullness in Pope's *Dunciad*) who receive special attention, beginning with the 1730 representation of the older Cibber as Sir Farcical Comic in *The Author's Farce*. 'I have as great a confusion of languages in my play as was at the building of Babel', boasts Sir Farcical. 'And so much the more extraordinary because the author understands no language at all', adds Fielding's stand-in, Luckless.

Later, in a satiric column, Fielding would accuse the author of *The Apology for the Life of Colley Cibber, Comedian* of murdering the English language. Ioan Williams argues that Fielding attacked Cibber's 'misuse of words he thought . . . connected with devious attempts to defend the reputation of Sir Robert Walpole . . .' as part of an effort to detect the 'ill use' of language that Locke broached in his *Essay Concerning Human Understanding* (Fielding 1970: xvi). Fielding's anti-theatrical writings against the Cibbers and other abusers of the English language might be regarded as malpractice suits instituted by a playwright who later became a lawyer.

Fielding both derides and celebrates the new literary market of the day, and the independent writer's role in it, in another episode of *The Author's*

Farce, where a scribbler named Scarecrow offers the publisher Bookweight a new literary product:

SCARECROW: Sir, I have brought you a libel against the ministry.
BOOKWEIGHT: Sir, I shall not take anything against them—(*aside*) for I have two in the press already.
SCARECROW: Then, sir, I have another in defense of them.
BOOKWEIGHt: Sir, I never take anything in defense of power.

The author portrayed in this funny, opportunistic exchange might be Fielding himself (not yet the staunch Opposition supporter he became later—still open to praising Walpole on occasion), except that the scribbler Scarecrow is not a playwright. The idea of selling a political stage satire to a publisher or producer was more in Fielding's line after 1735. He also tried to win Walpole's approval through dedication of a new play to the minister in 1732.

Whether his lapse into praise of Walpole was due to Fielding's need for patronage, or encouragement from the management at Drury Lane when his plays were staged there, the writer who became satirist-in-chief at the Haymarket did not always oppose the ministry in his plays. Arguments on behalf of Fielding as an early Brechtian find little support from this period of his career. A notable movement away from theatre of political protest took place in 1731–32, when he wrote *The Modern Husband* and dedicated it to Robert Walpole. Fielding's praise of Walpole is so fulsome it seems to be a joke or a caricature of a dedication; could the excessive praise be meant to undermine itself?

As the best Poets have owed their Reward to the greatest Heroes and Statesmen of their Times, so those Heroes have owed to the Poet that Posthumous Reputation, which is generally the only Reward that attends the greatest Actions. By them the Great and Good blaze out to Posterity, and triumph over the little Malice and Envy which once pursued them.

Protect therefore, Sir, an Art from which You may promise Your self such notable Advantages; when the little Artifices of Your Enemies, which You have surmounted, shall be forgotten, when Envy shall cease to misrepresent Your Actions, and Ignorance to misapprehend them. The Muses shall remember their Protector, and the wise Statesman the generous Patron, the steadfast Friend, and the true Patriot; but above all that Humanity and Sweetness of Temper, which shine thro' all your Actions, shall render the Name of Sir Robert Walpole dear to his no longer ungrateful Country.

Fielding's dedication proved prophetic. Walpole's 'posthumous reputation' has been shaped by the satire of the minister who chose not to protect the playwright. The first Minister is remembered (at least by those who read Fielding and quote his plays) as a statesman who was neither wise nor sweet in treatment of his literary opponents.

A number of circumstances about *The Modern Husband*'s February 1732 production at Drury Lane suggest Fielding was serious in his dedication, and sought to align himself with powerful, entrenched powers. The play's cast included the Cibber family dynasty: Colley Cibber, then poet laureate, as well as his son Theophilus, Theo's wife, Susannah Cibber, and the laureate's youngest daughter, Charlotte Charke. This wealth of Cibbers, combined with the play's dedication to the laureate's ally, argue that Fielding wanted patronage and a remunerative place in the cultural establishment. Colley Cibber by that time knew and entertained friends of the king and first minister, both on stage and off. Fielding would be no Luckless, if the Cibbers and Walpole could help him. They did not, it seems, reward the author sufficiently or win his lasting allegiance, considering his subsequent turn against them.

Nor is the play he wrote for the Cibbers now regarded as one of Fielding's finest. Colley Cibber as Lord Richly in *The Modern Husband* portrayed a wealthy rake, and the role might have been written especially for the well-known actor and rake; but the play did not flatter upper-class spectators—who would have been Cibber's friends and admirers. It showed husbands (Lord Richly and Mr Bellamont) prepared to sell the favours of their wives, and wives willing to betray the honour of their husbands when they were not busy playing card games. The exception, virtuous Mrs Bellamont, was portrayed by Susannah Cibber, whose husband later accused her in court of lacking virtue. 'A modern reader would think it had been better for [Fielding's] fame if he had never written such scenes', Frederick Lawrence remarked on the play's depiction of scandal (Lawrence 52). A highly moral critic writing in the nineteenth century, Lawrence found it implausible that such scenes would have been common, or welcome in Fielding's time, although the play ran for a respectable length (thirteen nights) when it opened.

Lawrence neglects to note that, a few years after *The Modern Husband*'s first performance in 1732, the cast of the play demonstrated the plot was not far-fetched, as debt-ridden Theo Cibber persuaded his wife to sleep with a wealthy gentleman, William Sloper, in exchange for payments to the pandering husband (Cibber). The adulterous affair became a national scandal. After arranging for his wife's alleged infidelity, Cibber took Sloper to court for personal damages. Trial witnesses recounted the sexual intrigue in sordid detail in 1738, and printed accounts of the testimony were circulated as pornographic literature. Perhaps *The Modern Husband*'s plot allowed Theo Cibber to rehearse in his imagination the practice of selling his wife's favours to Sloper or his equal, in which case Fielding's writing might be regarded as didacticism rather than satire. Then again, Theo Cibber did not need to perform Fielding's play to know that he was debt-ridden and could use a patron. His history of rakish living, gambling and wife-abuse started prior to Susannah's trysts with Sloper, and his role as a 'careless husband' may have been inspired by the example of his rakish father, Colley Cibber, who titled one of his plays *The Careless Husband*. The latter play was revived at Drury Lane just as *The Modern Husband* ended its run there.

One line in Act Five of *The Modern Husband* anticipates a critique of corruption and wealth Fielding offered in subsequent political satires. After Bellamont decides to protest Lord Richly's abuses of wealth and privilege, and his lordship's pandering, despite the risks of speaking out, he declares: 'Were you as high as Heraldry could lift you, you should not injure me unpunish'd. Where Grandeur can give Licence to Oppression, the People must be Slaves, let them boast what Liberty they please.'

The decorous language here lacks the plainer, more colloquial phrasing of criticisms voiced in Fielding's later stage satires; but the opposition to tyranny is consistent with his later playwriting. With this exception, *The Modern Husband* seems closer in style to Colley Cibber's plays, and their parade of fashionable fops and rakes, than to Fielding's best satires. The difference might be attributed to his writing Lord Richly's role specifically for the poet laureate—to give Colley Cibber a part equal to his earlier, famous role as Lord Foppington. Fielding was hardly endorsing Lord Richly's sentiments; as McCrea notes, 'Richly is a product of the new economic order that flourished during Walpole's long tenure, and Fielding's contempt for Richly is one thing we can be sure of in this otherwise confused effort' (McCrea 64). Once Fielding broke with the Cibbers, speeches given to such fashionable figures and elected officials in his plays became less Cibberian, more distinctively his own, even when he created characters meant to mock the Cibbers in his afterpieces. Fielding later had occasion to renounce what he called 'genteel Comedy . . . in which our Laureate [Cibber] has succeeded so excellently' with 'pretty, dapper, brisk, smart, pert Dialogue' that 'had some Years ago taken almost sole Possession of our Stage, and banished Shakespear, Fletcher, Johnson [Jonson], etc. from it' (Fielding 1742, 'Preface to *Plutus*'). Cibber's 'genteel Comedy' briefly seems to have taken possession of Fielding, too, in 1732.

The occasion for Fielding's break with this kind of theatre may well have been the actors' stage mutiny led by Theo Cibber at Drury Lane in 1733. The rebellion (discussed more fully in a later chapter) left Fielding at odds with Cibber Junior and other actors who joined the walkout. The satirist stayed on the side of Drury Lane's management, perhaps hoping his plays would continue to be staged there. When Theo Cibber returned from self-chosen exile a year later, and became the assistant to Drury Lane's new manager Fleetwood, Fielding was not rewarded for loyalty. Theo practically ran Drury Lane at a time the playwright had lost interest in flattering the Cibbers and their friend Walpole. Fleetwood declined to produce Fielding's new play, *Don Quixote in England*. Perhaps Fielding would have supported Walpole, or stayed friendly with the Cibbers and Fleetwood, if *Don Quixote in England* had won unstinting praise from them; but it is more likely that his theatre work was too innovative and anti-establishment for them. Certainly once he left Drury Lane, his plays became less conventional and more politically engaged than *The Modern Husband*. Hume questions how political [*Don Quixote in England*] really is 'because the "election" scenes Fielding added for topicality in 1734 vigorously blast the dishonesties of both sides', as if he must endorse one side or the other to qualify as a satirist (Hume 183). But a world of satire that included a character named 'Lord Both Sides' could accommodate multiple objects of ridicule.

Four Guineas for Charlotte Charke

Whereas Brecht depended on government support (and risked government objections) at his Berliner Ensemble, Fielding and co-manager James Ralph raised their own funds to support the Great Mogul's ensemble at the Haymarket. The popularity of Fielding's satires ensured that actors earned a decent wage. Charlotte Charke in her autobiography noted her generous salary was four guineas a week, and it continued for many weeks. Fielding may have been paying for the family name, securing a Cibber daughter as accomplice in his satire of her relatives; but in retrospect, we can see he hired a gifted artist who has won new attention from historians in the past few decades.

In other respects the unlicensed playhouse benefited Fielding's actors, too. Scouten writes that smaller theatres such as the Haymarket and Goodman's Fields had managers who 'worked closely with their players. At these smaller houses, too, a player learned co-operation with the other members of the troupe'. Fielding's company stayed together from one satire to the next, and some of them may have written plays when not rehearsing and performing. Writers in the ensemble included Charlotte Charke, Liza Haywood, and James Lacy. (Haywood turned Fielding's *Tragedy of Tragedies* into a musical, *The Opera of Operas*. Charke's writing is discussed later.)

Scouten also praises Fielding the manager as

a bold and shrewd contriver. . . . His experiments were numerous and lively . . . he used the curtain between the acts and sometimes between scenes, changed the lighting system, and revived induction scenes. . . . He continued production on days when acting was forbidden, performing not only on Lenten Wednesdays and Fridays, but also during Passion Week itself. A striking innovation was his device of offering two new plays on the same night. In his brief reign as 'Grand Mogul' he brought out an unusually large number of new plays (Scouten Part 3: cxxvi, lxxxvi–lxxxvii).

While he had none of Brecht's ambition to train actors in Epic theatre techniques, Fielding gave his actors training in satire by writing topical scenes for them: scenes that were non-naturalistic, non-Aristotelian and 'Epic' in their social criticism. (He mocked Aristotelian tenets of drama in his 1731 preface to *The Tragedy of Tragedies* describing a ghost as the soul of tragedy.) Some of these 'early Epic' plays include comic distancing and interruptions, 'Brechtian' moments where actors self-reflexively talk about acting, politics and their own managers. Ronald Paulson described Fielding's rehearsal plays with a summary that might (without knowing it) just as well have been a Brecht scenario when he wrote:

> . . . the unit of narrative is the scene as observed by spectators [on stage, portrayed by characters in the play], as well as by critics and by the author himself. There is already a script, but in the rehearsal situation the author and his audience can collaborate and make changes even at this point, aware as they are of the characters as actors in their roles and out of them (Paulson 1979: 125).

Brecht wanted his actors to perform in a way that indicated alternatives and changes were possible, and Fielding's rehearsal play format allowed for just such a presentation. In Brecht's words, an Epic theatre actor

> on the stage, besides what he actually is doing . . . will at all essential points discover, specify, imply what he is not doing; that is to say he will act in such a way that the alternative emerges as clearly as possible, that his acting allows the other possibilities to be inferred and only represents one out of the possible variants (Brecht 1964: 137).

The seemingly casual conversations in Fielding's rehearsal play structures, including those in *Pasquin* and *The Historical Register for the Year 1736*, also anticipated Brecht's Epic acting insofar as Georgian stage convention called for actors to address the audience, not one another. Direct address to spectators was practised long before Brecht or Fielding arrived on the scene, but the German author and director used it in a new way, writing stage directions for such addresses into scripts, and requiring actors to break the situational frame (the illusion of an imaginary fourth wall) that arrived late in the nineteenth century with conventions of naturalism and realism.

Some eighteenth-century spectators sat on stage. Garrick banished them from Drury Lane's stage in 1762, but it is quite likely that some of the people Fielding satirized in the 1730s sat on the stage, or near it, and audience members would have recognized the references to them. 'Thus all your acting / Leads back to daily life.' 'Do not step too far / From the everyday theatre, / The theatre whose stage is the street,' Brecht advised later in his poem 'On the Everyday Theatre'. If the targets of Fielding's satire dared not show themselves inside his playhouse, their faces still were known, and more so their actions, when they were alluded to, imitated and mocked at the Haymarket. 'One does not go to see the play, but the company', Lord Dapper tells Sourwit in *The Historical Register*; by 'company' he means the people in the audience, but in Fielding's theatre the actors on stage, and their impersonations of and references to those off stage, might also be major attractions. He hired Charlotte Charke for the role of Lord Place, who alludes to her famous father, the laureate, in *Pasquin*. Asked to secure a place for a voter who enjoys drinking sack, Lord Place responds: 'Odso, you shall be Poet-Laureate', since a butt of sack was one of the Laureate's rewards. 'I am no Poet, I can't make Verses', responds the voter. Charke as Lord Place would then have added: 'No Matter for that, you'll be able to make Odes . . . I can't tell you well what they are; but I know you may be qualified for the Place without being a Poet'.

Charke was not impersonating her father, merely questioning (through Fielding's lines) his abilities as a writer, and mocking her own knowledge of poetry. But the patronage-giver she impersonated might well have been one of her father's patrons. *The Grub Street Journal* berated Fielding for such topical satire, although it now might be read as praise, in a 22 April 1736 issue commenting on *Pasquin*'s characterizations:

> The surest way to render all such persons ridiculous, and consequently despised, is to introduce them personated upon the stage, and there openly acting those vile parts, which they daily act in a more clandestine manner upon the stage of the world (Cross 188).

Curiously, when the actor Samuel Foote won acclaim for his stage impersonation of prominent London citizens, Fielding wrote a column objecting to the practice. In *The Jacobite's Journal* for 30 April 1738, he 'indicted' 'Samuel Fut' (sic), and argued that:

Persons have been formerly ridiculed under fictitious Fables and Characters;
but surely since the Days of the Old Comedy, none, 'till your Time, have had
the Audacity to bring real Facts and Persons upon the Stage. . . . Mimicking
the Voice, Features, and Gestures of another Man, the meanest and vilest of
all Arts.

There may have been some jealousy behind this judgment, since Foote was
thriving at a time Fielding could no longer have new satire staged. For
Fielding to deny that anyone since the days of Aristophanes had brought
'real Facts and Persons upon the Stage' seems disingenuous, given the
many topical references to politicians and playwrights in his own plays.
Admittedly, Foote's satire was based more in physical impersonation and
vocal mimicry, less on analogy or 'fictitious Fables and Characters' than
Fielding's; but both authors referred to people who were in their audience
on occasion, and in prominent positions elsewhere.

No one watching *Eurydice Hissed* at the Haymarket in 1737 would have
missed its references to Walpole and the Cibbers, even if the references
were made through 'fictitious Fables and Characters' with names like
Ground Ivy (laureate Colley Cibber), Pistol (Theophilus Cibber) and
Pillage (Robert Walpole). Wilbur Cross argues that Fielding's attacks on
Walpole advanced 'by allegory, irony, ridicule. He adopted [especially in
Champion columns] the indirect method, suppressing names, he said,
because of his fears of the pillory' (Cross 263–64). Fielding's success as a
ministerial opponent peaked when *Eurydice Hissed* opened on 5 April 1737:
'the performance seems to have been a fathering of opposition forces', and
the Prince of Wales 'had much to applaud' in the satire, since the 'brief
Eurydice Hiss'd is the most thoroughly political, most steadily anti-Walpole
of Fielding's five plays of 1736–37', according to Cleary (Cleary 103).

While the short satire includes several depictions of bribery, the play
also makes an interesting case for popular support—not patronage or bribery of critics or claques– as a means to theatrical triumph and political
success. Wary of playhouses filled by the author's or manager's claque at
an opening, a character named Honestus in *Eurydice Hissed* argues that
'from the people's pockets come the pence, / They therefore should decide
what they will pay for' (Fielding 1967: 62). The implication is that both
theatre managers and political leaders should heed popular demand, and
not mislead the public. At this point (spring 1737), with extended runs of
his plays, Fielding could follow the recommendation made by Honestus:
'If you have merit, take your merit's due'. His worry about competition
from pantomimes, dancing dogs and rope dancers at rival theatres might
have been reduced as Fielding created popular theatre himself. In the end,
though, Walpole's censorship legislation stole the show, and politicized the
stage far more than any playwright.

Satirists Anonymous

Although it has been said that the Licensing Act was directed at Henry Fielding, and his plays seriously disturbed Walpole, Fielding was not the only author at the Haymarket under his management. As noted earlier, his satire was abetted by other playwrights whose company he welcomed, and by supportive audiences. The names of some authors were kept secret, or at least not published, possibly to protect them from adversaries; but titles of plays listed with anonymous authorship appear to have followed the examples Fielding set, and received his support. Goldgar observes that in 1737 'Fielding's company at the Haymarket began a whole series of plays presumably with anti-Walpole satiric twists' (Goldgar 154). He says 'presumably' because many of the plays are lost or were never typeset and published.

A Rehearsal of Kings; or, The Projecting Gingerbread Baker: With the unheard of Catastrophe of MacPlunderkan, King of Roguomania And the Ignoble Fall of Baron Tromperland, King of Clouts, opened at the Haymarket on Monday, 14 March 1737. It remains unpublished, author unknown. *Sir Peevy Pet*, a new one-act farce by author unknown, play not published, opened at the Haymarket on 17 March 1737. *The Female Free Mason* was performed at the Haymarket on 25 April 1737; little else is known about it besides the description: 'In which the whole Art and Mystery of Free-Masonry is delineated by the Admission of a Lady'. That evening was a benefit for Mrs Haywood, and perhaps she added the new piece to attract more spectators. *The Sailor's Opera; or, An Example of Justice to present and future Times*, featuring Mrs Charke as Kitty Cable, opened at the Haymarket on 3 May. The evening was a benefit for Charlotte Charke, and it could be she wrote the piece, described as 'a new Ballad Opera. Written in Honour of the Gentlemen of the Navy'. The text was not published. A new song, 'The Politician', was added to *The Historical Register* 'by way of Epilogue' on 6 May 1737. *The Lordly Husband* and *The Dragon of Wantley* opened on 16 May 1737; the first of these by author unknown, and not printed—the second, a burlesque by Henry Carey, became well known. *Fame; or, Queen Elizabeth's Trumpets; or, Never plead's Hopes of being a Lord Chancellor; or, The Lover turn'd Philosopher; or, The Miser's Resolve upon the Lowering of Interest* opened on 4 May, with no author listed. It was described as 'a New Satyrical, Allegorical, Political, Philosophical Farce', and may have been written by actor James Lacy; it was never published. (Scouten Part 3: 648–69)

Besides the already mentioned *Macheath turn'd pyrate*, a revised version of Gay's *Polly*, another play was scheduled to open late in May 1737: *The King and Titi; or, The Medlars*, allegedly 'taken from the History of Prince Titi, Originally written in French, and lately translated into English'. Again the text is not available; but its title suggests it too was a satire or allegory concerned with ruling powers. Shevelow speculates that it 'was most likely based upon a recent French work that vigorously mocked the warfare going on between the Prince of Wales and his parents' (Shevelow 244).

A Rehearsal of Kings was said to be performed 'By a Company of Comedians dropt from the Clouds, late Servants to their thrice-renown'd Majesties, Kouly Kan and Theodore', which could have been Charlotte Charke's way of referring to her father and brother. Colley and Theo become Kouly and Theodore. (Scouten Part 3: 648). This fury of creativity in the last days of the Haymarket under Fielding's management looks in retrospect like an effort to do and say everything that could be said and done on stage before legislators passed their censorship bill.

Other titles for Haymarket plays appeared in 1737 advertisements, and may have been early drafts of scripts Fielding withheld for further development. *The Battle of Parnassus*, in rehearsal on January 6 according to the *Daily Journal*, probably turned into *The Defeat of Apollo; or Harlequin Triumphant*, which opened at the Haymarket on 14 January with its author unlisted (Scouten Part 3: 628– 31). The play bearing that title was never published; but a bastard son of Apollo representing either Walpole, Theo Cibber, or Drury Lane patentee Fleetwood, appears in *The Historical Register for the Year 1736*. Medley refers to 'a bastard of Apollo' when the divine offspring is introduced in Act III of *The Historical Register*; the bastard might have been born in another play which no one claimed as their own. It could be that Fielding re-used or revised his January Apollo material here. The luxury of having his own theatre and actors would have allowed him to test and reutilize his own writing, as well as that of earlier authors. Here too an analogy with Brecht in his last years at the Berliner Ensemble seems appropriate, as the German author industriously reutilized old texts and premiered new ones in his advancement of Epic theatre.

Comparing the plays of Shakespeare and Beckett in his landmark book, *Shakespeare Our Contemporary*, Jan Kott remarked that it was 'odd how often the word "Shakespearean" is uttered when one speaks about Brecht, Dürrenmatt, or Beckett . . .' (Kott 131). By contrast, Fielding and his contemporaries have not often been described as 'Brechtian' authors until now. It may be odd to hear them so described, and yet the Great Mogul's players and his plays have more in common with Brecht than has been acknowledged, particularly when seen as practitioners of oppositional theatre who defy entrenched artistic and political states through their playwriting. And while Fielding's own plays may have had little or no impact on Brecht, the German author shared with Fielding an interest in the plays of John Gay, who provided each of his successors with a ballad opera to adapt (*Polly* in Fielding's case, *The Beggar's Opera* in Brecht's).

Fielding, Fo, Littlewood

Fielding's satires are rarely staged anymore. The topical references may limit their modern appeal. Forgetting the texts for a minute, we might ask whether there could be another Henry Fielding in twenty-first-century theatre. A writer who attracts government persecution for stage satire as an adventurous journalist attracts secrecy violation charges has yet to be seen. Perhaps the centres of provocative writing and theatrical discourse have shifted from live stage performance to electronic media, where contests are played out between 'whistleblowers' such as Bradley Chelsea Manning, Edward Snowden, Wikileaks's Julian Assange, (earlier, Daniel Ellsberg) and government officials who classify information 'top secret' before the startling information is revealed to the public on the internet or in newspaper stories. Mass-media outlets are less likely to broadcast scandalous satire or state secrets if they conflict with advertiser, government or corporation interests. Today playwrights could conceivably offer disclosures similar to those of Manning or Snowden or Wikileaks—a few actors and their director may be less circumspect about revealing such material than mainstream media—and could reach a wide public with the assistance of reviewers or lawsuits against them.

Dario Fo, the Italian satirist, accomplished breakthroughs along these lines in the past century with plays such as *Accidental Death of an Anarchist* (1970), based on legal transcripts and otherwise secret information about police brutality. Fo's countercultural satire offered the public entertainment and political insight it was not receiving from Italy's mass media in the 1960s and 1970s. He was harassed and threatened accordingly by government officials, including the United States Department of State, which banned him for a few years from performing in the United States.

Joan Littlewood, director of the Theatre Workshop and Theatre Royal in East Stratford, returned to the satiric practices of Fielding's era in 1970 in order to avoid legal prosecution. In a collaboration with *Private Eye* journalist and satirist John Wells, Littlewood staged a play attributed to eighteenth-century author and Drury Lane prompter William Chetwood. In a book on Littlewood, Nadine Holdsworth reports the proceedings:

> Threatened with legal action if she pursued her original plan to produce a drama documentary based on an inquiry into the Ronan Point disaster [the partial collapse of a residential tower block at Ronan Point in 1968], Littlewood and Wells concocted the story of Chetwood's non-existent play (Holdsworth 40).

The Wells-Littlewood play titled *The Projector* was said to be based on Chetwood's 1733 play, *The Mock Mason*. In fact, a play with the title of *The*

Generous Free Mason was written by Chetwood in 1730; but it had little to do with Littlewood's subject of substandard housing. As George Dorris noted in his account of the 'joke', Chetwood's original play concerned masons of 'the fraternal kind', while 'Miss Littlewood's "joke" involves building frauds, and therefore stone masons' (Dorris 265–66). She used the Georgian play title and author name to suggest her drama concerned a corrupt Dutch property developer named Van Clysterpump, one of whose buildings collapsed in 1733, so that the Stratford East play was not about a contemporary construction scandal. The ruse protected her from a lawsuit, and gave audiences a comic revue that evoked 'the songspiel style of *The Beggar's Opera* and the biting wit of Hogarth's paintings', according to Holdsworth.

Chetwood's original list of characters for *The Generous Free Mason* included the names of Noodle, Doodle (reused by Littlewood's group), and was performed at the Haymarket, as was Fielding's *Tom Thumb* (which also had Noodle and Doodle characters) around the same time. Stratford East's programme note for *The Projector* claimed a 1733 theatre riot broke out over Chetwood's *The Mock Mason* after ruffians were paid to riot by one 'Cornelius Van Dort, who had been attacked in contemporary pamphlets as "Tumbledown Dick" on account of the shoddiness of his tenement buildings'. That ironic, surreptitious reference to Fielding's pantomime (*Tumble-Down Dick*) allowed Wells and Littlewood to acknowledge their debt to the earlier satirist. The programme notes also list a series of songs ('I met a Maiden at the Fair', 'Know, my bright Virgins', 'The Buildings Are Falling') that might have appeared in an eighteenth-century ballad opera, and claimed that *The Projector* 'was one of several English plays with music inspired by the success of *The Beggar's Opera in* 1728, including *The Village Opera, The Grub Street Opera* and *The Beggar's Wedding*'. That lineage places the 1970 production in the company of satires by Gay and Fielding. The portrait of Georgian gentlemen on the 1970 programme cover was a counterfeit of a Hogarth-illustrated subscription ticket. The contemporary relevance of the play also was noted in the programme, which admitted that

> ever since 1968 when the tower blocks of flats at Ronan Point, a mile or so from the Theatre Royal, Stratford East, collapsed in mysterious circumstances, Joan Littlewood has wanted to present its story on the stage. Then John Wells came across, in a book of old plays published in 1751, *The Projector* by Chetwood, a play based on a situation with so many similarities to the 1968 story that we hope it will still appear topical.

The 1751 book of plays has yet to be found by anyone besides John Wells; but there is no denying that the play attributed to Chetwood recalled or rather anticipated the Ronan Point event—it seems to have been prophetic as well as satiric. It could be argued that Wells and Littlewood practised their own version of Brecht's *Umfunktionierung* on a ballad opera from Fielding's era; if taken at their word (which is not entirely reliable), they reutilized the play (at least its title) and made it contemporary simply by staging the original text—quite a feat, or perhaps I should say, quite a 'counterfeit'.

As long as inordinate wealth, corrupt governments and questionable business practices exist, there will be need for another Fielding, or another Littlewood and Wells, whether or not he or she arrives. Fielding wrote in a 1737 letter to *Common Sense*: 'I am far from asserting that all Government is a Farce, but I affirm that, however the very Name of Power may frighten the Vulgar, it will never be honoured by the Philosopher, or the Man of Sense, unless accompany'd with Dignity'. He did not assert 'all Government' is a Farce; but his phrasing leaves open the prospect that some Government (or absence of it) deserves the appellation—and provides a fine source of inspiration for future theatrical satire.

CHAPTER TEN

Fielding's London Merchant, and Lillo's

A brothel near Drury Lane theatre served as the setting for Henry Fielding's comic afterpiece, *The Covent-Garden Tragedy* (1732). A few years earlier, the same section of London was visited by John Gay's Macheath. The 1728 ballad opera refers to Vinegar Yard and Lewkner's Lane, sites that housed prostitutes near Drury Lane. Perhaps Gay's depiction of women who worked in these locations inspired Fielding's decision to write about them. But George Lillo's groundbreaking domestic tragedy, *The London Merchant, or The History of George Barnwell*, was a more immediate source of inspiration for Fielding's satire. It too featured a prostitute, Sarah Millwood. In response to Lillo's play, Fielding introduced prostitutes and a London merchant of his own, a flesh peddler named Mother Punchbowl in *The Covent-Garden Tragedy*.

Those who regard Fielding as an early Brechtian also might see his mock-tragedy's brothel scenes as precursors of Macheath's 'coffee-house' visits with women in *The Threepenny Opera*. Brecht noted that Macheath's 'regular and pedantically punctual visits to a certain Turnbridge coffee-house are habits, whose cultivation and proliferation is perhaps the main objective of his correspondingly bourgeois life' (Brecht 1979: 92). The formation of such bourgeois 'habits' was shown on stage by Fielding first, when he mocked the new middle-class morality Lillo had portrayed in 1731.

Thomas Lockwood in his recent edition of Fielding's plays sees *The Covent-Garden Tragedy* as a response to Ambrose Phillips's *The Distrest Mother* (a retelling of the Andromache legend). Simon Trussler suggests another influence—Lillo's—in his introduction to Fielding's 'burlesque':

> the setting of his *Covent-Garden Tragedy* in a brothel allowed Fielding to satirize false heroics by attributing them to ignoble characters and causes; to expose the moral falsity of poetic justice by extending its improbable mercy to pimps and whores; and, incidentally, to mock the newly-emergent form of domestic tragedy, that distant ancestor of nineteenth-century melodrama and the problem play (Trussler 172).

Trussler's incidental note on Fielding's mockery of 'the newly-emergent form of domestic tragedy' deserves further consideration. The most prominent domestic tragedy of the period, *The London Merchant*, originally featured Theophilus Cibber in the role of the innocent young apprentice, George Barnwell. A year later Fielding's 1732 afterpiece set in Covent Garden (the London district, not the theatre of that name) featured the same Cibber in the role of a far from innocent rake. Lovegirlo in *The Covent-Garden Tragedy* is not entirely different from Barnwell; both characters fall for women outside the circle of middle-class respectability. It was quite fitting for Cibber to originate both roles, since he personally had lived in both worlds, as a rake who knew the stews and as a famous son who knew the high life of London through his father Colley's wealthy friends.

While *The London Merchant's* dialogue included earnest praise for the new empire England was fostering through international trade, Fielding's play mocked local trade, namely the sale of women's sexual favours. *The Covent-Garden Tragedy* comically depicted petty squabbles over (to invoke Marx again) 'callous cash payment'. Disputes over money replaced traditional tragic conflicts over love and honour. One woman of the trade in Fielding's play rejected advances from Captain Bilkum, who would have 'bilk'd' her and not 'come down the Ready' by paying hard cash.

Thorowgood, the employer of apprentice Barnwell in Lillo's play, speaks with fervour about how 'It is the industrious merchant's business to collect the various blessings of each soil and climate, and, with the product of the whole, to enrich his native country'. His praise for the profits of trade, first spoken by the actor Bridgewater, is offset in *The Covent-Garden Tragedy* by Mother Punchbowl's lamentation, also spoken by the actor Bridgewater (impersonating a brothel madam), on the decline of her trade. Her business has seen better days and better clients.

> When I resolve the glorious Days I've seen,
> (Days I shall see no more)—it tears my Brain.
> When Culls sent frequent, and were sent away.
> When Col'nels, Majors, Captains, and Lieutenants,
> Here spent the Issue of their glorious Toils . . .
> Now we are sunk to a low Race of Beaus,
> Fellows unfit for Women or for War;
> And one poor Cull is all the Guests I have.

In one year Bridgewater went from the role of virtuous, thoroughly good merchant to that of a cynical brothel madam whose days of glory are gone. He was still playing the role of Thorowgood at Drury Lane in May, 1732, as late 29 May, three days before *The Covent-Garden Tragedy* opened at the same theatre with Bridgewater as flesh merchant Mother Punchbowl. Theo Cibber continued to play George Barnwell until that date, too, so the audience could see the same actors in ironically different roles. Fielding shows his audience the underside of trade, a marketplace where rakes and beaux pay cash (or have none and promise it) to Mother Punchbowl instead of Thorowgood. Punchbowl may have looked a lot like Thorowgood, if audiences recognized and remembered Bridgewater in both roles; but as a man playing a woman's part, he (or she) might have been taken less seriously—appropriately so since the play was a satire. Similarly, naive George Barnwell (Cibber) transformed into the rake Lovegirlo would have startled or amused spectators, depending on their sense of humour.

After one night, actors at Drury Lane called for an end of the play's run in 1732, according to a contemporary press account. 'The Covent Garden Tragedy will be acted no more, both the Author and the Actors, being unwilling to continue any Piece contrary to the opinion of the Town', said London's *Daily Post* on 5 June. Its treatment of prostitution did not please the audience, or appeal to its moral sentiments, possibly because the satire lacked a moral lesson like the one Hogarth gave in *A Harlot's Progress*, first published in April 1732—two months before *The Covent-Garden Tragedy* opened. The artwork's popular depiction of a prostitute's demise may have sped Fielding on to complete his afterpiece, and Theo Cibber to write his pantomime, *A Harlot's Progress*. Hogarth, in turn, owed some debt to Gay's popularizing of harlot imagery on stage in *The Beggar's Opera*, and acknowledged it with a portrait of Captain Macheath on the wall of a bedchamber in Plate III of *A Harlot's Progress*, as well as paintings based on a scene in the ballad opera.

In *The Harlot's Progress* Hogarth illustrates a young woman's decline and death; dissolute life is not rewarded. Lillo also offers a moral tale of vice and crime punished in his domestic tragedy. Fielding's afterpiece, by contrast, portrays exploited women far more favourably. None of Mother Punchbowl's 'lewd women' go to the gallows, unlike Sarah Millwood in *The London Merchant*. The bawdy satire ends in a 'sudden turn of joy', a truce agreed on by the feuding parties. The playwright counteracts the new genre of domestic tragedy by turning to traders less respectable than Lillo's, and letting them go unpunished for the most part. At a time when Lillo's tragedy had been playing for more than a year, and remained in the Drury Lane repertoire, Fielding dared to brush against the grain, and write an anti-domestic tragedy. He acknowledges the genre of tragedy in his play title and makes a reference to the 'Tragick Muse' in his prologue; but the play mocks tragic drama by undermining its rhetoric and averting catastrophe. He denied his audience the satisfaction of seeing vice punished and honest trade extolled. 'No fine Moral Sentences,' as Fielding noted in his mock-preface to the play.

Lillo opened *The London Merchant* with a prologue of fine moral sentences: a promise to show the Tragic Muse in a 'humbler dress'. Fielding in his prologue mimics Lillo: 'Nor King, nor Hero shall you spy', but rather 'Bullies, Bawds, and Sots, and Rakes, and Whores', presented since 'Examples of the Great can serve but few, / For what are Kings and Heroes Faults to you?' Going further than Lillo in lowering the social standing of his protagonist, Fielding constructs a world where money is not a source of tragic action, but an acceptable replacement for love and virtue, or at least a means to measure them. One of the prostitutes unabashedly professes her love of gold:

> STORMANDRA: Oh! I despise all Love but that of Gold.
> Throw that aside and all Men are alike

Her rival, Kissinda, would pay a man for his love:

> KISSINDA: And I despise all other Charms but Love.
> Nothing could bribe me from Lovegirlo's Arms;
> Him, in a Cellar, wou'd my Love prefer
> To Lords in Houses of six Rooms a Floor.
> Oh! Had I in the World a hundred Pound,
> I'd give him all . . .

> LOVEGIRLO: Wou'dst thou, my Sweet? Now by the Powers of Love,
> I'll mortgage all my Lands to deck thee fine,
> Thou shalt wear Farms and Houses in each Ear,
> Ten thousand Load of Timber shall embrace
> Thy necklac'd Neck.

Elsewhere Lovegirlo admits to Kissinda that to kiss her 'at a Shilling is not dear'. Parodic measurement of affection in shillings, pounds and loads of timber evidently did not amuse the audience at Drury Lane, nor did professions of love spoken by a 'woman of the Town'. Lillo's play, where a woman seduces a man to make him steal and kill, was far more acceptable to the public; it counselled young apprentices to avoid immoral women and not murder rich uncles for their fortune, as Barnwell did.

Reportedly a rake before his marriage, Fielding and actor Theophilus Cibber (a rake before and after his two marriages) must have enjoyed creating a stage hymn to their harlot-filled haunts. Fielding's depiction of other London merchants besides Lillo's trading in vice may have hit too close to home to amuse spectators. Some characters in the play were based on living Londoners, possibly opening night spectators. The play setting's resemblance to known neighbourhood haunts led *The Grub Street*

Journal of 2 June to propose that instead of performing *The Covent-Garden Tragedy*, actors should 'invite the audience to some noted Bawdy-house in Drury Lane'. A 21 June *Daily Post* letter defending the play, and signed by Mr William Hint, Candle-Snuffer, challenged the critics 'with the help of all your Dictionaries, to Wrest one word of it into indecent meaning'. Lockwood suspects that Fielding himself wrote the letter signed by the Candle-Snuffer; perhaps no one else would defend the author. In any case Mr Hint's defence was too little and too late to keep the play running (Fielding 2007: 352).

In retrospect, the afterpiece can be seen as one foray among many Fielding made against the reign of tragedy: whether it was old and bombastic or new and domestic, he preferred comedy. Lillo's investigation of 'the actualities of bourgeois life, the moral problems affecting the rising middle classes' was set 'within the framework of tragic drama inherited from the preceding century and suited for other aims', as Peter Lewis has noted (Lewis 209). The paucity of notable tragedians in Georgian England led Bonamy Dobrée to conclude that 'the age lacked the tragic sense . . . and, it may be that, denied its expression on the stage, [the age] found its expression in satire' (Dobrée 255). He might have added that the age found its expression in Fielding, who also suggested tragic forms were exhausted in his mock-prologue to *The Covent-Garden Tragedy*, which claims the 'new tragedy' (Fielding's own mock-tragedy) is 'the worst that ever was written. . . . One wou'd have guess'd from the Audience, it had been a Comedy: For I saw more People laugh than cry at it'. In fact, few may have cried, but not enough of the audience laughed to keep the play running beyond its first night.

Given the competition, Lillo's tragedy may have been the best his age had to offer its new middle-class audience. Its popularity may have been one reason Fielding chose to mock it. Lillo's depiction of merchants as upright, productive civil servants must have pleased their counterparts in the audience. Poor George Barnwell became a victim not only of Millwood's seduction, but also of a need to celebrate the law-abiding businessman's ethics personified by Thorowgood. At the beginning of Act Three, Thorowgood instructs his apprentice Trueman in the virtues of commerce, which he sees going beyond accumulation of wealth:

> Methinks I would not have you only learn the method of merchandise and practise it hereafter, merely as a means of getting wealth; 'twill be well worth your pains to study it as a science, to see how it is founded in reason and the nature of things; how it promotes humanity, as it has opened and yet keeps up an intercourse between nations far remote from one another in situation, customs and religion; promoting arts, industry, peace, and plenty; by mutual benefits, diffusing mutual love from pole to pole.

This advice on the commercial 'means of getting wealth' and 'mutual love' at the same time is hardly the lesson, or the kind of learning Brecht later disseminated in his *Lehrstücke* (learning plays) and anti-capitalist writing; nor would Brecht have countenanced the empathy that Lillo solicits for the errant apprentice Barnwell when the youth willingly accepts his death sentence. Rarely is 'mutual love' free from cash payment, crime or class differences in Brecht's plays. The same could be said of Lillo's tragedy, by the way, but Lillo is no Brechtian in his evocation of empathy and his Christian moralizing.

The German author might have been more sympathetic to *The Covent-Garden Tragedy*, with its mordant view of the flesh trade, as well as the satire of political economy voiced in Fielding's *Historical Register for the Year 1736*, where the Third Patriot announces: 'Look'ee, gentlemen, my shop is my country. I always measure the prosperity of the latter by that of the former. My country is either richer or poorer, in my opinion, as my trade rises or falls. . . .'

George Lillo's pro-trade patriotism in *The London Merchant, or the History of George Barnwell* begins in his preface, where the author dedicates the play to Sir John Eyles, a member of parliament and sub-governor of the South Sea Company. Lillo praises his patron for arriving at the South Sea Company when it was 'in the utmost confusion and their properties in the greatest danger'. Eyles heroically rescued the endangered company, or so the playwright implies. The dedication makes John Eyles a patron saint of traders without quite saying so. London audiences would not have heard that dedication in 1731 when Lillo's play was performed, nor would they have heard any reference to the South Sea Company in the play itself, which is set in earlier, Elizabethan times.

But the author's reference to 'the utmost confusion' hints at another financial scandal, different from the one portrayed in *The London Merchant*. The opening speech delivered by Thorowgood praises 'honest merchants'—like himself—and delights in the prospect for improved trade relations abroad. Only the dedication refers explicitly to the economic and political conditions of 1731, and economic troubles that began when the 'South Sea Bubble' burst, and investors lost great sums in 1720.

Characters in Lillo's play make no reference to those events, but the audience in London might have discerned additional, more timely meaning in merchant Thorowgood's joy that Spain has been handicapped in its trade, to the benefit of Elizabethan England. In the England of Lillo's day Spain again (in 1729) had become less of a threat to British trade after a new treaty permitted the English to continue their slave trade abroad in Jamaica and other ports without fear of Spanish interference. John Loftis argues that 'a load of dramatically irrelevant denunciation of the Spaniards' introduced by Lillo in the play's opening could be explained by the fact that 'the English merchants were among the strongest proponents of [going to] war with Spain' (Loftis 1963: 124). But the denunciation is not irrelevant, as it affirms English pre-eminence in trade. By 1730 Britain had the world's largest slave-trading industry. Hundreds of ships bound for Africa started in Bristol, Liverpool and London. Eyles opposed a reduction in such trade by the South Sea Company in 1732, when Spain offered to pay for a greater share of the market. By 1733 he had been replaced as sub-governor, after his stance against reduction in slave trade was overruled by others in the company. His fall, if you call it that, was linked to his insistence on unabated slave trade.

Should Lillo have written a new stage tragedy based on the Eyles case, a play in which a highly respected entrepreneur and elected official suffered for trading in slaves? When Lillo's preface to *The London Merchant* defined 'the end of tragedy' as 'the exciting of the passions in order to the correcting such of them as are criminal', he was not thinking of Eyles's slave trade advocacy as a crime, far from it. The patron of the play also was an investor in slave trade conducted by the Royal African Company.

Lillo devotes scant attention to the larger world of empire and colonial trade in which merchants participated. Profits from international sales, the luxury life derived from degradation and captivity of other human beings by large firms, receive little attention from *The London Merchant*'s characters. One exception is Millwood's description of herself and other women existing as 'but slaves to men'. Barnwell's seductress claims that she and other women are slaves because they 'have no property—no, not even in themselves' (I, ii). In this sense, perhaps her efforts to secure money of her own constitute a slave rebellion, one which draws Barnwell into a murder plot and ends with their capture and execution on the gallows. The ending has a curious, probably unintended parallel to the conclusion of Gay's *Polly*, where escaped plantation slave Macheath is reported to have been hanged for piracy and other crimes in the last act. Polly Peachum survives as a model of virtue, like some of Lillo's characters; only she is more conflicted, because she finds herself continually attracted to 'immoral' Macheath.

Lillo makes Millwood a villain, and part of her villainy can be heard in the speech expressing a wish to have her 'conquests complete, like those of the Spaniards in the New World, who first plundered the natives of all the wealth they had, and then condemned the wretches to the mines for life to work for more'. Her lines are the closest the play comes to a condemnation of colonial conquest, and yet Millwood dreams of a life in which she can conquer and enslave, rather than be a slave; what makes her admission particularly offensive (to a London audience in 1731) is that Spain, rather than England, stands as her model of imperial rule.

Millwood's servant Lucy offers another perspective on slavery when she asserts that men are slaves to women. Later in the play George Barnwell more or less enslaves himself to Millwood with her encouragement, as he steals and murders for her, and ultimately accepts the loss of his life as the price of having met her demands.

Another motive for Barnwell's crimes, want of money by Millwood, drives her to lead the youth astray. Few characters in the play escape the world of financial transactions around them. Even honest and virtuous Maria, enamoured of Barnwell despite his trespasses, comes to see financial exchange as a means of salvation. As if enough expenditure can purchase and redeem morality, she asks Trueman: 'If I should supply the money, could you so dispose of that, and the account, as to conceal this unhappy mismanagement from my father?'(Act III, scene i). Maria has the makings of a modern corporate executive, ready to treat Barnwell's 'mismanagement' as an uncorrected financial transaction, not a crime, only she lives too early, in an age where women had to depend on men such as Trueman to buy justice with cash. In the end, Maria's plan fails, as Barnwell willingly takes leave of his life, not only to uphold the law, but also to sustain the Christian world view that grants him 'heavenly mercy' along with his death (Act V, scene ii). The playwright sees a triumph of commerce here, too; he has Barnwell declare that 'future penitents [will] profit of [his] example'. Perhaps this affirmation of merchant class profit from tragedy is one reason that John Loftis thought George Barnwell, the merchant's apprentice, 'may be associated . . . with the Whig propagandists' assertion of the dignity of the merchant class', in a dramatic genre adapted 'to the social fact of the rise of the great merchants to high place', and for that reason 'regarded as a dramatization of the distinctively Whig conception of the merchant' (Loftis 1963: 125).

While George Lillo clearly meant to praise his patron Eyles's world of trade and industry and affirm its values with his moralistic tragedy, the play's depiction of wealth and commerce gone awry—the social deviations enacted by Millwood, Barnwell, and Maria—inadvertently attests to the underside of mercantile trade. Henry Fielding intuited some of those failings in his 1732 satire, *The Covent-Garden Tragedy*. Actress Kitty Clive, delivering the epilogue to Fielding's afterpiece, wittily summarized the future of a world where almost everything is for sale, including human beings:

> To be a Mistress kept, the Strumpet strives,
> And all the modest Virgins to be Wives.
> For Prudes may cant of Virtues and of Vices,
> But faith! We only differ in our Prices.

Procuring women at various prices for gentlemen, Mother Punchbowl too is a London merchant. The play featuring her, also John Gay's *Polly* with its escaped slaves, appeared on stage far less often than Lillo's domestic tragedy in the Georgian period. Bridgewater as the patriotic merchant was far better received than Bridgewater the procuress, whose impersonation of a woman was grotesque as well as comic. Perhaps the humour and early Brechtian social critique within Fielding's and Gay's plays can be appreciated more fully now, in an age when international trade agreements are subject to worldwide protests; marches and tear-gassed assemblies against World Trade Organization meetings constitute a new theatre—street theatre—that raises objections to rule by those men Polly Peachum once called 'the new Alexanders'.

CHAPTER ELEVEN

Literarization of Fielding's Plays

'A Modern Glossary' published in 1752 by Henry Fielding defines a number of key words and concepts that underlie his plays, as well as his novels and journal columns. It is difficult to take these terms seriously; but that is part of their value, as they induce scepticism and laughter in the reader. In our age of computer technology, when authors sometimes assemble 'key words' for their readers online, such words speed access to literature at the expense of its complexities. Fielding's glossary of terms tends to mock simplification and jar expectation. His 'key words' might be employed for the kind of 'literarization' Brecht sought in the theatre through projection of intertitles on a stage curtain. The projections, he said, would punctuate 'representation' with 'formulation,' and allow for complex seeing (Brecht 1964: 43) Fielding's comic non-compendium of terms also might be projected on a screen or curtain between scenes of plays in which some of his favourite words can be heard.

Here are some of his glossary definitions suitable for screen projection:

AUTHOR. A laughing Stock. It means likewise a Poor Fellow, and in general an Object of Contempt.

DRESS. The principal Accomplishment of Men and Women.

DULNESS. A Word applied by all Writers to the Wit and Humour of others.

NOBODY. All the People in Great Britain, except about 1200.

PATRIOT. A candidate for a Place at Court.

POLITICS. The Art of getting such a Place.

PROMISE. Nothing

ROGUE & RASCAL The Man of a different Party from yourself.

TASTE. The present Whim of the Town, whatever it is.

Offering a limited vocabulary (55 words), Fielding's glossary first appeared in the pages of his bi-weekly, *The Covent Garden Journal*. The fashionable words he defined in the 14 January 1752 issue of the journal were not offered as an explanation of his play texts; but any actor or director approaching Fielding's plays, or other comic drama and literature of the Georgian period, might want to share the some of these definitions with an audience before or during a performance.

Why not project Fielding's definition of AUTHOR on a curtain at the beginning of his 1730 satire, *The Author's Farce*? Luckless certainly qualifies as an AUTHOR; the protagonist is an impoverished writer held in disregard by booksellers, play producers, and his landlady. The political candidates in Fielding's *Pasquin* are PATRIOTS, in his sense of the term, and their rivals qualify as ROGUES and RASCALS. His definitions favour neither Whigs nor Tories in the attribution of place-seeking to a PATRIOT, and they allow that ROGUE and RASCAL can be found in either party. (Times have not changed in that regard.) The terms are not exactly neutral; they apply to nearly everyone who is a writer, politician, or fashionably dressed Briton, and fit many of the characters in Fielding's satires. His most exclusive term is also the most inclusive; by limiting a mere 1200 to his critique of political economy, when he contends that NOBODY except 1200 Britons is of any account the country, the rest of the kingdom's inhabitants are set free from accusations of elitism. (Today that elite would be considerably smaller in Britain and its former American colonies.)

Fielding found in these words meanings that were not necessarily common or widespread. The terms are taken from everyday life and conversation, but their compiler confers exceptional usage on them—which is to say he takes exception to their usual and unexamined meanings.

In his comic glossary, Fielding manages as Johnson did in his dictionary to introduce 'his own opinions, and even prejudices, under general definitions of words' (as Boswell once said of the dictionary author)— only he also chooses to leave out the general definitions and stress his own views of wealth, class, and fashion. Boswell called Johnson's display of such personal views an 'indulgence', but Fielding might have regarded it as a lexicographer's duty (Boswell 1923: 180, 181).

He also might have disagreed with Johnson's definition of 'Lexicographer, a writer of dictionaries, a harmless drudge'. Fielding was not a drudge but a judge by the time he compiled his glossary. No longer writing for the stage in 1752, he had not retired as a satirist. In fact, Fielding's glossary exemplifies its own definition of MISCHIEF: 'Funn [sic], Sport, or Pastime'. But the word collection is missing HUMOUR in its own sense of the word; for it offers no 'Scandalous Lies, Tumbling and Dancing on the Rope'. Scandalous Truths abound. It is tempting to invent a few more terms not in the original fifty-five.

ACTOR. Conversationalist known for speaking to eight-hundred people at once. Occasionally speaks to another character on stage.

CENSOR. Man who finds humour where others see none. (See HUMOUR)

FARCE. Reference to any government policy not your own, usually composed by rogues and rascals. (See ROGUE and RASCAL). Also a kind of theatre piece.

MINISTER. An ACTOR so conscientious he has been known to CENSOR a FARCE in which he appears as a character.

CHAPTER TWELVE

Tom Thumb Jones, Child Actress

As noted in Chapter Two, Brecht cast Asja Lacis in the role of a young man—young Edward—in his stage production of Edward II. *He was by no means the first director to engage in cross-gender casting, although he came up with a new way of describing the practice with his theory of alienation effects. Henry Fielding's use of a young woman in the role of Tom Thumb must have had a comparable distancing effect on his audience.*

English children had performed on stage before Fielding's *Tom Thumb* opened in 1730. In Elizabethan plays boys performed the roles written for women. When women were allowed to appear on the English stage after 1660, young girls took roles, too, notably in the Lilliputian companies that performed Gay's *The Beggar's Opera* after 1728. One Lilliputian actress was Peg Woffington, who began her career as Polly Peachum at the age of ten in Dublin. Later (and older) she performed adult roles opposite David Garrick, and became his mistress.

The first actress to take the role of diminutive *Tom Thumb* was one Miss Jones, a child whose parents also were actors in Fielding's Haymarket production of the play. The cast list credits Mr Jones as Lord Grizzle, Mrs Jones as Princess Huncamunca, and Miss Jones as Tom Thumb. The play opened at the Haymarket on Friday, 24 April 1730, in a double bill with *The Author's Farce* (which had opened on 30 March) with Mr Jones as Bookweight and Dr Orator. Mr Jones spoke the prologue to *Tom Thumb*, and Miss Jones delivered the epilogue (Scouten Part 3: 45, 54).

The idea of casting a young woman in the title role probably began with James Ralph, Fielding's collaborator, who also suggested Fielding should dramatize the story of Thumb, one of 'our most noted domestic Fabels, which must please an English audience'. Ralph initially recommended casting an opera singer, 'Cuzzoni in Breeches', and thought she 'would make a delightful Tom Thumb' (Battestin 1989: 86).

The play was exceedingly popular. While some critics speculate that 'Tom Thumb the Great' was meant to mock the 'great man' Robert

Walpole, the Minister saw the play three times at the Haymarket and never called for its prohibition. Battestin remarks that while it is 'amusing' 'to consider Tom Thumb the Great, played by a diminutive actress swaggering about the stage in hero's attire, as an ironic figure for the Great Man himself', if there are 'political jokes' in the play, 'they are either so good-humored that they gave no offence, or so recondite that they were lost on Fielding's original audience' (Battestin 1989: 88). Walpole withheld legal action against Fielding for seven years, and only took it after a number of other satires mocked him.

Even if it was not topical satire directed at Walpole, the portrayal of a 'great man', a hero and conqueror, by a child actress would have served as a distancing device, early Epic comedy insuring that contradictions of size and gender accompanied the contradictions of language in the play. At the same time as the farce mocked heroic tragedy and its verse through parody, it mocked conventional theatrical representations of stage heroes as full-sized men.

Hogarth's frontispiece engraving for the 1731 expanded version of the play, retitled *The Tragedy of Tragedies, or The Life and Death of Tom Thumb the Great*, shows Thumb as a very short figure, about a foot off the ground, dwarfed by the two women (Huncamunca and Glumdalca) who stand above him. The gender of Thumb is not easily discerned here. Huncamunca holds a candle up toward her rival for Thumb's affection, to see if Glumdalca's beauty poses a threat. Thumb is too short to see much of either woman except the hem of their dresses, and he looks down at the floorboards as the women tower above him. His helmet with a giant feather atop it makes him look even smaller by comparison.

No eyewitness accounts of Miss Jones's performance as Tom Thumb survive. Nor do we know her age, her height, or her first name. But audiences might have heard a mother's reference to daughter, and vice versa, in some of the original lines. When Tom proclaimed 'Huncamunca's mine', it could be heard as Miss Jones expressing affection for her mother, Mrs Jones in the role of the Princess:

TOM THUMB: Trust me, my Noodle, I am wond'rous sick;
For tho' I love the gentle Huncamunca,
Yet at the Thought of Marriage, I grow pale . . .
[yet] she shall be mine;
I'll hug, caress, I'll eat her up with Love.

A daughter could say such things about her mother. Spectators might have laughed at that in-joke, as well as the plot Fielding wrote. For most of the play, Thumb and Huncamunca refer to one another without meet-ing. Hence lines such as Huncamunca's 'O, Tom Thumb! Tom Thumb!

Wherefore art thou Tom thumb?' And later, from Tom Thumb: 'Where is the Princess? Where's my Huncamunca?'

Besides parodying *Romeo and Juliet*, the separation of the pair allowed for a joyful reunion when they met. Mother embraced or cradled daughter at the same time as the Princess embraced Tom Thumb. Or perhaps they kept a respectful distance between them while Huncamunca blushed at the King's words. When the couple meet for the first time, the King encourages them to wed and 'propagate, / 'Till the whole Land be peopled with Tom Thumbs'. Thumb agrees; he will 'Endeavour so to do'. It almost could be mother speaking to daughter when Princess Huncamunca claims Thumb makes her blush with his talk of their wedding night. Apologizing for such talk, Thumb's words to the king's daughter could also be those of a child addressing her mother: 'I know not where, nor how, nor what I am, / I'm so transported, I have lost my self.' The next response from the Princess is not exactly what a mother or a princess would say—but rather a witty playwright's rejoinder: 'Forbid it, all the Stars; for you're so small, / That were you lost, you'd find your self no more.' The presence of Fielding—or his words—here may overshadow anything said or done by mother, daughter, princess or Thumb. Wordplay is a central action throughout Fielding's parody of bombastic tragedy.

Still, those watching the play in 1730 would have seen a child speaking onstage in Thumb's role, which could explain why Lord Egmont, who wrote a few comments in his diary after attending the Haymarket in April, 1730, noted that 'The author is one of the sixteen children of Mr. Fielding'. Fielding probably was only one of thirteen children (as Battestin notes); but the Earl's thoughts about children after watching *Tom Thumb* might follow from a consciousness of the child at the centre of the comedy. *Tom Thumb* is not to be mistaken for children's theatre, or a play about a child; but there is a playfulness about its language that anticipates the 'children's verse' and so-called 'nonsense' written by Edward Lear and Lewis Carroll. The Queen of Heart's 'Off with their heads' would almost fit into a scene of *Tom Thumb*, as Carroll too mocks royalty and its authoritative speech.

When Fielding revised and retitled his play *The Tragedy of Tragedies* in 1731, Miss Jones was replaced by 'Young Verhuyck'. Perhaps the girl had grown too tall or too old, but she continued to perform in Fielding's plays: as Miss Sneak in *Don Quixote in England* (1734), and as Aurora's Maid in *Tumble-Down Dick* (1736). Both Mr Jones and Miss Jones became members of the Great Mogul's Company of English Comedians directed by Fielding at the Haymarket in 1736–37.

The original cast for *The Historical Register for the Year 1736* lists Miss Jones in the company of Mrs Charke, Mrs Haywood, and Mrs Lacy, as Ladies who gossip about Italian opera and attend an auction. When Medley, the playwright within the play, is asked, 'What are these ladies

Fig. 4   Hogarth's illustration of Tom Thumb and his rival admirers, published in the 1731 edition of the play, *The Tragedy of Tragedies*.

assembled about?' he answers, 'Affairs of great importance, as you will see'. The affairs they discuss involve the famous Italian opera castrato, Farinello, his children and how 'it must be charming to have a child by him'. These same ladies acquired 'great importance' in another way, as the four actresses appeared in Fielding's most popular plays, and two of them may have written satiric plays for the Haymarket repertoire. While Miss Jones is not the most renowned of the four, she deserves some small praise for introducing 'affairs of great importance' to the English stage, and advancing with Fielding from the conquests of Tom Thumb in 1730 to the conquests of Farinello in 1737. (Her first name was never listed in the playbill; but if actors in Fielding's playhouse had been in the habit of addressing their child actor as Tom and Miss Jones, she also might have been known to some of them as Tom Jones.)

CHAPTER THIRTEEN

A World on Fire

As a playwright Henry Fielding encountered some strong objections to his work, after his stage satires agitated the ministry of Robert Walpole and its supporters in the press. Despite many charges levelled against him, the author was never accused of predicting climate change, or anticipating an age of extreme weather in his lifetime; but today, as our century begins to experience a marked increase in droughts, wildfires, hurricanes, floods, and record high temperatures, a scene in Fielding's 1736 pantomime, *Tumble-Down Dick, or Phaeton in the Suds*, reads like a brief, comic jeremiad against global warming disasters. After the apprentice lantern carrier Phaeton falls, and loses control of the sun-like source loaned by his father, a Countryman complains: 'Oh Neighbors! The World is at an End; call up the Parson of the Parish; I am but just got up from my Neighbor's Wife, and have not had time to say my Prayers since.'

> FIRST COUNTRYMAN: The World at an End! No, no, if this hot Weather continues we shall have Harvest in May. Odso, tho', 'tis damn'd hot! I'cod, I wish I had left my Cloathes at home.
> SECOND COUNTRYMAN: S'bud I sweat as if I had been at a hard day's work.
> FIRST COUNTRYMAN: Oh, I am scorch'd!
> SECOND COUNTRYMAN: Oh, I'm burnt!
> THIRD COUNTRYMAN: I'm on fire! [*Exeunt crying Fire*]

England does not burn up, since Neptune, emperor of the sea, arrives to rectify the climate crisis. But the brief eruption of extremely hot weather is a curious development in the text. It is tempting to see Fielding as a prophet of the planet's currently rising temperatures, complete with scorched earth zones and weather-ruined harvests, although we usually attribute the crises to trapped carbon gases and not Phaeton's fallen lantern.

Reports of extreme heat were recorded in the eighteenth century. When David Garrick drew record crowds to his Dublin performances in the summer of 1742, spectators fainted and some may have died of heat prostration or distemper. Davies writes: 'The excessive heat became prejudicial to the frequenters of the theatre; and the epidemical distemper which seized them, and carried off great numbers, was nicknamed, the Garrick fever' (Davies 1780, Volume I: 52). That illness (discussed more fully in Chapter Twenty) might have been caused by poorly-ventilated, crowded conditions in a theatre not built for summer shows, and not by Garrick's heated acting. But another report of temperatures rising—in the theatre world during the summer of 1733—suggests Fielding may have been responding to a known atmospheric challenge: 'Unseasonably hot weather descended' on the city of London that summer, and 'horse-drawn carts trundled up and down the streets, spraying water in an effort to settle the dust'. Several theatres advertised that 'Care will be taken to keep the House cool' (Shevelow 164). Records of the temperatures in England during the spring of 1736, when the pantomime played, were by no means high: 51 degrees Fahrenheit in May, 60 degrees in June. (Statistics come from a chart that can be found at http://www.rmets.org.uk/sites/default/files/qj74manley.pdf_) However, a late May 1736 advertisement for the Haymarket, where Fielding's parodic play had opened, declared: 'This is much the coolest House in Town' (Scouten Part 3: 588). Heat was anticipated.

If not written for an overwarm playhouse, Fielding's scene with the world on fire might have reflected religious views of the day. There is a touch of Biblical parody in the dialogue, as if Hell has finally ascended to earth to torment the sinner who slept with his neighbour's wife, and the idle man who sweats as if he worked hard. The sun is said to take 'devilish large leaps' like a man going 'a Fox-Hunting', another linkage of hellish punishment to the lifestyle of an idle class. Fielding was not averse to mocking wealthy, adulterous and fashionable dramatis personae in his satires. He also must have heard a few hellfire sermons. Evangelism was soon to spread around the country, and Fielding might have responded to some of its early fiery language, or comparable sermons that preceded Methodist preaching. A number of his writings question whether religion serves any useful purpose. His comic glossary published in 1752 defined 'Religion' as 'A Word of no Meaning; but which serves as a Bugbear to frighten Children with'.

The scene of intemperate weather was also a local and comically English response to the Roman myth in which Phaeton carries his father's lantern. *Tumble-Down Dick* was created in part to parody depiction of the same mythology in a pantomime titled *The Fall of Phaeton, or Harlequin a Captive*, which opened two months earlier at Drury Lane. John Rich, manager of Covent Garden, and a champion of pantomime, also was one of the targets of Fielding's play; the satirist was not fond of pantomime in general. *Tumble-Down Dick* might be called an anti-pantomime; it mocks the very form it embodies, and takes aim at producers of pantomime. As the Battestins note, in this parodic pantomime 'Rich is introduced as "Machine", who arrogantly presides over the rehearsal of the inane Ovidian entertainment he has devised' (Battestin and Battestin 203). Since Fielding's play opened at the Haymarket, he was free to ridicule his rival pantomimes at the Patent playhouses, and he did so in *Tumble-Down Dick*.

If this scene of the world on fire were enlarged today with songs ('There'll be a hot town in the old town tonight', etc.) and more dialogue, its staging might startle contemporary audiences. As a new, globally-warmed variant of Georgian pantomime, the sketch could be staged in tandem with a fragment of Beckett's *Happy Days*—the scene where Winnie's parasol catches fire in her sun-scorched terrain. Or a few lines from Beckett's play might be inserted in Fielding's. Winnie could sit in for the 'Neighbour's Wife', wave to her burning countrymen, and ask: 'Shall I myself not melt in the end, or burn . . . Do you think the earth has lost its atmosphere?' (Beckett 38). Fielding's scene also could be staged as curtain-raiser to performance of Beckett's play in its entirety, to open an evening of theatre for a world on fire. Lines from Brecht's poem about Buddha and the burning house would fit the bill as well. The Buddha recalls: 'I opened the door and called / Out to them that the roof was ablaze, so exhorting them / To leave at once. But those people seemed in no hurry' (Brecht 1976: 291).

CHAPTER FOURTEEN

Fielding's Cibber Letters: Counterfeit Wit, Scurrility and Cartels

Never printed in a book until now, the letters introduced and published below reveal that Henry Fielding and James Ralph co-authored a counterfeit autobiography of actor Theophilus Cibber. The volume they wrote and attributed to 'Mr. T . . . . C . . . . .' contains satiric criticism of theatre censorship, cartels, and Colley Cibber's autobiography. The book and letters they wrote responded to the era of monopolies and a managerial dynasty in the theatre (discussed at length in Chapters Nine and Sixteen), and can be seen as literary acts of resistance initiated by early Brechtians. Readers are advised that questions have arisen about the authenticity of the eighteenth-century letters printed here; but the documents seemed too important for their publication to be delayed any more than 275 years.

Since *An Apology for the Life of Mr. T . . . . C . . . . ., Comedian*, was printed in 1740, little has been written about this counterfeit autobiography beyond paragraphs and footnotes debating whether Henry Fielding penned its account of the life of Colley Cibber's son. Later commentators agree that the initials 'T.C.' in the title stand for Theophilus Cibber, an actor who had to postpone plans for his own autobiography because an impostor stole his prospective readers. 'Theo. Cibber himself had proposed to publish his own Life by subscription, but by the advice of some friends he dropt the design' once the book by his stand-in came out (Genest IV: 531–32). Cibber had no idea who wrote the book. Besides offering amusing anecdotes about his life in the theatre, the counterfeit autobiography's 144 pages consider events that would have been quite important to stage artists of the period: namely, the 1737 theatre censorship law that Theophilus and his father Colley Cibber endorsed, and the prospect of a new theatre cartel controlling performances at London's licensed theatres, with casting and play selection dictated by a few theatre managers like the elder Cibber.

The book's objections to cartels and censorship can be viewed in retrospect as defence of free speech at a time—not entirely different from

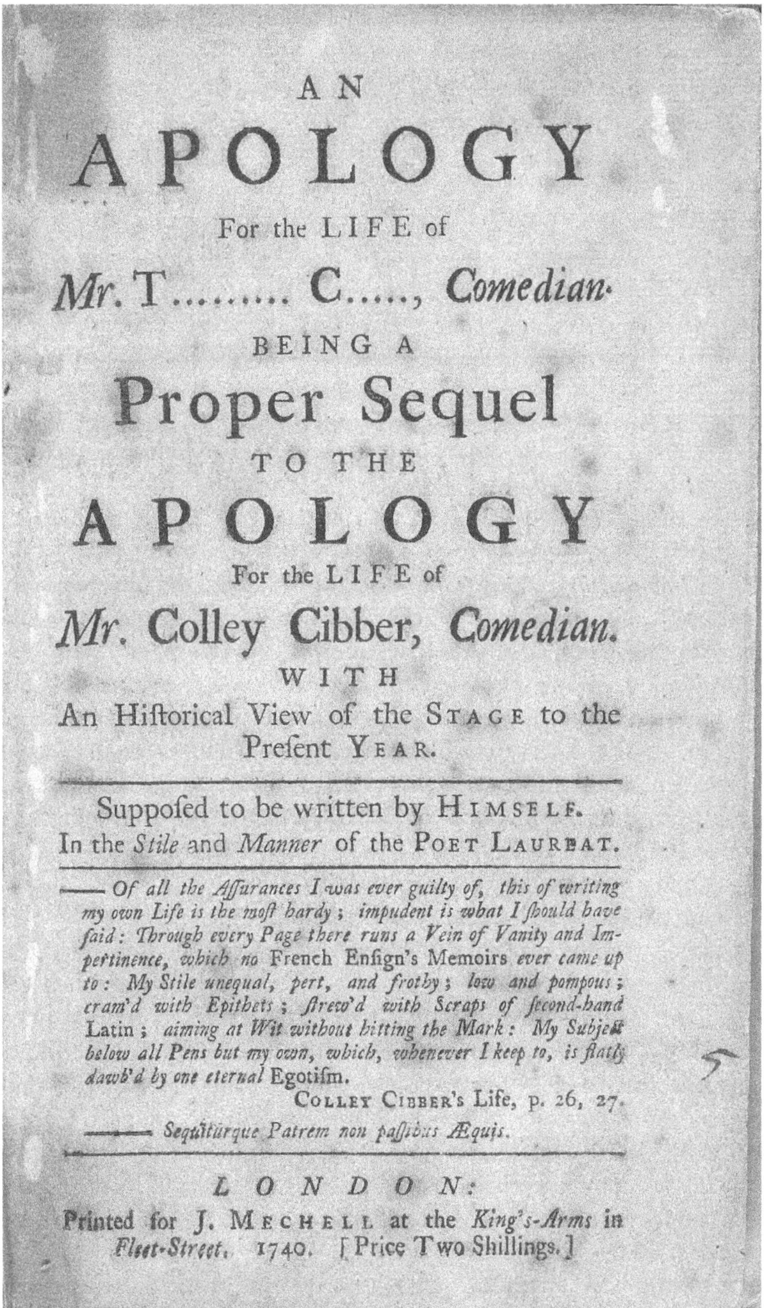

AN
APOLOGY

For the LIFE of

Mr. T......... C....., *Comedian.*

BEING A

Proper Sequel

TO THE

APOLOGY

For the LIFE of

Mr. Colley Cibber, *Comedian.*

WITH

An Historical View of the STAGE to the Present YEAR.

Suppofed to be written by HIMSELF.
In the *Stile* and *Manner* of the POET LAUREAT.

—— *Of all the Affurances I was ever guilty of, this of writing my own Life is the moft hardy; impudent is what I fhould have faid: Through every Page there runs a Vein of Vanity and Impertinence, which no French Enfign's Memoirs ever came up to: My Stile unequal, pert, and frothy; low and pompous; cram'd with Epithets; ftrew'd with Scraps of fecond-hand Latin; aiming at Wit without hitting the Mark: My Subject below all Pens but my own, which, whenever I keep to, is flatly dawb'd by one eternal* Egotifm.

COLLEY CIBBER's Life, p. 26, 27.

—— *Sequiturque Patrem non paffibus Æquis.*

L O N D O N:

Printed for J. MECHELL at the *King's-Arms* in *Fleet-Street.* 1740. [Price Two Shillings.]

Fig 5.   Title page of the book by Mr T . . . . C . . . . .

our own—when men of wealth and influence sought to make speech a profitable commodity subject to their control. The eighteenth-century theatre history recorded in *An Apology for the Life of Mr. T . . . . C . . . . ., Comedian* pretends to see stage satire and cartel practices from the perspective of one of their victims, Theo Cibber. It also frequently quotes a victimizer, poet laureate Colley Cibber, not known for kindness towards his son or rival theatre artists. The title page promises

> a proper sequel to *The Apology for the Life of Mr. Colley Cibber, Comedian*, with an historical view of the stage to the present year, supposed to be written by himself in the stile and manner of the poet laureate.

In fact this sequel to Colley Cibber's autobiography is an improper sequel—unauthorized, also cheeky in its admission of lies, betrayals and trampling over others by the Cibbers in theatre and politics.

Whoever counterfeited T . . . . C . . . . .'s *Apology* probably kept his (or their) identity secret to avoid reprisals from Cibber father and son and their allies in first Minister Walpole's offices; such reprisals could end careers, as Walpole proved in June, 1737 when the Licensing Act went into effect. The legislation kept satire like Henry Fielding's off the stage. Before the Act passed, as already noted, Fielding had become quite popular for his political satires at the Haymarket; *Pasquin, The Historical Register for the Year 1736*, and *Eurydice Hissed* all attracted enthusiastic audiences, mocked men of wealth and influence, and greatly displeased Walpole's regime, judging from the pro-ministry critics who attacked Fielding's plays in the months before he was effectively banned from the stage. After June, 1737, Fielding had ample motive to co-author Mr T . . . . C . . . . .'s *Apology*, as the newly discovered letters printed below suggest.

Prevented from continuing to stage satire at the Haymarket, Fielding moved more actively into the medium of print, not yet controlled by the government. Through the counterfeit *Apology*, he was able to resume in a thorough, extended form (much longer than a journal column, and more durable than a news sheet) his comic criticism of the Cibbers and Walpole. Here, as in a stage satire, adversaries could be discussed, even 'captured' and impersonated to comic effect, as their prejudices and their widely-circulated pronouncements—such as those in Colley Cibber's *Apology*—were mimicked. In one of the letters that follows, Theophilus Cibber calls the theft of his persona a kidnapping.

Attributing base ambition, self-love and support of theatre censorship to Theophilus and his father, the counterfeit autobiography led some readers to take its admissions at face value; others, to see in the act of impersonation another, second, shared level of deception perpetrated by a satirist. Theophilus himself said the *Apology* 'did in fact pass for his with many readers' (Coley 423). Henry Fielding joked about the volume—without overtly calling it counterfeit or signing his name to a column discussing the new volume—in the 12 August 1740 issue of the periodical *The Champion*. There he cited 'the learned Lord *Scriblerus*' Notes to 2nd *Dunciad*', without mentioning that Lord Scriblerus was another counterfeited identity (devised by Pope, Swift, Gay, Arbuthnot), as he introduced readers to the *Apology for the Life of Mr. T . . . . C . . . . ., Comedian*. He also wryly reprimanded the book's reputed author, Theophilus Cibber, for quoting so much of his father's autobiography, and in that way 'taking away the Life of another', precisely the offence perpetrated by the counterfeiter who called himself Mr T . . . . C . . . . . (Coley 424). Colley Cibber's own memoir, which preceded Mr T . . . . C . . . . .'s by a few months, remains a historically significant document; the poet laureate's account, as Peter Thomson noted, traces 'the shift in acting brought about by theatre architecture between the post-Restoration "Stuart" age and the Hanoverian age' (Thomson 2013). At the same time as Colley Cibber's *Apology* advanced theatre history and commented on the actors of his era, it also promoted his own career. The prominent actor-manager and playwright's preening probably disturbed his parodists, who quote him, then undermine his standing and his son's with admissions they attribute to the Cibbers in *An Apology for the Life of Mr. T . . . . C . . . . ., Comedian*. The anonymous creators composed a counterhistory, as they revised and added to the poet laureate's prior historical view of the stage, and expanded the discussion of state censorship Cibber father and son supported. The confessions attributed to Cibber Junior (as Theophilus was known at the time) also mocked his opportunism and his small fame as an actor best remembered for the role of Pistol in Shakespeare's *Henry IV, Part II*.

State Secrets Sold by Grub Street

The most compelling pages of T . . . . C . . . . .'s *Apology* engage in a subtle, ironic defence of Henry Fielding's theatre, through passages written by someone who was there at the time of crisis, and aware of the artistic freedom endangered. The confessions of 1740 claimed to offer a government insider's view of Fielding's stage satire. 'As this [1737 Licensing] Act is of such importance to the Theatres, and the passing of it caused great Debates in both Houses it may be proper to consider the Cause and Reasons given for having it enacted, in relating which, I may give some curious Anecdotes and State-Secrets, which Mr. C. Cibber has omitted', T . . . . C . . . . . promises readers in return for their two shillings (Mr T.C. 1740: 90–92). Mr T . . . . C . . . . . then quotes Colley Cibber's unflattering reference to 'a broken wit', that is, to Henry Fielding, and considerably expands on the father's justification for censorship of Fielding and others. The 'State-Secrets' revealed centre on a political stage satire titled *The Golden Rump* (introduced in Chapter Nine). As noted earlier, the play was never staged and never published, but allegedly read by the Prime Minister and other legislators who found its scatological humour and references to the King's posterior so offensive they rallied around the new censorship law. T . . . . C . . . . . provides an insider's knowledge of this now lost play; he suggests it was written at Walpole's request ('by a certain great Man's own Direction'), and given to the Minister by a theatre manager (Giffard at Goodman's Fields) in exchange for a promise of 'Great things'. *The Golden Rump* was attributed to Fielding by Horace Walpole; it would be quite fitting if Fielding deflected such false attributions with one of his own initialled T . . . . C . . . . . (Battestin and Battestin 1989: 226) In his *Memoirs of King George II*, Horace Walpole also claimed he had in his possession an 'imperfect copy' of *The Golden Rump* found among his father's papers; but the copy has yet to be located in Walpole family archives.

Until now, it has been difficult to establish who wrote Mr T . . . . C . . . . .'s life story, because even in print exempt from the Lord Chamberlain's censorial eye, satirists often found it advantageous to conceal their own names. Legalized fury at printed satire erupted in July of 1737 when a journal printer was arrested and his office ransacked after publication of a facetious essay signed with Colley Cibber's initials. It is possible another wit wrote the controversial essay for *The Craftsman*, but Martin Battestin awards Fielding the honour. The 2nd July *Craftsman* article pseudonymously written in the first person voice of the poet laureate claimed he was ready to censor old plays as well as new ones, and wished to be appointed 'Supervisor of all Plays', including Shakespeare's and Jonson's, which in his view might be subversive texts. 'Nobody, without Vanity, is fitter for this Office than Myself', the poet laureate claimed in his alleged letter to *The Craftsman*. In fact Cibber and son earlier had shown no hesitation in cutting and revising Shakespeare's plays to make them (in their view) more suitable for the Georgian stage (Battestin 1989: 234).

The writer who impersonated Cibber Senior in *The Craftsman* wisely signed the article with the initials 'C.C.P.L.'—for Colley Cibber Poet Laureate. This choice saved the writer (but not his printer) from a jail sentence. As late as 1939 a scholar was uncertain whether Colley Cibber himself wrote the 1737 article. 'It seems more likely that Cibber did not write it than he did', concluded E.L. Avery (Avery 103). The authorial use of initials provided similar protection when "T . . . . C . . . . ." was named author on the title page of his *Apology*. No one was arrested for writing the book.

The Cibbers might well have suspected Fielding of composing the unflattering family portrait. During his theatre career he personally witnessed many Cibber family activities recounted in the rogue *Apology* and in the letters appended to this chapter. Theophilus performed in a few of Fielding's plays, notably *The Covent-Garden Tragedy* and *The Tragedy of Tragedies*, and some of the satirist's plays were produced at Drury Lane under Colley Cibber's management, before Fielding managed his own company at the Haymarket. These professional associations did not deter Fielding from mocking both Cibber father and son on stage for their alliance with the Ministry of Robert Walpole and for the elder Cibber's discouragement of young authors while a manager at Drury Lane. In *The Author's Farce*, Colley Cibber's stand-in, Marplay, rejects Luckless's new play by informing him: 'Sir, it will not do . . . there is nothing in it that pleases me, so I am sure there is nothing in it that will please the town.' In fact, the town liked *The Author's Farce* very much. For a 1734 revival of the play at Drury Lane, Fielding added Marplay Junior, a caricature of Theo, who seconds Marplay Senior's abusive decisions.

The conflict between Fielding and the Cibbers is inseparable from the history of competition between theatres, and between theatre managers, in the period from 1730 to 1750. Drury Lane served as an artistic home for the Cibbers during some of this period. Their competition included theatres run by the Rich family (father Christopher at Lincoln's Inn Fields, then son John Rich who founded Covent Garden Theatre in 1732–33), as well as smaller venues such as the Haymarket where Henry Fielding's company thrived from 1736 until June of 1737. Theophilus and his sister, actress Charlotte Charke, both for a time participated in actor rebellions against Drury Lane management; but he then returned to the fold.

While the actor rebellion is discussed more fully in Chapter Sixteen, it should be noted here, to help explain one of the appended letters. Theophilus became a mutineer in response to the threat of increased management control over actor choices and salaries, which alarmed him as it later alarmed his double, Mr T . . . . C . . . . . In a 1733 letter to Drury Lane Manager John Highmore, when he led actors against management, Theo Cibber (not to be mistaken here for Mr T . . . . C . . . . .) asked: 'Is there not now subsisting a CARTEL between the Patentees of Covent-Garden and Drury Lane, very prejudicial to every performer? . . . such Agreements . . . shall reduce the Income of every Performer to a very small Pittance, and render the Actors the only Slaves in Great Britain . . . Slaves to those who are born their Fellow-Subjects' (Conrad 85). This fear was later confirmed by the playwright Benjamin Victor, who in 1761 recalled: 'friends to the Seceders [who left Drury Lane in protest in 1733] urged that the actors were a free people and not to be sold with the Patent, as slaves with a plantation in the West Indies' (Genest III: 402). While comparing themselves to plantation slaves may have been an over-the-top, exaggerated claim, the protesters were after all actors used to employing heightened language in scenes of distress. Mr T . . . . C . . . . . echoed these charges against management in the 1740 *Apology*.

Theophilus Cibber Against Cartels

For all the faults that led satirists to mock him, Theophilus Cibber had his admirable side, shown when defence of the rights of others coincided with self-interest. His objection to cartel agreements affirms Conrad's view that in 1735, it was not the threat of increased censorship that alarmed actors like Theo, but rather 'the tyranny of the patentees and patentee cartels' who ran Drury Lane and Covent Garden. Here young Cibber's fears may have been exacerbated by the fact that his father sold his shares in Drury Lane, leaving the son (and daughter Charlotte) less secure at that establishment. In the autobiography attributed to Theophilus, the actor voices concern over his loss of favoured standing. When Highmore sold his control of Drury Lane to Fleetwood, writes Mr T . . . . C . . . . .

> We at the Hay-market [not Fielding's space that season, but rather the temporary home of rebel actors led by Theo Cibber, 1733–34] were under a most terrible Consternation; we looked on ourselves as Persons who were never to enjoy that Liberty [of sharing managerial decisions at Drury Lane] we had so strenuously endeavoured to obtain: For this Conjunction of the Patentee Masters must have compelled us to have returned under their Management (Mr T . . . . C . . . . . . 1740: 97).

Theo's anxiety over loss of professional standing is also mentioned in one of the letters assembled here, as Fielding's friend James Ralph expresses a fear that Theophilus will write an autobiography before his impersonators do, and 'claim Hereditary Stage Rights and boast once more about the Glorious Revolution he led against theatre managers in 1733'. Instead, the counterfeiters recorded these sentiments for him, with their own exaggerations and recriminations added.

Curiously, a letter in which Theophilus Cibber discusses the counterfeit *Apology* appears in the documents assembled here, too. Exactly how it entered the file of the correspondence written mostly by Fielding and his friend James Ralph is troubling. But it could be that the printer of Mr T . . . . C . . . . .'s *Apology*, Mechell, to whom Theo Cibber's letter was addressed, received it first and then sent it on to Fielding, who as co-author of the rogue autobiography would have been intrigued by Theophilus's complaint, and saved it along with his own letters on the topic.

Besides offering evidence of Fielding's involvement in writing Mr T . . . . C . . . . .'s *Apology*, the seven letters printed here include a reply from Theo's sister, Charlotte Charke, who had been cast in satires that Henry Fielding wrote and staged at the Haymarket. Charlotte's participation in plays that mocked her father, brother and Walpole would have pleased the Prime Minister's opposition. Colley Cibber himself disowned his daughter, as she acknowledged in an autobiography published under her name in 1755. Probably Charke's habits of dressing like a man and living with a woman off stage disturbed the poet laureate as much as his daughter's stage roles. But she remained a rebel on stage and off for most of her life. As recounted more fully later in this book, she joined her brother in the 1733 rebellion against Drury Lane's management, and after that Charke appeared in two plays about actor rebellion against managers—*The Stage Mutineers* (written anonymously in 1733) and her own satire, *The Art of Management; or Tragedy Expelled (*written in 1735*).* Her anti-establishment choices as an actress, author and rebel may had led Fielding to ask Mrs Charke if she would co-author the T . . . . C . . . . . *Apology.* She declined the invitation in a letter printed here.

   Another important player in the cast of letter writers is James Ralph. Ralph was a manager and shareholder at the Haymarket, also co-editor with Fielding of the journal, *The Champion*, from 1739–41. An American-born writer, James Ralph travelled to London with his friend Benjamin Franklin, and became active in the city's theatre and politics by 1730. Although his name is hardly mentioned in most theatre histories, Ralph worked productively with Fielding behind the scenes at the Haymarket, and gave him the idea for his popular stage comedy, *Tom Thumb* (1730).

   Behind the scenes, where Ralph stood, is also where the authors of *An Apology for the Life of Mr. T . . . . C . . . . ., Comedian* stayed for several hundred years. Until now no one has conclusively proven who wrote the mock autobiography of Theophilus Cibber. The previously unpublished letters that follow confirm, if genuine, that the 1740 book was co-written by Henry Fielding and James Ralph. Their exchange of letters begins with a discussion of the memoir Colley Cibber published, then considers the theatre careers of Cibber's son Theo and his daughter Charlotte. One letter concludes in the name of Hercules Vinegar, a pseudonym Fielding used; but someone else could have used it, too. Other letters place the initials H and J—for Henry and James—in their closing. No one except Charke and Theo Cibber sign their own names to the correspondence. But the letters as a group point toward Fielding and Ralph as counterfeiters of young Cibber's *Apology.*

The Counterfeitable Man

In *The Counterfeiters*, a study of Augustan satirists, Andy Warhol and their legacy, Hugh Kenner argues that 'the concept of the counterfeitable man was the [Augustan] age's characterizing achievement' (Kenner 27). Kenner's book looks at counterfeit identities shaped by Swift, Pope and Defoe. He neglects to mention Mr T . . . . C . . . . .'s *Apology* as a variant on the same sensibility. Perhaps it is not the same, insofar as the *Apology*'s authors counterfeit confessions of a man who at the time was quite alive and visible onstage (unlike Swift's Lemuel Gulliver or Defoe's Robinson Crusoe). In any case the writers of Mr T . . . . C . . . . .'s *Apology* demonstrated that Theophilus Cibber's voice was counterfeitable, and quite suitable for mimicry. (Later Brecht would show how one man can replace another in his play *A Man's a Man*, and renew some of these eighteenth-century themes with new variants.)

As the source of comic mimicry, Theo Cibber unwittingly won a place in the repertoire of eighteenth-century stage rakes, fools and rogues, and the *Apology* gave it to him, as did the placement of Pistol (a character based on Theo Cibber) in the stage plays mentioned in one of the letters appended here; these plays include *The Stage Mutineers* (unsigned, attributed to Edward Phillips), *The Historical Register for the Year 1736* (by Fielding) and *The Beggar's Pantomime* (attributed to Henry Woodward).

While I am pleased to be able to introduce readers to a transcribed copy of Fielding's Cibber letters on the occasion of their first publication in a book, I have to admit some doubts about their authenticity. I do not know where they were kept for a few hundred years. They came to my attention through a typed transcription of the originals displayed on an internet website (geocities.com/~lostfielding) that was captured in a screenshot by an unknown scholar around 1997. I have tried to find the website that matches the screenshot, and consulted web historians at the Internet Archive in San Francisco; but 'geocities.com/~lostfielding' seems to have fallen off the World Wide Web. I am told a site no longer maintained online is called a 'ghost', a term highly appropriate in this case, considering Henry Fielding's own fondness for ghosts. In his play *Tom Thumb* the title character, swallowed by a cow, reappears on stage to declare: 'Tom Thumb I am—but am not eke alive. My Body's in the Cow, my Ghost is here.' Perhaps the Ghost of Henry Fielding now wanders the World Wide Web, and materializes occasionally in the form of personal correspondence. Readers are invited to add to this correspondence, by reporting any online sightings of Fielding's ghost, and to share any other findings that confirm the names of the men who impersonated Theophilus Cibber in 1740. I have modernized the spelling of the ghostly 'originals' in the texts that follow.

Fielding's Lost Letters

30 March, 1740

My dear Henry,
I hear your friend the Laureate has written *An Apology for the Life of Colley Cibber, Comedian*, and it is to appear in Print this week. As if we have not heard enough of his Foppish Prating in stage plays, we now are likely to see Booksellers provide Cibber with another platform on which to display himself as Sir Robert's Favorite Poet. Is there no way to stop the man from his Fawning Performances? Of course I am not advocating curtailment of his Liberty, as the Minister would. But if we do nothing, soon Cibber Junior, denied old Colley's share of the Patent at Drury Lane, will write his Life Story also, to claim Hereditary Stage Rights and boast once more about the Glorious Revolution he led in 1733. If we must hear more from the Cibber family, I would rather listen to Mrs. Charke again; have her personate the old man or her brother Theo in all their Vanity, as she did so admirably under our direction at the Hay-Market, and in her own Puppet Theatre. Shall we write a new book in her name—*An Apology for the Life of Mrs. Charlotte Charke, Puppeteer*?

At wit's end, Ralph

10 April

To the honorable James Ralph, Wit's End, London,
As much as I admire Mrs. Charke's performance in Breeches, and her excellent Puppet staging of *The Covent-Garden Tragedy*, I am inclined to read and therefore write a version of the Life of Mr. Theophilus Cibber, rather than that of his sister. First of all, to render his Life Story comic would not take Great Imagination—he could almost do it himself, so much Humour can be found in the tales of this wife-pandering Pistol. There was a reason we cast him as the Rake in *The Covent-Garden Tragedy*; Debauchery and Bombast are his special calling. A parody of young Cibber—Pistol by name—keeps appearing in new plays—viz. *The Stage Mutineers*, *The Historical Register*, *Tumble-Down Dick*, *The Beggar's Pantomime*. And like his father, the lad has played on a much larger Stage than Drury Lane, as Advisor to a Minister in Whitehall, I am told. Indeed, those who should know aver that the old gentleman's Muse has been dead some time, and the Laurel (the Heir Loom of the Family) has fallen down on the head of the son. What do you say we write the son's Apology before he can?

Hercules Vinegar

17 April

Dear Mr. Vinegar:

I thank you for the invitation to contribute to the planned *Apology for Mr. T .... C ....., Comedian*; but I find myself too much in my brother's Debt (more than fifty pounds sterling) to do anything that could undermine his Income, and prevent him from affording Loans to me in the future. Besides which, he has undermined his own Reputation so effectively he needs no assistance from you or me. As you ask, I will not tell Theo about Rumours a new book is to appear in his name; I might, if I knew the names of the Authors, but you never told them to me. Is our Mutual Friend Mr. Fielding one of the Literary Assailants? When I first met him I took the part of Lord Place in his play called *Pasquin* at the Hay-Market, and I was engaged at four guineas per week; I also played Hen the Auctioneer in his *Historical Register*, and I should be delighted to work with Fielding again, especially for those Wages. Until then I remain your servant,

Mrs. Charlotte Charke

22 April

Most revered Hercules,

I have now scribbled some fifty pages of *An Apology for the Life of Mr. T--- ----- C-----, Comedian*, and I am sending them on for your Improvement. We had best not sign our Names, or even our usual Pseudonyms, to this Great Book, lest its subject come after us with a Pistol. He is a terribly hotheaded young man, more so than the Fools he portrays on stage. If his own Initials grace our Title Page, I imagine the Braggart will claim he wrote the book himself, and leave us alone.　　J

1 May

Dear J,

I do not want TC to claim credit for the Authorship of our Comedy, and for that reason cannot sanction this Plan further unless we make some of the stories so Abhorrent that even Mr. TC will deny them. His Confessions must include an admission that CCPL ensured the Licensing Act would drive certain Wits out of the Theatre, and leave more space for his own Meager Works. (The Minister will not be amused by the boast, but so much the better.) The said Confession also should reveal the lad's enormous Restraint, viz. He did not renounce CCPL as a Blood Relative when the old man declined to pass on Management of Drury Lane to his

Truculent Son. The worst offence is not the son's, but CC's, for enabling his Heir's entry into Theatre in the first place. The father who sees himself as a Master of Dramatic Art surely must be held accountable for the arrival of such a young Prince of Folly on his Stage. Perhaps CC tried to prevent that by selling his Theatre shares to Highmore; if so, it was but another failed Plot, one TC foiled with his own bumbling Counterplot. I could not have written a better Farce myself.   H

12 May

Dear H,

You must be careful not to credit Mr. TC with the Authorship of a Farce better than yours, or he will soon be echoing your praise in all our favorite Taverns. I differ about the need to make his words Abhorrent; he has already done that for us. We need invent little, simply report the Stories we heard about TC in language as Craven as his own. Even then I fear readers will find it too far-fetched, too full of Self-Love, and think the work is all Fiction; such is the Danger of writing in Cibberian. I have taken the pages you sent me, inserted my Contributions, added selections from CC's memoir, and asked our printer Mechell to typeset them as fast as he can. The Volume should be in print by July. Mr. T . . . . C . . . . . will have to cancel plans for writing his own Life Story (plans I heard him tender only last week) once our Edition arrives at the Bookseller's. But we do him a great favor by placing his Name in print. Apologist Junior should be flattered that so much Attention is devoted to his Life; his *Apology* may even outsell his father's, although I would not want him to receive a Penny of our Advance. There will be an Advance, won't there? One Man of Letters to another,   J

12 July 1740

Dear Mr. Mechell,

By now I have been reported the Author of half the Scurrility, Treason and Base Whiggishness in the Kingdom, as the writer of an *Apology* released by your printing house. I am far from thinking whoever has aspersed me, by signing my initials to this volume, had a Design of doing me an Injury, when it was only an idle childish Levity. But whoever has stolen my good Name—and my now famous Initials—does both you and me a Disservice. He makes you a Kidnapper who has taken over my life without my consent; and I would not be known as the author of so Witty a volume as *An Apology for the Life of Mr. T . . . . C . . . . .,* lest friends and neighbors begin to expect Satire from me regularly. I am a most Choleric fellow, and protest that the Humour of this new *Apology* frequently forces me to laugh aloud at myself.

Theophilus Cibber

Postscript

Poor Theo Cibber continued to suffer unknown verbal assailants years after the publication of the counterfeit *Apology*. In 1752, he published an advertisement—practically an arrest warrant—for another unknown adversary:

ADVERTISEMENT.

> AS I find there are People in the World capable of hearkening
> to, and receiving the grossest, and most improbable
> Falsehoods, as Truth; and having fatally experienced the Error
> of negligently suffering such Scandal to pass unnoticed, or
> unanswered, I now think it an indispensible Duty to myself and
> the Public, to prosecute such Vilifiers as the Law directs;—in
> order, therefore, to bring such Vilifiers to Justice, I hereby offer
> a Reward of Five Guineas, to any Creditable Person, that will
> bring legal Proof of any Inventor, Propogator, Writer, Printer,
> or Publisher of any scandalous Libel, *&c.* against me
> THE. CIBBER. *Octob.* 20. 1752.

However, the much-maligned actor was not above authorship of vilifications himself. During 1739–40 Theophilus engaged in pseudonymous journalistic writing for the pro-Ministry *Daily Gazetteer*. According to Cross, attacks Fielding penned under the name of Hercules Vinegar elicited replies from one Ralph Freeman, pseudonym for 'a "legion" [of writers] which included Theophilus Cibber', and 'Freeman was a master of vituperation'. Probably Ralph Courtville, not Theo Cibber, wrote the best of Freeman's lines. In October 1740, Fielding as Hercules Vinegar announced the publication of a new book, *An Apology for the Life, Actions, and Writings of Ralph Freeman, alias Court Evil, Esq* (Cross 266–68). Once again Colley Cibber's memoir title became the basis for a parody. Although the parody of Freeman was not printed, its prospective sponsor was named in print: 'T. C., Publisher-General of the Ministerial Society'—another invocation by Fielding of the memoirist with Theophilus's initials (Cross 283). In the counterfeit 1740 memoir T . . . . C . . . . . boasts that he had a hand in Ministry journals: 'I wrote *Country Correspondents* and *Gazetteers*, to create Merit with the M------y

[Ministry], which we [son and father], might at a proper Time make use of.' Such self-serving Cibberian journalism gave satirists another reason to mock Walpole supporter Theo.

Ironically, the stage plays that parody Pistol, and other forms of humour directed at Theophilus, may be what most vividly preserve his theatrical career, and his fear of a theatre cartel. His impersonators, those who mocked young Cibber and his father, hid their own names in pseudonyms, signifiers of a world where writers won their liberty by joining the ranks of Swift's Drapier, Fielding's Scriblerus Secundus, and Mr T.C., Comedian. Henry Fielding belongs in their satiric legion, as a co-creator of Mr T . . . . C . . . . .'s *Apology*, and as the last unlicensed playwright in England.

Brecht was not so reticent about claiming authorship, even of works he did not write, as we will see in the next chapter.

CHAPTER FIFTEEN

Bertolt Brecht Writes *The Beggar's Opera,* Fielding Rewrites *Polly*

One of Brecht's most audacious statements on his playwriting first appeared in the 9 January 1929 edition of an Augsburg newspaper. Introducing readers to a play that had opened in Berlin, he wrote: 'Under the title *The Beggar's Opera, The Threepenny Opera* has been performed for the past two hundred years in theatres throughout England' (Brecht 1979: 89). The implication is that Brecht wrote *The Beggar's Opera*, or that it differs from the play he wrote primarily in title. Was the playwright joking, or did he see so much continuity between his work and John Gay's that he considered them the same? He admitted that the original music had changed over two centuries, and there was a new score; but 'we still . . . have the same sociological situation', he wrote, because people still were 'living off morality', not 'leading a moral life'.

Perhaps Henry Fielding would have cited a continuity between his work and Gay's, too, if his adaptation of John Gay's *Polly* had been permitted to open in May 1737. Fielding retitled his version of the play *Macheath turn'd pyrate; or Polly in India*. After May he could have said (anticipating Brecht) that despite the different titles, the same play has NOT been performed for nine years, since *Polly* was first banned in December 1728.

A continuity of satire, its continuation by one author after another, might also be found in the impact that Marx had on Brecht. As quoted earlier, Walter Benjamin noted:

> Marx, who was the first to illuminate with criticism the debased and mystified relations between men in capitalist society, thereby became a teacher of satire; and he was not far from becoming a master of it. It is with Marx that Brecht has gone to school (Benjamin 1977: 84).

But Marx himself went 'to school' with a few eighteenth-century satirists, including Laurence Sterne and Henry Fielding, whose comic writing the political economist enjoyed. Marx's daughter, Eleanor, noted in an 1858 letter that 'Marx read and reread Walter Scott; he admired him and knew him almost as well as he knew Fielding and Balzac' (Marx 1983: 50). His reading of history and economics, more than his reading of literature, influenced Marx's views of England; but without saying so explicitly, he sided with Fielding in a reference to eighteenth-century British government curtailment of liberty, its repeated 'reaction against the people' that had 'driven more than one popular writer, like Cobbett, to look for popular liberty rather in the past than the future'. Writing about the history of the East India Company, Marx described the period as a time

> when the Whigs became the farmers of the revenues of the British Empire, when the Bank of England sprang into life . . . The era of apparent liberty was in reality the era of monopolies . . . authorized and nationalized by the sanction of Parliament (Marx 1971: 174, also quoted in Chapter Nine).

In this 'era of monopolies', the curtailment of play production at small theatres like the Haymarket served the two large licensed theatres, Drury Lane and Covent Garden, at Fielding's expense. Despite the loss of liberty he risked as a stage satirist, he persisted, and tried to open *Polly* in 1737. That effort is reconstructed in the pages that follow.

Fielding Rewrites *Polly*

A printer's devil raced into the theatre waving a playbill at Henry Fielding. Fielding waved back, paid the small boy two pence, waited for the ink to dry, and held the paper up so the assembled actors could read:

HAY-MARKET   **30 MAY**

The Great Mogul's Company of Comedians
presents

Macheath turn'd Pyrate;
or, Polly in India

Never Before on a London Stage

Very much taken and improv'd
From the famous Sequel of the
late celebrated Mr. Gay. With a
New Prologue for the Occasion
Delivered by Mrs. Charke

Also **The King and Titi; or The Medlars**
A New Farce taken from the History of Prince Titi

Seats at 2s except Boxes 4s
To begin at exactly Six O'Clock

The cast stared at the new play title while Fielding spoke: 'As you can see, ladies and gentlemen, Pirate Macheath and Polly Peachum take the stage in ten days, if we have any liberty left among us'.

Mr Fielding's announcement did not reassure his actors. The assembled cast was rather tired. The previous night they had performed *Eurydice Hissed* and *The Historical Register for the Year 1736* to great applause, then caroused at Henry's favourite tavern (The Wild Boar) until two. They drank small beer, listened to the playwright review the night's audience, and toasted the outstanding spectators (a promising young actress from Dublin, a critic who had laughed out loud twice, a distressed Whig legislator). The actors then retired for a few hours, and morning arrived too soon. Fortunately the lights were not bright this noon inside the Little Theatre in the Haymarket, only a few tallow candles burned in the chandelier.

'Have you invited Mr Walpole to the *Pyrate*'s first night? Last time he attended a play by Gay he sang along', Mr Roberts snorted. The handsome actor dressed in pirate hat raised his sword and burst into song. The entire cast joined in the lyrics from *The Beggar's Opera*:

> When you mention vice or bribe
> 'Tis so pat to all the tribe
> Each cries—That was leveled at me.

'That's what he sang, by Gad, although Bob Booty can't carry a tune to save his life', confirmed Roberts, as he replaced the sword in its scabbard.

'The Minister loved the lyrics—they were all about him. But he didn't like being compared to a highwayman, that's why he banned Mr Gay's next play. Which was not *Macheath turn'd Pyrate*', Fielding said as he again silently read the playbill. It reminded him he had to write a new prologue.

'An attractive title, sir. You think the Ministry won't know the play was banned years ago because you changed the name?' asked Mr Lacy, who then answered himself: 'It's still about an outlaw who's more popular than the Minister'.

'All the ladies in London admired Captain Macheath when he first stood on stage. Thank goodness he escaped a hanging', crooned Mrs Haywood. 'The ladies'll flock to see him turned pyrate, too, even if Mr Lacy plays the rogue this time.'

Mrs Lacy placed a restraining hand on her husband's and replied: 'Perhaps you'd rather see the Minister play the pyrate. I'll take Mr Lacy any day'.

Mr Lacy: 'I can carry a tune'.

Fielding shook his head: 'I wouldn't give Walpole the role. He has the criminal element about him, he has a mistress or two, but he's no comedian'.

Mr Roberts: 'He'll be here all the same on May 30, with most of his police guards in tow'.

Fielding: 'We can only seat eight-hundred'.

Mr Lacy: 'You must insert the vice and bribe lyrics into *Pyrate*, Henry, let the Minister sing them again'.

Fielding admitted: 'The lyrics already have been inserted, Mr Lacy, along with several new speeches about the coming war with Spain, and Cibber's dismal acting at Drury Lane. Still Mr Gay's *Polly* remains intact, almost a virgin, her porcelain beauty improved by a few cosmetic changes. I speak of the play, not the actress'.

'She's a mere child of nine, born in '28', said Mrs Haywood, 'if only Mr Gay were alive to see his *Polly* now'.

Mr Lacy: 'That Walpole should outlive Gay'.

Mrs Hayward: 'Let's hope our *Pyrate* outlives the Minister'.

Mr Roberts: 'The Great Man's final days are near. With our opposition . . .'

'We could all be transported to Jamaica ourselves . . .' suggested Mrs Charke. The late arrival doffed her top hat, smoothed her trousers and bowed.

Mr Fielding: 'Enter Polly Peachum, looking ever so much like a young man who escaped West Indian slavery by donning the plantation owner's best suit'.

'You've seen these clothes before, Henry', said Charlotte, 'I wore them on stage as Hen the auctioneer last night'.

Mr Fielding: 'Ah yes, the never ending breeches roles. All the same, you might buy some clothes of your own, Mrs Charke, leave your costume here after the curtain call'.

Mrs Charke: 'I can't afford this finery on my wages . . .'

Mr Fielding: 'I know, a young daughter to support, with no father around'.

Mrs Charke: 'Thank goodness *he's* gone'.

Mr Fielding: 'And an insatiable craving for ornate men's clothing, neck high in foppery, 'tis a sad case'.

Mrs Charke: 'Or is it a farce?'

Mrs Hayward: 'The lamentable history of Charlotte Charke, alias Mrs Tragic. Alias Polly Peachum last seen among Indians in the New World'.

Mrs Charke: 'Polly in India is a great role, madam, I'd play this role for pennies . . .'

Mr Fielding: 'I thought that's all we paid . . .'

Mrs Haywood: 'But she gets to chase Macheath every night. That's worth something'.

Mr Lacy: 'Thank you, dear Haywood. It is an adventure, this new play'.

Mrs Haywood: 'It's a declaration of war'.

Mr Fielding: 'When the pyrates attack the colonials?'

Mrs Charke: 'When Henry Fielding defies the Ministry's ban'.

Mr Fielding: 'This is not the play they banned. I revised and improved Mr. Gay's dialogue'.

Mrs Charke: 'Don't forget my new afterpiece about the Prince of Wales. Titi'.

Mr Fielding: 'I'll remember it better after you finish writing it'.

Mrs Haywood: 'She's taking sides with the Prince against his father. And her own Father'.

Mr Roberts: 'They won't let it open'.

Mrs Charke: 'They can't condemn the play before I complete it, can they?'

Mr Lacy: 'They'll close us down for the Polly billing alone. Can't you keep Gay's name out of it, Henry?'

Mr Fielding: 'Mr Gay won't object if we use his name'.

Mrs Charke: 'He might turn over in his grave, but he won't object'.

Mr Fielding: 'It has to be credited to Gay. The playbill's already printed'.

Mrs Charke: 'Yes, I see you have a new prologue for me'.

Mr Fielding: 'Soon. An Ode to Polly Peachum. And I don't mean Lavinia Fenton'.

Mrs Haywood: 'When Miss Fenton played Polly Peachum men fought for tickets.

For in her Polly all the muses shine.

Her charms transport, the listener pines

When dear Miss Fenton sings her lines'.

Mr Fielding: 'In her distress I forget my own

Domestic crisis, bills unpaid

Excise taxes and declining trade.

Instead of these her fate I moan'.

Mrs Charke: 'I hear Miss Fenton will attend our first night with the Duke of Bolton'.

Mrs Lacy: 'She could steal the show just by sitting in a box'. [*She slowly eases herself onto a stool with the airs of a duchess in a huge hoop skirt.*]

Mrs Hayward: 'You ought to advertise that. Returning at last, Miss Fenton has not been seen on the English stage since 1729'.

Mr Fielding: 'And *Polly*, our play. Never rehearsed since 1728, unless we begin soon. Places for scene one, please'.

★   ★   ★

Inside an old oaken Whitehall office, the under-appreciated actor Theophilus Cibber (alias Pistol, alias Cibber Junior, the laureate's son) sat for his third hour, waiting to confer with a Minister's assistant about the dangers of *Polly*'s alias *Pyrate*'s opening at the Haymarket.

A dour, lean assistant wearing a bird's nest of a grey wig apologized for the delay: 'The Minister has been posing for an oil portrait, sir; as you are an actor, you must understand how time-consuming these artistic matters can be. I could bring him a message and save you the trouble of waiting any longer'.

Cibber: 'It is personal and might I add rather urgent, sir. Mr Cibber the laureate asked me . . .'

'Colley Cibber? The poet laureate?'

'No less', he confided while smoothing his huge moustache.

'Why didn't you say so? Has the laureate written a new ode to honour the Minister? He's dismayed by those other poets who have nothing kind to say about him.'

'But that's exactly why I'm here', said Cibber Junior.

'Oh, the Minister will be so pleased. When he has time to hear it.'

'I'm not here about a new poem, it's a new play. By one of those opposition writers.'

'Oh dear. Not another satire by Mr Fielding.'

'Worse. A new play by John Gay', warned the actor.

'The man is dead. I attended the funeral to make sure.'

'His banned play is very much alive, opening at the Great Mogul's playhouse in the Haymarket, in nine days. It's not my theatre.'

He held up a purloined copy of the playbill.

'The Great Mogul? Some foreign potentate invading our stages?'

'A fancy name for Fielding and his troupe of troublemakers.'

'You are not one of them, I gather.'

'Too good for them. My sister, Mrs Charke, performs with Fielding.'

'She is a troublemaker. All breeches and wind.'

'She was not so bad at Drury Lane (my theatre). She's to take on Polly Peachum.'

'Not your wife Susannah?'

'My wife lacks the innocence for the role, she now plays the infidel with an adulterer named Sloper. But that's not to my purpose here. You need to know the first night of *Polly*, now called *Macheath turn'd pyrate*, is already sold out. And they haven't submitted a script to the Lord Chamberlain.'

'The Lord Chamberlain banned *Polly* in 1728. The ban has not been lifted. Must we read it again?' asked the assistant, who once saw a copy of the play for sale in a bookstall, but never read it, knowing it would turn him into a sensualist and a Tory.

'No sir! I would not ask that of you, only a word with the Minister when he is free. So you will let the Minister know I was here?' Cibber quipped as the assistant tried to show him out. The actor posted his copy of the playbill on the other side of the thick wooden door as he left, so his warning would not be forgotten.

First, before he stepped out Cibber heard the assistant address the back of his head: 'Certainly. The Minister has the greatest respect for your father'.

Alone on the cobblestones, stepping over a gin-sodden teenager, Theo Cibber wondered whether the Haymarket would refund the price of his two tickets (8 shillings) if *Pyrate*'s opening night was cancelled.

★   ★   ★

William Hogarth etched the final fine lines of a new engraving. This one was almost too small to exhibit; a hand-sized subscription ticket. Even if larger, it would not be displayed on the Ministry's walls, unless the opposition won a majority. Not likely, given the Minister's hold on legislators used to generous bribes. No, the engraver designed this portrait to go on a ticket for *Macheath Turn'd Pyrate*'s benefit night. The black pyrate Macheath and his crew lifted their glasses to the authors Gay and Fielding. Polly Peachum poured their libations, with a few Indians in the same tavern smoking tobacco. Through their open door the distant harbour could be seen. In front of a ship portly Robert Walpole stood in iron chains, a convict transported to the New World. Walpole was a Lilliputian, barely visible; it was not a flattering image of the Great Man. One collector of Hogarths would buy a ticket with no intention of attending the author's benefit; he just wanted the picture. It would hang in his family's gallery for 200 years. Walpole heard about the engraving a few months later; he would have liked a copy to use as evidence in court, but not one could be found.

★   ★   ★

Wearing a brown taffeta hoop dress over her breeches, Mrs Charke stood near the prompter's box, and held a wrinkled sheet of paper up to the light as she recited the new prologue:

> When last you saw our heroine Polly
> She'd married the great man Macheath
> For love, or was it an act of folly?
> Her husband now transported as a thief
> To the West Indies, Miss Peachum pursues
> Him across the seas, risks all dangers.
> The woman in his thrall cannot choose
> Her course. So Polly walks among strangers,
> Indians, pyrates, slave traders,

A few native born, many invaders.
Though you cross an ocean you'll understand
The language these foreigners command.
Their world's far from the Thames and yet
It sounds so much like England.

Seated in a box close to the stage, Fielding appraised her speech: 'Fine delivery, but a few lines are missing'.

He scrawled the lines on a tobacco wrapper and handed them to the prompter. The prompter's voice rose from beneath the stage floor:

Prompter: 'It sounds so much like England
And London. But without our ministry,
'Tis a far better city'.
Mr Fielding: 'I couldn't have said it better myself. Again please'.
Mrs Charke repeated the new lines with a flourish.
Mr Fielding: 'Now the drop with the island scene falls open, blue sky and green palm trees. Enter Mrs Trapes. That's your cue, Mrs Haywood. Look at Charlotte'.

Liza Haywood lifted her flowing white gown and stepped forward to stare at Mrs Charke, who curtsied on cue.

Mrs Haywood: 'Bless my eye-sight! What do I see? I am in a dream, or is it Miss Polly Peachum. Mercy upon me! Child, what brought you to this side of the water?'

Mrs Charke removed herself slowly from the larger woman's full embrace: 'Love, Madam, for I have heard my husband now inhabits this island'.

(In fact Charke's own husband had fled to Jamaica; the lines were quite personal. But she had not chased after him or missed him.)

Mrs Haywood: 'Macheath was here, sentenced to plantation service. But the great thief robbed his master, ran away and turned pyrate. I hear he also married a transported slave, one Jenny Diver, and she's gone with him, my dear. You must give over all thoughts of him, for he is a very devil to our sex. But here you may begin life anew; a young lady of your beauty hath the wherewithal to make her fortune in any country'.

Mrs Charke (*apparently weeping*): 'Would I had never known that thief; he stole my heart and I have yet to recover it. Why have I a heart so constant?'

Mr Fielding: 'Prompter, have you those new lines for Mrs Haywood?'

The prompter's voice again rose from the floorboards: 'Polly: Why have I a heart so constant?' Mrs Trapes: 'Constancy's hardly the fashion in England, or here, dear girl. You must learn to live with the times. Here pyrates rather than ministers ravage the country. Plantation owners plunder the land, too, and buy their women. That's as close as we come to romance'.

Mr Fielding: 'Add that new song here'.

Lyrics were passed to Haywood, harpsichord music accompanied as she sang:

> Love now is nought but art
> 'Tis who can juggle best.
> To all men seem to give your heart.
> But keep it in your breast.

Mrs Charke joined in:

> In wives and politicians
> The genius is the same;
> Both raise their own conditions
> On others' guilt and shame.

Together:

> With speeches full of surprise,
> A wife her husband supplies,
> And the woman who is wise
> Keeps her schemes unknown.
> The side she's on is her own.
> A minister in her home.

Mr Fielding: 'You're both in such fine voice, let's skip to Polly's lyrics at the start of Act Two. Mrs Charke if you would begin with the new lead-in'.

Mrs Charke: 'Your improvement on Mr Gay'.

Mr Fielding: 'Would he were here to write it himself'.

Mrs Charke: 'I find the Indians here to be honest, courageous, peaceful. Life in their wig-wams is so different from that Whig-wearing tribe in England'. (*She sings:*)

> I hate those coward Tribes,
> Who by mean sneaking bribes,
> By tricks and disguise
> By flattery and lies,
> To power and grandeur rise.

'Henry, you've outdone yourself.'

Mr Fielding: 'The best lines are John Gay's'.

Mrs Charke: 'The tribe on this island chooses a more honourable way of making a fortune. I refer to the tribe of Pohetohee.

> They were never drawn
> Their truth to pawn
> Untaught to fawn
> They heroically go on
> Without flattery or lies
> Under West Indian skies.
> Honesty their cause supports
> Far from the fraud of England's courts.'

Mrs Haywood: 'I can't understand why his play was banned'.

From the prompter's box the answer rose up in song:

> By flattery and lies,
> The favoured writers rise
> To oversee their fellows.
> Old Walpole has his spies

Mr Fielding: 'Well done, old mole. We'll keep that in'.

Mr Lacy: 'Excuse me, sir, there's a Mr Theophilus Cibber here to see you. Insists he cannot wait. He comes direct from Whitehall'.

Mrs Charke: 'My brother. Beware the would-be laureate'.

Mr Fielding: 'Bring him in, Lacy. You'd better exit, Charlotte, I don't want your brother to see any of the show until he pays for his ticket'.

Mrs Charke as she exited could be heard singing: 'I hate those coward tribes, those Whig-wearing men with bribes. To unlicensed plays they never subscribe'.

Mr Fielding: 'We were just singing about you, Mr Cibber'.

Mr Cibber: 'The honour is all mine'.

Mrs Haywood: 'I wouldn't say that'.

Mr Fielding: 'Our play has already been cast, sir, though we appreciate your readiness to serve as one of our comedians'.

Mr Cibber: 'But I make no such offer, I could not possibly perform in one of your plays, or Mr Gay's. It would wound my father deeply. Your words have wounded him before, and the minister too'.

Mr Fielding: 'Rare praise for a satirist'.

Mr Cibber: 'As father often said, against contempt and scandal, words heightened by the skill of an actor, infusing dangerous sentiment into the multitude, there is no immediate defence'.

Mr Fielding: 'Would it were so. In any case, our new play is set in the West Indies. Far from the London you and your associates haunt'.

Mr Cibber: 'Your highwayman hero is rumoured to look just like the minister'.

Mr Fielding: 'You will have to buy a ticket to determine that, sir, although in all candour, I find our lead actor more handsome and wittier than any man in office. And all of our actors keep their listeners awake, more than I can say for some legislators'.

Mrs Haywood: 'Perhaps that is why the Whigs are so critical of our theatre'.

Mr Cibber: 'You may soon have no listeners at all, sir. I come as a friend to warn you. Do not open this play'.

Mr Fielding: 'A play you and the ministry have never seen on stage'.

Mr Cibber: 'I have read Mr Gay's *Polly*. We have all read it. The book sold quite well'.

Mr Fielding: 'And yet your friends were not shamed into resigning. Perhaps it is not such a powerful satire after all'.

Mr Cibber: 'Ah, but as the laureate—'

Mr Fielding: 'Your father'.

Mr Cibber: '—indeed . . . has said even the most harmless of plays can move men to seas of tears, and gales of laughter, if actors deliver their words with genius'.

Mr Fielding: 'You dare accuse my company of genius? We are artists, no more and possibly less'.

Mr Cibber: 'The law may flatter your actors with an arrest warrant, sir. I hope not to see that'.

Mr Fielding: 'If you don't want to see it, stay home. For all others we sell tickets at the coffee house next door. A few places for *Macheath turn'd pyrate* remain unsold. Go to the Wild Boar if you want to buy them. In any case, I advise you to go'.

Mr Cibber: 'I need no tickets to see trouble arising here, Mr Fielding'.

Mr Fielding: 'I suspect it will follow you out the door. Watch your step, Mr Cibber, too late'.

Cibber backs out, trips, recovers, asks 'who put that prompter's box there?' and exits without applause.

★   ★   ★

Mr Potter, the owner of the Little Theatre in the Haymarket, did not want the government to close his playhouse. The property was too profitable, full houses meant Fielding could pay the rent, even if Potter raised it because the price of bribes was rising. Since he had no licence for stage plays, Potter relied on bribes and ministerial neglect to keep the Haymarket open.

But the bribes demanded were exorbitant, and Fielding's satire was attracting too much attention. If the Minister didn't notice the nightly crowds, Fielding's rival managers would. The Cibbers and the Riches wanted no competition.

If he could replace Fielding with another remunerative client who had friends at court, that might save the day. He heard young Cibber was looking for a space. Ever since he led an actor rebellion in 1733 Cibber Junior had wanted a company of his own. Potter had rented the theatre to young Cibber and his mutineers during that period, before they returned to Drury Lane. It would be a blow to the father to see his son leave Drury Lane again; but perhaps Theophilus Cibber could take Fielding's place at the Haymarket. He claimed to have friends in the Minister's office, maybe they could get his theatre an official patent.

'They call him Pistol', Potter told himself. 'I could rename the building Pistol's Playhouse. That'll please him. But Colley Cibber will have a fit.'

★   ★   ★

Colley Cibber was about to have a fitting. His new black velvet breeches had to be taken out at the waist.

'It's that butt of sack they give the laureate', he explained to his tailor, 'all that sugar in the sack has to go somewhere'. The tailor wasn't particularly sympathetic; Cibber could keep his old, less portly shape by sharing the sack, offering tailor and hair stylist a glass once in a while; but that solution never occurred to the poet. The alteration was made in his waist size, not in his meagre hospitality.

Mr Cibber: 'Once I had the perfectly fitting clothes of a starched fop it was hard to stop. I owe it to my fame as Lord Foppington to stay stylishly suited'.

Tailor: 'Or have a tailor who'll fit the suit to the man'.

Mr Cibber (*taking snuff with pleasure, offering a pinch*): 'Well-said young man. Do I detect the wit of a playwright in your repartee?'

Tailor: 'I was a promising poet once, sir, but your son turned down my script when he ran the Haymarket Summer of '33. Said I was only fit to sew the buttons on his waistcoat, and so I did. Still do'.

Mr Cibber: 'My son's an idiot. The Haymarket's now the house where Henry Fielding runs riot. You might show him your play; the man's mad enough to stage anything, as long as it maligns the ministry and me'.

Tailor: 'Oh I couldn't malign you sir'.

Mr Cibber: 'Your respect for my position is greatly appreciated'.

Tailor: 'It ain't respect for you, it's my 'spect for that fellow Fielding. Nobody can write better than that one. I spent an evening in the Haymarket gallery laughing at some fellow on stage named Fibber. A poet too big for his breeches. Where'd Fielding ever get that idea? Oh hey, you don't think . . .'

Mr Cibber: 'Even my tailor mocks me! Out! Get thee to a gallery'.

Tailor: 'All my pins, remember'.

Mr Cibber: 'Out, out'. (*The pins are removed.*)

Tailor: 'But your breeches . . .'

Mr Cibber: 'Let them go'. (*The pants fall as he exits.*)

Tailor: 'Even so have the great fallen'.

★   ★   ★

Lovely Miss Lavinia Fenton, former actress still capable of attracting a crowd, peered out her coach window as it bounced along the cobblestones toward the theatre district. The Duke of Bolton had arranged for her to watch Fielding's company rehearse. He wouldn't allow her to go back on stage, and he wouldn't marry her until his current wife passed away; but he would accommodate every other whim she could dream of, and some that never occurred to her. Who else would have secured her a private preview of *Macheath turned pyrate*?

If she had stayed on professionally in the theatre, she might still be portraying Miss Peachum herself. *The Beggar's Opera* could have run forever; its sequel might also live a long life. Now some young upstart, a daughter of Colley Cibber, was playing Polly. 'Zounds I hope she's not as pretentious as her father on stage. I wonder if she'll end up with her portrait on fans and fire screens, as I did. She's hot, they used to say.'

Once she had stepped inside the dimly lit theatre, Miss Fenton could see a handsome actress in breeches and waistcoat impersonating the new Polly.

'She's no Adonis, no Venus either', thought Fenton, as she watched another actress portraying Jenny Diver mistake Miss Charke's Polly for a young man.

Jenny: 'How many women have you ever ruin'd, young gentleman?'

Polly: 'I have been ruin'd by women, madam. All the women I ever knew were mercenary'.

Jenny (*flirting*): 'But sure you cannot think all women so'.

Polly: 'Why not as well as all men? The manners of the courts are catching'.

Jenny: 'But we are not in London now. The Ministry's ways cannot reach this far. Besides, a young woman should know how to avoid ruin. (*sings*)

Man may escape the rope and gun;
Nay, some have outlived the doctor's pill;
Must he who loves woman must be undone,
Is her sweetness sure to kill?'

Polly: 'You would share women's greatest secrets with me, Madam?'

Jenny: 'I would share more than that. And I do what I please without shame or restraint'. (*kisses her*)

Polly: 'Had you a husband, this embrace would be most unwelcome to him'.

Jenny: 'But not to you, I trust'.

'My Polly was never untrue to Macheath', Miss Fenton whispered to Fielding, who now stood beside her, 'but then we live in modern times. Truth's as scarce in love as in government'.

'Here we tell all', said Mr Fielding, 'until the curtain falls'.

Miss Fenton: 'Mr Gay would applaud you'.

Mr Fielding: 'It is his play after all'.

Miss Fenton: 'You have added a few words'.

Mr Fielding: 'But we removed nothing Mr Gay wrote. That would curtail his liberty and we'll have none of that'.

Miss Fenton: 'You have no fear of ministry intervention?'

Mr Fielding: 'No fear, only expectation'.

★   ★   ★

Standing in a tavern, glass in hand, as if posing for a portrait, young David Garrick regaled an actress with the tale of his journey from Lichfield two months earlier. He travelled with his tutor, Mr Samuel Johnson: 'We had but one horse between us, and Mr Johnson kept saying: "I finally understand why Richard would trade his kingdom for a horse. No one should have to walk from Lichfield to London, except a horse."'

The young woman laughed: 'You should tell your tutor that no one in London recites *Richard III* anymore. The only history play people talk about is *The Historical Register*'.

'What's that?'

'Henry Fielding's new farce at the Haymarket. It has a pack of politicians, a pack of patriots, a pack of ladies, a pack of beaux. I'm one of the ladies. Come along tonight, maybe Fielding will be there, too. He directs our troupe, the Great Mogul's Company of Comedians. I can get you standing room in the wings.'

'Yes, you must. It will be my first appearance on a London stage.'

And so it was.

*   *   *

After the day's rehearsal, Mrs Charke walked back to her rented room, kissed her partner Mrs Brown, read her daughter a sonnet from Shakespeare (Number 23 which begins 'As an unperfect actor on the stage, / Who, with his fear is put besides his part'.). A brief collation of tea and black bread prepared her for playwriting that continued late into the night. Ever since *The Art of Management* was staged two years earlier, she had been drafting a sequel. Once again she would return to the stage as Mrs Tragic, the comically irate actress who triumphed over thespian adversaries. The new play featured a government minister who cried at Mrs Tragic's protests against his misguided authority.

> MRS TRAGIC: 'And shall Tragedy be silent now? Nay, you shall feel the mighty Vengeance which my Wrongs have rais'd within my Breast. With Hercules Vinegar the comedian I'll go, and jointly plot the ruin of our Foe.'

'That's my name for Fielding', she whispered in an aside to her sleeping daughter, Kitty.

> MR VINEGAR: 'Do they think us no more than Fools or Clowns, who will not dispute their Power; none here are bound to obey them. Let us have the general Voice to complete our Happiness. To ease our past Anguish, by entreaty sway, is to enjoy such Bliss as never can decay.'

'Fielding would never resort to these childlike rhymes', Charlotte admitted to her daughter, still asleep, 'but then he doesn't read his plays to his children, as my father did'.

> MRS TRAGIC: 'No more shall Folly rule the Stage,
> When liberty and justice mark the age.'

'I hear they are freer in the New World, perhaps you will live there one day', Charlotte predicted to Kitty. Her daughter heard, and went to the colony of Virginia in 1758.

*   *   *

Mr Potter handed his companion a cheap glass of gin and an expensive lawyer's contract. Theophilus Cibber was inebriated, out of snuff, and almost ready to sign.

'You'll rename the theatre Pistol's Playhouse?' he asked once again.

'It says so right here in the third paragraph. And I'll repaint the interior, just as I did for you in '33.'

Mr Cibber (*raising his half empty glass*): 'I was ever so bold as Pistol, a devil-may-care of the first order. Falstaff never saw the like, Shakespeare neither'.

Mr Potter: 'You and Mr Shakespeare will share the stage again'.

Mr Cibber: 'His ghost'.

Mr Potter: 'You mean the ghost of Hamlet's father?'

Mr Cibber: 'So you've seen him too? He looks a lot like my father. Grey wig down to his shoulders, hoary old poet'.

Mr Potter: 'I've never seen the laureate in that play'.

Mr Cibber: 'P'haps I'll let him try it. Pistol's Playhouse presents Theophilus Cibber as the Prince of Denmark. My father as the ghost. Mrs Clive the Queen. Susannah, my wife, can play Ophelia'.

Mr Potter: 'That would make her mad'.

Mr Cibber: 'Yes, my sister would be better in that role. My wife will have to play elsewhere. So will Fielding's company'.

Mr Potter: 'I'll evict the current tenants if the government doesn't arrest them first. Just drink your gin and sign on this line, Mr Pistol'.

*   *   *

When he heard Lord Chesterfield would defend the players in Parliament against the ministry's latest plans, Fielding jokingly offered to draft a few lines of a speech for his Lordship. Chesterfield laughed and accepted the offer, hence his Lordship's surreptitious visit to the Haymarket. He walked into the rehearsal wondering if that was Lavinia Fenton who had just walked out. 'Is she ready to play Polly Peachum again, what a peach she was in that role. If she's left the Duke of Bolton, perhaps I ought to interview her about free expression over a quiet dinner', he thought, 'no, the Duke would never let her go, and I have to write an appeal tonight, or Fielding has to write it'. The speech would be heard in the House of Lords, a new audience for Fielding's wit; one not entirely favourable to the first reading—the playhouse censorship bill would pass despite his Lordship's objections.

*   *   *

The printer's apprentice sat in front of Fielding, next to a table piled high with manuscripts. The boy peered at their titles, plays he had never seen printed, although the Haymarket had put them on stage: *A Rehearsal of Kings; or, The Projecting Gingerbread Baker: With the Unheard of Catastrophe of Macplunderkin, King of Roguemania*; *The Sailor's Opera; or, An Example of Justice to present and future Times*; *Fame, or Neverplead's Hopes of Being Lord Chancellor*; *or, The Miser's Resolve upon the Lowering of Interest.*

Meanwhile the playwright scribbled his preface to *The Historical Register* and *Eurydice Hissed*. As he had promised a lawyer friend, his preface denied the play represented anyone in the Ministry; it vowed the play's characters were only 'a set of blundering blockheads', and its alleged patriots 'a set of cunning, self-interested fellows, who for a paltry bribe would give up the liberties and properties of their country'. No one could mistake these characters for the men in power . Even if men in power gave out the paltry bribes, they had no need to take them—though he didn't write that down. He left out some humorous accusations, the printer was impatient; he wanted to print the plays before their author was arrested.

Fielding handed the boy the newly written pages, and a full script of another play, and advised: 'Please tell Mr Roberts that I'm sending another text for him to set next week. It's called *Macheath turn'd pyrate*. To be sold when the play opens'.

★   ★   ★

Theophilus Cibber stood in the shadows of a theatre alley and watched two women of the night decipher the playbills on the wall. Said the first woman: 'Hey now, what say we go over to Drury Lane and buy cheap seats for the play by 'enry Fielding? There's always cordial men there, full of laughter'.

'But his play's at the Haymarket. Look here, love.'

'No, says 'ere on this poster *The Miser*, that's his, with *The Beggar's Opera*, Theatre Royal, Drury Lane, May 24th. And his *Mock Doctor* the next night, while *Eurydice Hissed* plays at the Haymarket.'

'So he's playing two theatres.'

'No. Another *Mock Doctor* same author, at Covent Garden later in the week. And his play *The Intriguing Chambermaid*, will be at Drury Lane May 27.'

'Four plays in three playhouses. It's that new drink, coffee, drives some men to reckless self-endangerment.'

'Eh now, wot's that? You been seeing 'enry's plays?'

'A few but there's five if you count that new *Historical Register* at the Haymarket. I couldn't get into that one, no cheap tickets left.'

'This Fielding fellow's taking over all London's playhouses.'

'He's a popular man. I seen him once in the Wild Boar surrounded by actors.'

'Every actor in London's taking his parts.

(*Seeing Cibber step out of the shadows:*) Well, maybe not every actor.'

Both women retreated from Theophilus, whose face was red hot; his breathing, heavy. He gaped at the couple and choked out the words: 'I was in his plays once; but they shouldn't allow Fielding to speak so much, so freely, too freely'.

'It's a joyful noise, better than the pantomime, if you can get a seat.'

'Here are two tickets for you, then, ladies. No charge.'

'*Macheath turn'd pyrate*. Opening soon?'

'So they say. Play number six. I won't be able to attend.'

'Thank you Mr. Cibber Junior; may you be as famous as your father.'

★   ★   ★

Henry Fielding filled his pipe with tobacco, lit the tiny black flakes, and puffed with content. 'At last John Gay will have his play on', he mused. 'It's no longer entirely his, I added a few lines, Charlotte did too, but these days Shakespeare gets rewritten, why shouldn't John Gay?'

In his diary he added: 'John Gay never completely left London; *The Beggar's Opera* can be seen at Covent Garden this week, his early farce, *The What D'Ye Call It* (a great title for a play) is at Drury Lane. *Macheath turn'd pyrate* alias *Polly* will have him playing in London's finest three houses. Full houses, too.'

★   ★   ★

Robert Walpole dusted his wig with powder. A small cloud of the white substance rose in the chamber, causing his already bewigged guest to cough ever so politely.

'No argument whatever can be alleged to support the bringing of politicks on the stage', Walpole confided, as he crowned himself with the immaculate white wig.

The cloud settled and a brief silence ensued, as if the other man in the room had to wait for a prompter to cue him. No prompter spoke, but Colley Cibber realized he was expected to say something: 'Absolutely. The stage must remain unimpeachably moral, which leaves no room on it for politicks. Which is not to condemn politicks as immoral, nor even condemn the politicians; but they become irreparably rebellious when guided by Henry Fielding's pen. The poets, not the politicians, are to be blamed for the scandals on stage.'

'Wonderfully phrased, Mr Cibber. I can see why you remain our poet laureate. I may quote your words in Parliament, if you'll permit me.'

'It would be a great honour, sir; for while we keep politicks off-stage, I see no reason not to let a few of my best lines entertain the House of Lords. If their Lordships won't go to the theatre, I will go to them.'

'Not too many other venues will be open to them, once my bill passes', concluded Bob Booty.

*   *   *

They filled the house completely. Before the Licensing Act passed, rehearsals of *Polly* continued until the Great Mogul's actors arrived one morning and saw their theatre filled with bricks and lumber. They couldn't walk across the stage. The wings were overloaded with old scenery; the new backdrop of a blue sky over Jamaica had been blackened. Potter, the owner, hired men to move a construction site inside late at night. Of course the stage could be cleared, the house could be cleaned, the sky repainted blue, but not soon enough to open on schedule. And then the Licensing Act passed. Beginning 21 June 1737, government censors would have to approve everything spoken on stage. *Macheath turn'd pyrate* would not be approved, and the unlicensed Haymarket could not re-open. Mrs Charke, unable to get roles on a London stage, unassisted by her famous father and her less famous, not at all wealthy brother, started her own theatre for puppets, all exempt from the Lord Chamberlain's control. The puppets at Punch's Theatre performed three plays by Henry Fielding, and three by Shakespeare. Theo Cibber found a source of income more promising than theatre; he was taking his wife's wealthy lover to court, to sue for damages. Henry Fielding kept writing—not stage satires—but so far there were no censorship laws to prevent his publication of those new books called novels. John Gay's *Polly* was performed for the first time in London forty years later, 19 June 1777.

Coda: Henry Fielding, Puppeteer and Magistrate in 1748

Henry Fielding could not be completely banished from the stage. He was back in a theatre again by 1748. Almost no one saw him there, because the satirist was hidden inside a puppet booth. Madame de la Nash's Breakfasting Room had no need to comply with censorship laws, for it sold no theatre tickets, only breakfasts twice a day, each featuring a free Punch and Joan show. The evening show came with a rather late breakfast gratefully imbibed by patrons who slept until 5 p.m. after a hard night of carousing. For their shillings the customers were served tea, coffee, or a cup of chocolate, and 'Gratis with that Excellent old English Entertainment, call'd A PUPPET-SHEW. . . . With all the Original Jokes, Farts, Songs, Battles, Kickings, etc.'

Madame de la Nash, also known as Mary or Mrs Fielding to her friends, served the breakfasts in a house on Panton Street, near the Haymarket in

London. Mr Fielding, a lawyer soon to be appointed Justice of the Peace for Westminster, would put down the pages of *The Jacobite's Journal* he was writing and take up the voice of King Henry II and his Queen, while manipulating puppets who looked remarkably like Punch and his wife Joan with small paper crowns on their heads. Unscripted references to the news of the day, and greetings to alleged criminals in the audience would enter into the dialogue, much to the delight of spectators. 'That puppet called me a thief' said one amused Whig legislator to his mistress. 'Indeed, sir, and well he should; that's my chocolate you're drinking', replied the mistress, who told a columnist her name was Polly Peachum.

Theophilus Cibber was not pleased by Fielding's return to the stage. To compete with the satirist, he revived Fielding's own *Author's Farce*, including the puppet play within it, without the scene that mocked Theophilus and his father. Fielding's 1730 farce with dialogue for puppets played at Covent Garden under Theo's direction. He had the puppet 'Nobody' dressed to look like Henry Fielding, and the audience knew it as they watched Nobody sing to the tune of 'Black Joke'—

> Of all the men in London town,
> Or knaves or fools, in coat or gown,
> The representative am I.

But Fielding was immune from comic prosecution at this point. He held a court of his own with the Panton Street puppets. When another antagonist, the actor Samuel Foote, wrote that 'an arrant Impostor' was seen on Panton Street impersonating 'Henry Fielding' and 'officiating as Jack Ketch to a Puppet-Show', Fielding in turn held a mock-trial where a puppet judge sentenced the rogue 'Samuel Fut' to 'Scorn and Contempt, as a low Buffoon'.

Perhaps the popularity of these mock-trial sentences, as well as the 'Court of Criticism' Fielding convened in satiric London journal columns, led to his appointment as a Justice just as the 1748 puppet theatre season ended. He also had been paid a substantial book advance that June for the manuscript of a novel titled *Tom Jones*. After his triumph as novelist and his judicial appointment, the magistrate was not seen again on stage—or behind the curtain of a puppet booth—although some of his more conventional plays continued to be performed in London.

No theatre censor could end Fielding's life as a writer of comic dialogue. One exchange he published in a July 1748 issue of *The Jacobite's Journal* may well have been tried out first inside the satirist's puppet booth, where the author himself played all the parts. Walpole and his successors could not stop this conversation.

PRISONER'S COUNCIL: What is the Difference, pray, between Satire and Abuse?

THOMAS SCANDAL, ESQUIRE: I won't answer you.

MRS GRACE (*next witness*): I likewise bought the Poem of the Defendant, expecting to have read some pretty Things in it . . . Something to make one laugh at some People. I never was more deceived in my Life.

P. COUNCIL: So you expected Abuse, too, Madam?

MRS GRACE: I cannot help saying, I did.

P. COUNCIL: I am sorry a Lady should have such a Taste.

MRS GRACE: Sir, I am a true Englishman, (*here was a great Laugh*). Englishwoman, I mean; and I shall always relish Satire against any of the present Copulation of Ministers. (*Here was another great Laugh, but the Lady afterwards explained her Meaning to be Coalition.*)

Thus Henry Fielding opposed the Copulation of Ministers, left the legitimate stage for Madame de la Nash's puppet theatre, and spoke with the voice of a true Englishwoman.

CURTAIN

CHAPTER SIXTEEN

Stage Mutineers

And just when they seem engaged in revolutionizing themselves and things, in creating something that has never yet existed, precisely in such periods of revolutionary crisis they anxiously conjure up the spirits of the past to their service and borrow from them names, battle cries and costumes in order to present the new scene of world history in time-honored disguise and borrowed language.

Marx, *The Eighteenth Brumaire of Louis Bonaparte*

On 27 July 1733, theatre history turned into farce, complete with old costumes and worn battle cries, when a comic afterpiece titled *The Stage Mutineers* opened at Covent Garden. The play was based on a rebellion that began at the end of May. 'A considerable Body of malcontent Players', led by Theophilus Cibber at Drury Lane, 'enter'd into a mutinous Association against their Masters . . . in a State of Hostility; which hath prevented any Plays being acted there', according to the London *Craftsman* of 2 June.

The defiant actor mutiny against theatre management took place 120 years before Marx linked history to farce in *The Eighteenth Brumaire of Louis Bonaparte*. Attributing a few of his words to Hegel, Marx contended that 'all facts and personages of great importance in world history occur, as it were, twice . . . the first time as tragedy, the second as farce' (Marx 1963: 15). His attribution of theatrical form to political action 'in time-honoured disguise and borrowed language' was anticipated by Charlotte Charke and her brother Theophilus Cibber, both 'stage mutineers' who rebelled at Drury Lane against their employers. The differences between labour and management had not yet been resolved in July when *The Stage Mutineers* opened, and actors on Covent Garden's stage mocked the uprising that took place off stage at Drury Lane. Had Marx not been preoccupied with other economic issues when reading in the British Museum, he might have reviewed this labour dispute and given it a footnote in *Capital* (perhaps in his reference to 'workers' combinations' about which more will be said later); but this mutiny deserves more than a footnote in the annals of theatre history.

By 1733, London's theatre scene was dominated by managers of the two royally licensed theatres: Drury Lane and Covent Garden. Other, lesser theatre houses were not officially sanctioned, and by 1737, after passage of stringent theatre censorship laws, the smaller houses including Henry Fielding's Haymarket space had to close. The dissident actors in 1733 questioned casting and hiring practices that left them at the mercy of a few managers. Conrad notes that by March 1733, Theo Cibber had persuaded nine other Drury Lane actors to join him in 'taking over the Drury-Lane lease on a nineteen-year term. Nominally under the Duke of Bedford, this lease involved small payments to each of thirty-six renters for each acting night in the theater' (Conrad 60). Young Cibber and his cohorts had a legal claim to stay in the playhouse from which Drury Lane's manager John Highmore locked them out; they rightly charged Highmore with 'violating a recent lease which put the conduct of the theatre in the charge of certain players'. Actors had been involved in management before Highmore's reign, when three of them (Colley Cibber, Robert Wilks, Barton Booth) served as Drury Lane's managers and Patent co-owners. When Booth sold his share to Highmore, Cibber Senior 'disdaining to work on equal terms with such inexperience . . . delegated his part of the management to his son, Theophilus' (Farnsworth 162–63). Cibber's son lost these managerial privileges soon after his father sold his share to Highmore, and this displacement gave young Cibber cause to lead a rebellion against the new owner; but it was not merely self-interest that motivated Cibber Junior to rebel, or so he said. With the new man in charge, Wilks deceased, Booth and Cibber Senior out of office, with the recent lease ignored, actors were no longer part of Drury Lane's management. After they were locked out of the house, the rebel artists regrouped, called themselves 'the Company of Comedians of His Majesty's Revels', and rented the Little Theatre in the Haymarket. There the new company opened in September with Congreve's *Love for Love*, and gave Drury Lane a run for its money. Their group was said to be a cooperative and more democratic than Drury Lane in its administration, although the integrity of the rebels was questioned from the start by London newspapers, and later in *The Stage Mutineers*.

The satiric tenor of *The Stage Mutineers* questions Theophilus Cibber's activities and allegiances, but the work also inadvertently acknowledges his radical labour demands and dream of a commonwealth for actors at the same time as it mocks the advocate of artistic autonomy. For all his faults, young Cibber might even be considered an eighteenth-century Brechtian, along with other mutineers and satirists, as his concerns anticipate a call to join with the discontented that Brecht voiced in his poem, 'Address to Danish Worker Actors on the Art of Observation':

Whom then, actors, should you obey?
I'd say: the discontented . . .
From all the struggles waged
Make pictures
Unfolding and growing like movements in history.
For later that is how you must show them on stage.
The struggle for work.
Bitter and sweet dialogues between men and women,
Talk about books,
Resignation and rebellion,
Trials and failure.
All these you must later show
As historical processes.

(Brecht 1961: 17, 19)

While it shows discontented actors on stage, *The Stage Mutineers* is not an entirely accurate representation of theatre history. It distorts and exaggerates situations, as any disrespectful satire might. Considered along with other background information, the actor rebellion that the play mocks becomes more understandable and justifiable.

Fig. 6.   John Laguerre's 1733 engraving of *The Stage Mutiny*, with Theophilus Cibber in the centre leaning backward. The actress to his right may be Charlotte Charke. Colley Cibber at far right holding bag of money. Centre banner declares 'Liberty & Property'.

Objections to theatre mismanagement and lack of democracy faced by actors before the 1733 mutiny were recalled later by Henry Fielding. In a 1752 newspaper column he wrote of 'the Case when that famous Triumvirate, Booth, Wilks, and Cibber were in the Management; who, by discountenancing, and keeping back any Actor of apparent Genius, left such a Set of wretched Strollers behind them, at their Departure, that our dramatic Entertainments became contemptible' (Fielding 1963: 198). Although he chose not to take the side of the rebels in 1733, Fielding here conceded that Drury Lane managers had not treated performers well before the mutiny. His reference to the 'contemptible' Entertainments that followed also reflected Fielding's own discomfort with pantomime and fairground acts that were becoming popular in the 1730s, particularly at Covent Garden, the same house that mocked him along with Theo Cibber's rebels in its production of *The Stage Mutineers*.

Besides its representation in a stage play at Covent Garden, the 1733 revolt won attention in the press, and was depicted in comic engravings by John Laguerre and William Hogarth. (Hogarth more or less copied and miniaturized Laguerre's print in his own 'Southwark Fair' engraving.) A likeness of Theo Cibber as Pistol, wearing a tricornered hat and looking like a handsome pirate, figured prominently in Laguerre's June 1733 engraving. The woman shown at his side may be Charlotte Charke, who played no more than a supporting role in her brother's rebellion. (The female figure in the engraving has also been identified as the Drury Lane actress, Mrs Heron.) Charke not only took part in the original 1733 walkout, she also joined its comic re-enactment when she portrayed the mutineer Mrs Haughty in the July 1735 Lincoln's Inn Field revival of *The Stage Mutineers* two years after it was first staged. Her participation in this production took place around the time Charke was writing *The Art of Management*, which opened on 24 September 1735; the experience of playing Mrs Haughty must have helped her shape the comparable role of Mrs Tragic in her own afterpiece about actor rebellion.

Charke's new farce, *The Art of Management; or, Tragedy Expell'd*, mocked another manager at Drury Lane, Highmore's successor, Charles Fleetwood. When her play opened, Fleetwood tried to buy all the newly printed copies of it and destroy them, but the text survived. Fleetwood also sought to have the opening disrupted, judging from a *Daily Advertiser* report on 26 September that Mrs Charke was 'very much applauded' despite efforts by 'young Clerks' to shout her down. Her mutiny onstage was met with one from hired protesters in the audience. A close reading of Charke's play indicates that she was inspired not only by actual events, but also by the earlier comedy, *The Stage Mutineers*, which is attributed to Edward Phillips.

The impact of Cibber's 1733 mutiny was short-lived; most of the Drury

Lane rebels were back in the same theatre they left by March 1734. But the issues raised by the dispute reached a wider public—as did the stage production—through newspaper reports and letters from actors and management. The theatre's management published a list of actor salaries to contest the rebels claims that they had been underpaid before they seceded. The fact that Theo Cibber had been paid five pounds weekly and his actress wife four pounds weekly even when ill was supposed to prove his rebellion unwarranted. Cibber responded by publishing a letter to Highmore that claimed he and others received less than management contended, and aired other grievances. Another response to management's claiming it paid respectable wages was delivered by one of the two conniving managers in *The Stage Mutineers*: 'Let us lower their Stipends, and make 'em humble by making 'em poor'. The parsimonious manager's partner in the Phillips play objects, and claims the actors are 'ready to rebel: One Step more wou'd make 'em all Patriots; Liberty and Property wou'd be the Word'. Hardly flattering to the managers, the scene also cast comic aspersions on English merchants who used the same slogan to protest Walpole's tax plan earlier in the year. (More about the merchant protest later.)

Covent Garden's satire of stage mutiny in 1733 did not favour rebel actors in depiction of their lockout, as all the faults and vanities of their profession became objects of ridicule. The prologue to *The Stage Mutineers* announced that everything in the theatre was fair game:

> Our Bard would fain some Novelty pursue;
> And hopes this Theme will please, because 'tis New.
> Long to your Sight the Stage has partial shown
> Some Fools of all Professions—but their own:
> Long has she laugh'd at Follies of the Age—
> Laugh, in your Turn, at Follies of the Stage:

While not the first satire of the period to turn its attention to the follies of the stage, *The Stage Mutineers*'s mockery of the acting profession advanced beyond the earlier rehearsal play comedy by Buckingham (*The Rehearsal*), and beyond Fielding's mimicry of tragic bombast and well-known authors in *Tom Thumb*, *The Tragedy of Tragedies* and *The Author's Farce*. Laughter at earlier drama (particularly one play by Fielding, as will be seen) was elicited by *The Stage Mutineers*. But some of the 'Novelty' introduced was indeed new, and not just about earlier plays, because it concerned the folly of actors forming a 'combination,' a new form of organized labour.

Actors to the Barricade

In his history of eighteenth-century England, Roy Porter notes that before the (anti) Combination Acts of 1799 and 1800 made formation of worker associations a crime, 'the most powerful London combinations' were run by journeymen tailors and stay-makers, with carpenters, joiners, construction workers and wool-combers also creating early forms of union (Porter 88). A combination of actors receives no mention in his account, or in Marx's discussion of combination laws in *Capital* (Marx 1976: 583, 901). Nor does E.P. Thompson refer to an actor combination in his masterful study, *The Making of the English Working Class*, where other early assemblies of workers are documented. At one point Thompson quotes a Leicester stocking-weaver's praise of tradesmen who unite: 'Look at other Trades! They all Combine, (the Spitalfields weavers excepted, and what a Miserable Condition they are in). See the Tailors, Shoemakers, Bookbinders, Gold beaters, Printers, Bricklayers, Coatmakers, Hatters, Curriers, Masons, Whitesmiths. . . .' (Thompson 1966: 238). Actors do not make the cut. Historical record honours tailors for forming the first combination in England in 1720 (Perkins 28). While only thirteen years later, the 1733 combination of Drury Lane actors seems to have been overlooked by labour historians and theatre historians.

Hardly writing this play to document labour history, but rather seeking to mock theatre workers and their protest, the author of *The Stage Mutineers* introduced the word 'combination' as a term meant to alarm. The Wardrobe Keeper in the play warns theatre managers that 'the best Part of the Company have left the House, and I have heard, are now in Combination'. Warned by this report, the theatre managers resolve to guard the entrance of their building, barricade the doors, and 'Let loose the Dogs of War'. The barricade holds, the rebel actors are unable to enter the building, and they retreat in humorous, non-violent defeat. 'We march'd our Troops, but found the Enemy had firmly barricado'd up the Gates, nor cou'd we, Sirs, by all our Arts provoke the dastard Spirits to the Fight', laments Truncheon, one of the embattled stage mutineers. 'We went— we saw—we bullied,—and we returned', adds his cohort Pistol, slightly amending Julius Caesar's boast that 'We came, we saw, we conquered'. Marx might have enjoyed this parodic reference to the Roman empire, had he read it, as it anticipates his own assertion that 'the Revolution of 1789 to 1814 draped itself alternately as the Roman republic and the Roman empire' (Marx 1963: 15). The theatricality and mock-Roman heroics of the 1733 revolt were augmented by actors in all the roles.

The comic battle report delivered in *The Stage Mutineers* is based on a more sombre event. London's *Daily Post* reported on 29 May 1733 that three days earlier, at Midnight on Saturday last several Persons arm'd took Possession of the [Drury Lane theatre], by Direction from some of the Patentees, and lock'd up and barricado'd all the Doors and Entrances thereunto, against the whole Company of his Majesty's Comedians, as also against Mr. Cibber, jun. nothingwithstanding he had paid to one of the Patentees several hundred Pounds for one third Part of the Patent Cloathes, Scenes, &c. and all Rights and Privileges thereunto annexed, for a certain Term not yet expired' (Scouten Part 3: 394).

Much like the rebels led in the play by Pistol, the rebels at Drury Lane led by Theo Cibber found themselves locked out of their theatre, but as noted earlier, unlike the rebels in the stage comedy, Cibber's following decided to rent the Haymarket and performed there for much of the 1733–34 season. Their revolution for improved working conditions and wages did not end at the barricades. In a lengthy open letter to Highmore, Theo Cibber at one point declared: 'We have been often told the Patentees will starve us poor Devils the Players into Compliance with their Wills. Excuse me, Sir, that can't be. We must and will eat.' Hogarth's version of Laguerre's engraving of 'The Stage Mutiny' included a banner that echoed Cibber with the slogan 'We eat', although it was hardly endorsing the declaration, as it unsympathetically showed both factions on the same stage. The rebels did not starve, because they attracted audiences to their new plays at the Haymarket; in fact, 'the same plays were acted much better in the Haymarket' and their competition compelled Drury Lane's owner to sell his holdings (Genest III: 403–04).

Losing audience income as well as actors, Highmore sold his shares to a successor (Fleetwood) who invited the rebels back to work under more friendly management. Theo Cibber and his followers accepted the offer, and Cibber became the equivalent of a modern manager, as assistant to the new owner. That ending could not be portrayed in *The Stage Mutineers*, because the play opened in July 1733, many months before the 'theatric wars' at Drury Lane had been resolved. The play did not tell the whole story of the mutiny, but it was quite timely when first performed for twelve nights during July and August of 1733.

Author Declines to Take a Bow

Despite its popularity, *The Stage Mutineers* remained a play of unclaimed authorship. When published (1733), the play's title page attributed the writing to 'a gentleman late of Trinity-College, Cambridge'. Attribution of authorship to Edward Phillips is largely based on a reference printed in the 1740 *Apology for the Life of Mr. T . . . . C . . . . .,* where Theo Cibber allegedly discusses his life and art, including the satire of him in

The Stage Mutineers. Mr T . . . . C . . . . . claims the 'young Spark, who was just come from Trinity College at Cambridge, to set up for an Author in Town . . . had just before wrote a Farce, call'd the *Mock-Lawyer*' (Mr T.C. 1740: 17). This attribution, if reliable, would mean the young spark was Edward Phillips; his ballad opera, *The Mock Lawyer*, opened at Covent Garden in April of 1733. It is quite possible that Covent Garden's manager, John Rich, was delighted to stage a new satire about a labour dispute at his competitors' theatre just months after Phillips arrived; perhaps he even commissioned the play to make Drury Lane and its popular author, Henry Fielding, look foolish. One character in the play is based on Fielding, as will be seen shortly. Another, later production by Rich of a play by Phillips that mocked Fielding adds credibility to the likelihood of their 1733 collaboration; a few scholars argue that Rich commissioned Phillips to write *Marforio*, a satire on Fielding's *Pasquin*, for performance at Covent Garden on 10 April 1736. The anti-*Pasquin* play advertised as 'a Theatrical Satyr: being a Comi-Tragical Farce, call'd The Critick of Taste: or, a *Tale of a Tub*' closed quickly, and never was published; but its list of characters included the Great Mogul and Drawcansir (both pseudonyms for Fielding), which suggests it made unkind references to the author of *Pasquin*. Quite possibly both *Marforio* and *The Stage Mutineers* were attacks on Fielding written by Phillips at Rich's invitation, as part of a continuing war between the poets; he might even have reused some of *The Stage Mutineers* in the unpublished *Marforio*. John Rich's role as producer of the anti-Fielding satires would have served his own economic and theatrical interests. The man who produced John Gay's first ballad opera, and made enough money from it to build the new Covent Garden theatre in 1732, Rich had a motive to encourage new ballad opera satires such as *The Stage Mutineers*, since it reduced respect for a leading satirist (Fielding) who was not his theatre's author, and who disliked the pantomimes Rich was producing. This also could explain why *The Stage Mutineers* focuses on a play by Fielding that failed after one night at Drury Lane; Rich was laughing at his rival theatre's disaster.

Fielding's Plebeian Tragedy Lasts One Night

Fielding recovered from the one-night debacle of June 1732, and achieved a notable success during the 1733 London theatre season with his new Molière adaptation, *The Miser*, at Drury Lane. It opened on 17 February. Fielding's satisfaction with his own work became a target of satire in *The Stage Mutineers*, where a self-praising author named Crambo, a caricature of Fielding, boasts he has written a text that will be 'a comedy of comedies', 'an opera of operas', and 'a tragedy of tragedies', the last of which was the title of an earlier Fielding farce. Actresses in *The Stage Mutineers* refuse to perform Crambo's newest work, which is clearly not a version of *The Miser*; the play they reject is 'filthy' and too 'low' and 'plebeian'. Their objections to the unnamed script fit Fielding's one-night satire, *The Covent-Garden Tragedy*, which opened and closed at Drury Lane on 1 June 1732. As noted in Chapter Ten, Drury Lane's own actors called for an end of its run, according to one press account. 'The Covent Garden Tragedy will be acted no more, both the Author and the Actors being unwilling to continue any Piece contrary to the opinion of the Town', said London's *Daily Post* on 5 June. The editor of *The Grub Street Journal*, commenting on this report, added: 'For unwilling Read unable' (Scouten Part 3: clxvii). The actors objected to a mock-tragedy set in a brothel, where whores argued and customers fought over them. Its first presentation offended some Drury Lane patrons, too. In a letter defending the play, Fielding (who signed as 'Philalethes' in the *Daily Post* on 31 July) noted that 'Three Ladies of the Town made their exit in the First Act' (Cross 137). This departure may have inspired one in *The Stage Mutineers* where three actresses make their exit from the stage, after telling Crambo that his new comedy is too 'low' and 'filthy' for them to perform in it. The actress Squeamish protests that the play in which she is cast has 'all over Faults—Such Enormities, such Language. . . . For the Part is so naughty filthy a Part', and her description fits the roles Fielding wrote for the female characters in *The Covent-Garden Tragedy* (if you are a prudish actress who objects to portraying a prostitute). Pistol (Theo Cibber's stand-in) in *The Stage Mutineers* supports Mrs Squeamish's refusal to take so 'low' a part. 'We wo'not play it', he says of the drama authored by Crambo. The actors in *The Stage Mutineers* who demand more control over casting of their parts could be echoing those at Drury Lane who were unable or unwilling to perform *The Covent-Garden Tragedy* for a second night. Fielding's antagonists (Rich and Phillips) would not let him forget this failure.

The complaints Squeamish and Haughty raise about 'low' characters also echo serious objections made to Lillo's play, *The London Merchant*, which Fielding parodied in his *Covent-Garden Tragedy*. A 21 August 1731 article in *The Weekly Register* reported that while 'The Play of *George Barnwell* [Lillo's *London Merchant*] is given out for the Seventeenth Night, and, 'tis possible, may run the Remainder of the Season', 'the Characters were so low, and familiar to Life, so apt to excite Ridicule and Contempt, that none but a masterly Hand could have overcome the Prejudice' ('Some Remarks on the Play of *George Barnwell*', reprinted in Loftis 1960: 33). Could it be mere coincidence that *The London Merchant* was performed on a double bill with *The Stage Mutineers* at Covent Garden on 4, 10, and 17 August 1733? Was Squeamish offered the 'low' role of Millwood, the prostitute in Lillo's play? Or was she was offended by the role of the prostitute Kissinda in Henry Fielding's parody of Lillo? Without question not Lillo but Fielding as Crambo is the author whose work Squeamish and Haughty reject.

Pistol sides with the defiant actresses, and the resulting confrontation between the stand-ins for Fielding and Theo Cibber nearly culminates in a duel, as Pistol draws his sword, ready to fight over the playwright's 'Catastrophe', which he regards as 'Unjust repugnant to Theatric Laws'. (These accusations of improper playwriting quite effectively mock the vocabulary of Georgian critics and playwrights.) The duel is averted when one of the managers advises Crambo to 'retire to the Coffee-House a little, or we shall have a Tragedy here indeed'. Crambo retreats accordingly. *The Stage Mutineers* cannot be taken as an accurate historical record of events at Drury Lane, but it hints that the actor rebellion might have been incited by Fielding's playwriting and actor discomfort with it, as well as other indignities experienced by the performers. The fact that the satire also attacks Theo Cibber, a frequent performer at Drury Lane before the 1733 lockout, further supports the proposal that *The Stage Mutineers* was produced by Rich at Covent Garden to ridicule his Drury Lane rivals.

One modern study of Fielding's plays entirely misses the significance of references to Fielding and Cibber in *The Stage Mutineers*. After Robert Hume dismisses the play as 'a silly afterpiece', he suggests that Fielding should have rewritten it as 'a better version of Covent Garden's topical farce, called something like *A Commonwealth in the Haymarket; or, The Mutineers*' (Hume 162, 171). If Fielding had rewritten the play, it would no longer be a third party's satire of both Cibber and Fielding, unless he chose to mock himself, which he did later in *Eurydice Hissed* (1737) but not at this point in his career. The 1733 audiences watching Crambo and Pistol argue in *The Stage Mutineers* probably would have recognized them as caricatures of Fielding and Theo Cibber, would have known why Rich was producing the play, and may even have been familiar with the title of the unnamed play over which the characters disagree.

Not all depictions of 'low life' on stage were badly received in this period. When Theo Cibber's pantomime, *The Harlot's Progress*, opened at Drury Lane on 31 March 1733, the scenario loosely based on Hogarth's engravings was well received (This success of pantomime at a rival theatre would be another reason for Rich, the pantomime king, to commission a play mocking Theo Cibber.) The far less popular *The Covent-Garden Tragedy* probably was inspired by the same engravings Hogarth issued in April, 1732; but Fielding was more sympathetic to his Drury Lane denizens, all of whom survive and thrive in his so-called 'tragedy', than Hogarth was in his moralistic scenes of venereal disease and death. Theo Cibber appears not to have objected to the 'low' and 'filthy' humour of *The Covent-Garden Tragedy* when he performed a lead role in 1732; Wilbur Cross argues that Cibber (with assistance from Fielding) defended the play in a 21 June 1732 letter to the *Daily Post*, where he wrote that 'wretched low stuff' was to be found not in Fielding's comedy but rather in *The Grub Street Journal* that was attacking the playwright (Cross 133). Cibber's departure from Drury Lane with the actors who accompanied him began eleven months later, in May 1733. Neither the differences between actors and management that May, nor the departure of actors from Drury Lane can be attributed with certainty to production of Fielding's comedy the prior summer. But it is quite likely that Rich encouraged the writing of *The Stage Mutineers* and its unflattering depiction of characters representing Cibber and Fielding as an attack on two prominent Drury Lane artists.

The rivalry shown between the two artists (as Crambo and Pistol) was not invented; they feuded for years. Sometime between February, when Theo Cibber staged Fielding's version of *The Miser*, and May when actors were locked out of Drury Lane, a break developed between the two. Fielding stood with Drury Lane's managers during the lockout, and in January 1734 he gave them a revised version of his *Author's Farce*, with new scenes mocking Theo Cibber and his father. His play showed the characters Marplay Sr and Jr discouraging and dismissing the work of new, rival authors, and revising as their own plays by other authors. Their efforts to control the play market do not incite rebellion in the revised *Author's Farce*; but Fielding's writing against Cibber father and son suggests they were seen as obstructionists who secured their stage empire from incursions by the likes of Fielding. Cibber Sr was still poet laureate, with friends at court; and his son, after ending the walkout, became very active in the patent theatre scene as Drury Lane's Acting Manager.

It is possible that Fielding sided with Drury Lane's management during the mutiny to ensure continued production of his plays. *The Miser* was performed there as late as 16 May 1733 (on the same bill with Cibber's *The Harlot's Progress*) before the season abruptly ended on 27 May. 'We are assur'd that there will be no more Plays acted this season [at Drury Lane]', reported the *Daily Post* on 29 May, in its account of the theatre's doors being 'lock'd up and barricado'd' 'by Direction from some of the Patentees [managers]'.

The Mock Author: Edward Phillips

The Livery Rake, a new ballad opera by Edward Phillips, opened a few weeks earlier at the same theatre on 5 May. The writer who later allegedly ridiculed the dissident actors first saw some of them perform his new play (although Cibber was not in the cast). Perhaps both he and Fielding were dismayed that the actors locked out toward the end of May had endangered the run of their plays, although *The Stage Mutineers* was not flattering in its depiction of theatre managers, either.

One other significant dispute took place before the opening of *The Stage Mutineers*. The play's reputed author appears to have been at odds with Henry Fielding over *The Mock Lawyer*. In April and May of 1733, not long before the lockout, *The Grub Street Journal* accused Covent Garden manager John Rich of stealing a play from Fielding's friend, James Ralph; the play became Phillips's *The Mock Lawyer*. Fielding 'told Mr. Rich, that it [the play] was Mr. Ralph's; and that he [Ralph] had shewed it to him [Fielding] before'. Ralph later informed *The Grub Street Journal* that he was the one who had given his script to an intermediary who gave it to Phillips; so it was not stolen (Battestin 1989: 643). The misunderstandings and accusations revealed in newsprint at the time suggest another motive for Rich to produce Phillips's unflattering depiction of Fielding as the author of 'dull unmeaning Nonsense'. If in fact Phillips wrote such speeches for *The Stage Mutineers*, and left his name off the script, he may have wanted to protect himself from further attacks by the playwright he was attacking, or from future loss of patronage by Drury Lane. The rivalry between Fielding and Phillips can also be sensed in the latter's authorship of *The Mock Lawyer*, a play with a title that sounded like a sequel to Fielding's *The Mock Doctor*; while not exactly stealing Fielding's plot, which came from Molière, Edwards became a 'mock' author after Fielding made such mockery in play titles profitable.

If Phillips was inside Drury Lane's quarters for rehearsals of *The Livery Rake* in May, he may have run into Fielding, and heard him express confidence in Drury Lane's management, as Crambo does in *The Stage Mutineers*: 'In faith we have nothing to fear, Gentlemen; the Parts are excellently cast and properly dressed, and now, ye critical Rogues of the Pit, I defy ye'. Then the rebels defied him, and so did Edward Phillips.

Charlotte Charke, another mutineer locked out of Drury Lane, was not particularly averse to *The Covent-Garden Tragedy* or *The Stage Mutineers*. She later staged Fielding's afterpiece as a puppet play in her own theatre. Also as noted earlier, she appeared as the actress Haughty in a 1735 revival of *The Stage Mutineers*, even though she seems to have been one of the mutineers mocked by the play in 1733. Later she would perform in Fielding's satires about theatre and politics, *Pasquin* and *The Historical Register for the Year 1736*. In the theatric wars that developed between Fielding, Phillips, Theo Cibber, and various theatre managers, Mrs Charke consistently took roles that were opposed to abusive managers, on stage and off. Perhaps she would play as cast—but in plays by Fielding, Phillips, and herself, her roles tended to oppose or mock men in power. As the rebel daughter of a famous father, her voice received special notice when she spoke out against the kind of pro-government, pro-establishment authority her father represented as poet laureate, imperious theatre manager, and ally of Robert Walpole.

The Last Mutineer: Henry Fielding

Henry Fielding also became a stage mutineer late in this sequence of events. When Theo Cibber returned to Drury Lane in 1734 as a deputy manager, Fielding lost the prestige he had there. His new play, *Don Quixote in England*, was declined by Fleetwood in favour of a pantomime featuring a fairground giant, Mynheer Cajanus. Fielding's comedy opened to acclaim that April at the Haymarket, and according to Wilbur Cross, *Don Quixote* marked 'Fielding's return to direct political satire, from which he was compelled to keep clear while writing for Drury Lane. Once back in the Haymarket [where *Tom Thumb* and other farces had played], he regained his old freedom . . . He introduced three new scenes in the course of which Don Quixote becomes a candidate for Parliament and thereby a means for exposing the bribery in country elections' (Cross 157–58). The political satire here was not as extensive or as pointed as it would be in later years, but it marked a change in Fielding's career. Once he moved into a smaller, unlicensed theatre, where he had more control over play production, the satirist was free of Fleetwood and assistants like Theo Cibber. The route led him to follow young Cibber's rebel company with his own, the Great Mogul's Company of English Comedians, so-named in 1736. Before that date, Charlotte Charke briefly ran another independent group, the Mad Company of Comedians at the Haymarket in the summer of 1734. One of the first women to manage a theatre company in England, she also performed the role of Macheath in *The Beggar's Opera Tragedized*, Lovemore in Fielding's *The Lottery*, Minerva in *Penelope* (a new ballad opera, author unknown), Harry in *The Humorous Election* (a new opera, author unknown) with her Mad artists. Her company featured some of the actors who worked with Fielding later in his Great Mogul's Company, and on several occasions all roles in her productions were performed by women (Conrad 42).

One independent acting company followed another which followed another, all in the Haymarket's theatre space. Like the later political actors Marx mentioned, these Georgian adventurers were able to 'conjure up the spirits of the past to their service'. Following other stage rebels to the Haymarket, Fielding cited Aristophanes's example to defend his own political comedy against critics in 1737 (Fielding, *Common Sense*, 21 May 1737). As noted earlier, his political discontent was shared by full houses of theatregoers by 1736. The public's applause for Fielding's dissident, satiric voice, and its willingness to pay his increased ticket prices must have led Walpole to sense that this was no mere stage mutiny focused on theatre conditions, but an increasingly popular and public assembly against the Ministry.

Fielding's later stage satires also constituted a kind of actor rebellion against the Cibber dynasty (Charlotte Charke exempted). Cibber Senior and Junior both received comic misrepresentation in *The Historical Register for the Year 1736* (April 1737), where Pistol declared himself entitled to the position of 'Prime Minister theatrical'. His boast recalls one made by Pistol in *The Stage Mutineers*, where he vows to 'seize upon the Theatre. / Then crown'd with Conquest arrogantly great, / Like Caesar's, rule the mimic World in State'. In 1737 audiences again heard a battle cry borrowed (from Phillips, by Fielding) and spoken in Pistol's name. However, times had changed. Cibber Junior's days of rebellion were over by the season Fielding brought Pistol onstage in 1737. The upstart had returned to Drury Lane and become its Acting Manager. He was a 'Prime Minister theatrical' of sorts, and no better liked by Fielding's crowd than that other Prime Minister, Walpole.

Derrida's Spectres, Phillips's and Charke's

The July 1733 and April 1737 borrowings of battle cries and costumes from colleagues who rebelled against Drury Lane managers were not the conjuring of dead revolutionaries discussed in 1852 by Marx, and more recently in 1993 by Jacques Derrida writing on the spectres of Marx. Instead, in 1733 and 1735, and then again in 1737 with Pistol's return, stage artists borrowed and parodied the behaviour of fellow actors briefly engaged in a labour dispute. These parodic plays responded to conflicts between actors and theatre managers who were very much alive, and would have seen the depictions of themselves on stage; the emphasis here, while still illuminated by Marx's vocabulary, has to be placed on the battle cries and costumes of dissident theatre professionals, not deceased historical personages such as Robespierre or Danton, to whom Marx referred.

Costume pieces are not only worn but contribute to the humour of these Georgian stage farces; their playwrights joke about diadems and feathered hats, the poor players' signs of nobility, to which the actors bid farewell when in danger of losing their occupations. Efforts to keep their occupations motivate the battle cries heard on stage and off. In *The Stage Mutineers* and Charke's *The Art of Management*, characters based on Theo Cibber and Charlotte Charke become living legends; their serious struggles for independence turn into farce. They share a quality Derrida finds in Marx's exegesis of the transition from history to farce: 'the anachrony of a revolutionary present haunted by its antique models'. Almost as soon as they were staged, the Georgian parodies of actor revolution became 'haunted' antiques, comic history plays 'haunted' by the still living actors they mimicked, and the labour organizing so far ahead of its time as to be 'out of joint'. They also employ some 'antique' words of Shakespeare and parody the bombast of other writers in their battle cries. In Derrida's words, 'the anachrony or untimeliness will not be erased'. In fact, it increases as the plays age. '"Untimely", "out of joint", . . . the spirit of the revolution is fantastic and anachronistic through and through' (Derrida 140). While Derrida draws on *Hamlet*, the 1733 and 1737 rebels draw most notably on *Othello*, as we will see.

Fantastic and anachronistic in the time of the role originators, these Georgian farces about mutiny can be seen as comic refusals of the serious and radical impulses they initially parodied. Traces of the original impulses to rebel can be found in the play texts, words and signs of actor discontent that were not erased or destroyed, despite one manager's efforts to destroy Charke's text the week it was printed, and other efforts to turn the mutiny of 1733 into stage comedy.

While comic in language, and while they caricature the actual events on which they are based, Phillips's and Charke's plays hold within them a serious narrative: theatre workers demand concessions from management in exchange for their artistic labour, in 'Combination' long before actor unions won recognition. Or as Derrida notes, citing Marx's German reference to the phantasmagoric: 'It is nothing but the definite social relation between men themselves which assumes here, for them, the fantastic form [*die phantasmagorische Form*] of a relation between things' (Derrida 194). The stage farce's 'fantastic form', its utopian dreams of an actors' commonwealth, employs mock-tragic costume pieces, hyperbolic battle cries and invective, and comic names that underscore the traits of *The Stage Mutineers*'s characters: Madam Haughty, Mrs Squeamish, Miss Crochet, Mr Pistol and Mr Truncheon.

Furious Discords Reign

The name-calling continues in Charke's play, *The Art of Management*, where a theatre manager named Brainless cuts expenses by firing dedicated actors, notably Mrs Tragic, and replaces them with fairground acts—clowns and trained animals—indicative of an era when pantomime and fairground entertainment were gaining popularity at the expense of serious drama. Mrs Tragic protests such changes. Her tirades, exaggerated in their language, turn tragic rants into unintentionally comic monologues. Her encomium to victory after the rebels triumph over management also moves from rant to comic variants of bombast. After Brainless is arrested for debt, Tragic congratulates her brother, Headpiece (based on Theo Cibber), on his triumph:

Now,
No more shall furious Discords reign;
No more for Justice shall we plead in vain;
For thou, no less the Hero, than the Player,
Shall crown each Wish and chace away Despair;
No longer Actors on their Heads shall stand,
Nor obey a bullying Deputy's Command.
Now to thy Honours, let each raise his Voice,
And in choral Symphonies rejoice . . .
[*Next she breaks into song:*]
No more shall Folly rule the Stage,
My Hero will our Hearts engage . . .
Thus happy in thee
From Tyranny free,
From Fools and Bullies relieved.
Who when they enslaved
The worthy and brave
They mostly themselves deceived.

Despite a few songs in it, the play is not a ballad opera, not a tragedy either, and 'Thus happy' at the end, with song from a jubilant Mrs Tragic, whose triumph would seem to render her name inappropriate.

Charke's Mutineers Triumphant

While *The Stage Mutineers* can be seen as a document of a failed actor rebellion, Charlotte Charke's sequel, *The Art of Management*, constitutes a more rebel-friendly revision. She lets the insurgent artists avoid the failings of their predecessors, and walk out on foolish managers with more success. Her play might be subtitled 'The Stage Mutineers Triumphant'. Mrs Tragic, Charke's own role, has some of the play's best comic speeches, and even as she mocks her own excesses, the fiery rebel leader finds ample cause to protest tyrannical theatre management after she is fired without just cause:

SQUIRE BRAINLESS [Manager]: Good morrow, Sir. Mrs. Tragic your Servant, you look mighty well, I hope you are so.
MRS. TRAGIC: And dar'st thou hope, thou Blockhead, Tyrant, Ravisher of Merit's Right.
HEADPIECE: For shame, nor let your Tongue good Manners so far exceed.
BRAINLESS: Pray, madam, what is the Meaning of this tragical Rant, sure you are mad, or talk in your Sleep.

MRS. TRAGIC: Ha! Not mad; but bound more than Madness is. Deprived
Theatric Rights; confin'd to that of low Degree.—Prithee, let me
rave, nor dare disturb the Solemn Purpose of my Soul. . . . I'm
amaz'd to think that e're
Stupidity shou'd sit upon Theatric Throne!
I had been happy had Scene-men, Candle-Snuffers,
Or, Bill-stickers, been Masters there, so I had
Nothing known; Oh! Now farewell the proud haughty Strutt,
The Salary that makes Actresses extravagant and proud;
Farewell the spangled Robe, and the tir'd Page, whose
Akeing Legs that rowl, and Players Pride has oft
Supported. O farewell, the Diadem and Crown that
Make shrill Voices squabble for Parts of Queens.
Oh! Farewell all Pride, Pomp, and Circumstance of Self-Conceit
Farewell, all, for Tragic's Occupation's gone!

The comic rant here borrows from several other sources, as will be seen
shortly. After this speech of farewell, Charke's portrait of rebellion allowed
Mrs Tragic to outlive her ranting lament and celebrate a triumph. The
plot was kind to her brother Theo, too; Catherine Shevelow regards the
portrait of Headpiece (Theo) reconciled with Tragic as a sisterly dream
of family harmony and reconciliation, although the father figure (Colley
Cibber) is nowhere to be seen. The restoration of 'Theatric Rights' may
have been inspired by Theo's brief period of glory during and after the
1733 rebellion (Shevelow 209).

Shevelow also suggests that Truncheon's expression of caution to Mrs
Haughty in *The Stage Mutineers* could be a comic tribute to Charke and
her original 1733 walkout at Drury Lane (Shevelow 166). Truncheon
tells Haughty: 'Enough, enough, my Amazonian, my Female Patriot, who
wildly talk'st of Liberty and Freedom.' Rather than accept his quieting
of her with faint praise, the irrepressible Haughty replies: 'Wildly I talk
because I am a Woman, / But tho' a Woman I'm inspired with Liberty, /
And in her Cause have boldly plac'd my Standard . . .'

Haughty without question is a defiant woman, and her outspoken role
may have been inspired by Charke herself, who performed these lines in
the 1735 revival of *The Stage Mutineers*. No character in the play, including
Haughty, is exempt from some ridicule in the course of the action. But at
the same time as the play mocks Haughty and other actresses for the taking
of liberties, sometimes trivial ones, *The Stage Mutineers* pays tribute to their
independence and tenacity. One of the female characters declines to give
in, even when romantic overtures are employed to bring the actress into
the rebel camp. Miss Crotchet decides to leave Pistol after his rebellious
plot fails.

PISTOL: And wilt thou leave me too?

CROTCHET: I cannot see how it can be for my Interest to stay.

PISTOL: Shall sordid Interest out-balance Love?

CROTCHET: Why in Love should not Women act on the same Principle
as the Men.

In *The Stage Mutineers* scenario, actresses such as Crotchet and the
'Amazonian' Haughty fare reasonably well, but Pistol is repulsed both in
his rebellion and his romance. His occupation as actor and his reputation
as a lover are both endangered. Theo Cibber differed from Pistol in this
regard; he did succeed for a time in 1733 and after. His sister's fantasy of
victory in *The Art of Management* does more justice to her brother's story
and her own than the ending of *The Stage Mutineers*. Both plays portray
actresses whose comic determination and outspokenness honour the
artistry of Charlotte Charke.

Pistol and Mrs Tragic Rewrite *Othello*

While the two staged versions of rebellion by Drury Lane actors differ in
many details, their shared concern surfaces in the repetition of a singular
phrase parodying Shakespeare. Here they are similarly 'haunted by [an]
antique model' of tragic language. The phrase can be heard first in a
lament by Pistol in *The Stage Mutineers*: 'Farewell, for Pistol's Occupation's
gone.' His self-centred sense of loss was echoed two years later by Mrs
Tragic in Charke's 1735 play (in a speech already quoted): 'Farewell all,
for Tragic's Occupation's gone.' Both speeches parody their antecedent
in Act Three, scene iii, of *Othello*, where the title character informs Iago:
'Farewell! Othello's occupation's gone.'

The Georgian theatre mutineers (or their plays' authors) parody
Shakespeare, whose tragic hero bids farewell to 'the plumed troop, and the
big wars'. Othello is defeated not by enemy soldiers but his own suspicions
and jealousy, and Iago's deceptions. Pistol in *The Stage Mutineers* is no
Othello as he bids farewell to 'the plumed Crest and the big Buskin' of his
stage costume; the Georgian actor's dream of heroically taking over a stage
through a combination, forming a commonwealth of actors, and ruling a
new theatre empire collapses in comic debacle. In *The Art of Management*,
Mrs Tragic like Pistol in *The Stage Mutineers* is a mock-tragic figure, an
artist for whom loss of the chance to perform tragedy, and the new prospect
of unemployment, become sources of tragic posturing. When Charke's
character bids farewell to 'the Diadem and Crown that / Make shrill Voices
squabble for Parts of Queens', her lament haunted by an antique model is
twice removed from *Othello*, and it parodies two prior scenes (Othello's
and Pistol's) of militaristic male pride. Here, to borrow again from Marx

on Louis Bonaparte, we have 'heroes without heroic deeds', actors who first must save their endangered careers if they are to perform heroic deeds on stage in the future.

For both Pistol and Mrs Tragic, it is not Desdemona but their own stage career that they jealously guard, so it will not turn into an occupation 'gone', with actors deprived of rights and voice. At the time these plays portrayed them, actors of the period had good reason to be anxious about managerial policy; employers were paternalistic, arbitrary, late in paying salaries. Cartel agreements between Drury Lane and Covent Garden management at times meant an actor fired from one theatre would not be hired by the other. In both mutiny plays, managers given cartoon dimensions hardly deserve the compliment of being termed tyrannical, as they bluff, bluster and lose control of their acting company. Against such mock-tyranny the stage rebels raise their voices in a parody of tragic language that follows the example Henry Fielding set with his popular afterpiece *Tom Thumb* in 1730; but the mutineer plays also employ the parody of tragedy for topical satire of theatre labour disputes. Behind the comic rhetoric of their farewells to an occupation lies a more serious anxiety, anticipation of hardship by actors left to the mercy of Drury Lane's management.

The fact that Charke and her brother had earlier enjoyed the support of a famous father, then lost his overbearing presence when he sold his share of Drury Lane's theatre, may have contributed to their sense of insecurity, as well as a newfound sense of freedom—in a theatre no longer dominated by their family's patriarch. Later in her theatre career, Charke would become a destitute actress, a single mother without steady employment, desperate to support herself and her young daughter. (Her father declined to reconcile with her at that point.) She hid from bailiffs and spent time in prison, as did her brother Theophilus, whose debts were due to gambling and self-indulgence. In 1744 efforts by both brother and sister to skirt the strictures of the Licensing Act were deterred by a Middlesex Grand Jury's call for justices to 'apprehend all "Players of Interludes, Plays, and Drolls"' (Scouten Part 3: liv–lvi). The comic farewells of 1733–35 anticipate their later situations in a profession that did not guarantee steady employment to most actors, and still doesn't. As actress Kitty Clive wrote in a 1744 pamphlet:

It is pretended by the Managers, that they have the same Right to discharge an Actor that a Master has to turn away a Servant, than which nothing can be more false and absurd; for, when a Master dismisses a Servant, there are many thousands besides to apply to; but when the Managers dismiss an Actor, where are they to apply?

Kitty Clive chose not to follow Theo Cibber out of Drury Lane when he led other actors away in 1733; but she personally could not stand Cibber, according to Shevelow's reading of the situation. So she stayed on along with her friend Henry Fielding.

Ruling the Mimic World

The 1782 *Biographia Dramatica* entry on *The Stage Mutineers* finds the play favouring the rebels:

> As in all disputes of this kind, both sides are generally to blame, I shall not here attempt to enter on the merits of the cause, but content myself with observing that the Farce under our present consideration seems to be written in favor of the performers (1782, Volume II: 354).

Compared to Charke's play, *The Stage Mutineers* seems less sympathetic to the rebels, as noted earlier; it shows conceited, petulant stage artists refusing to perform in a play they find beneath their standards. (If the unnamed play is Fielding's *Covent-Garden Tragedy*, they misunderstand the aims of its allegedly low humour.) In any case, their complaints concern more than a single play. The actor named Comic wants to be given all the 'Tip Top' comic roles, and the actress Miss Lovemode wants more fashionable costumes. The dance master Coupée asks for pearl-coloured stockings and red shoes. (Incidentally, his request is quite similar to a request for 'pearl-colour'd stockings and red-heel'd shoes' attributed to a singer in the 'Introduction' scene of John Gay's *Polly*; could the author of *The Stage Mutineers* be borrowing from Gay, whose rebellious singer named Crotchetta found her character 'so low that she would rather dye than sing it' at the start of his second ballad opera?) Mutinous Haughty will take no role but that of Empress or Queen. Squeamish wants 'a Liberty to supervise [her] Part'. Pistol has personal ambitions, too. As he leads the revolt, it becomes clear that the actor could turn into the arrogant ruler of a theatre empire, but instead finds himself 'Dethron'd in Empire, and despis'd in Love . . .'

Pistol's mock-tragic farewell to the profession would have amused audiences who knew Theo Cibber as the thwarted heir to his father's powerful position in management at Drury Lane. A line in the play about Pistol inheriting a poet laureate's crown of leaves received cheers and encores from the 1733 audience, according to an account in *An Apology for Mr. T . . . . C . . . . . :*

> Towards the last Scene the Author had introduc'd a Sale of theatric Goods, and one of the Properties put up to be dispos'd of, was APOLLO's crack'd

Fig. 7. Theophilus Cibber as the Antient Pistol.

Harp, and wither'd Crown of Bayes—Upon which a Character on the Stage reply'd,—Oh, Pray lay that aside for Mr. Pistol, he will claim that by heredi-tary Right—This immediately put the whole House in a Roar,—and Encore, Encore, was all the Cry (Mr T.C. 1740: 18).

Pistol in *The Stage Mutineers* has high regard for himself, but also sees his prospective triumph as everyone's; with him in charge, the stage would know greatness again. This view was shared (without the comic tenor of it) by Theophilus Cibber himself, judging from a 1756 pamphlet in which he recalled the off-stage rebellion and his company's season in exile at the Haymarket in far more reverential terms than those used by the author of *The Stage Mutineers* or the writer of Mr T . . . . C . . . . .'s memoir:

'Twas in the Month of September, in the memorable year 1733,—myself, and a large Body of Comedians, found a happy Asylum in this little Theatre [the Hay-Market], protected by a generous Town, against the despotic Power of some petulant, capricious, unskillful, indolent, and oppressive Patentees; . . . They had more Money than Knowledge of what they traffik'd for. . . . 'Twas here [in the Little Theatre in the Hay-market] we set up our Standard of Liberty; 'twas then we affix'd that Motto [Liberty]—And oh! The bles'd Remembrance of those golden Times!

For a time in 1733–34, Cibber and his cohorts at the Haymarket won public support for their season, which is to say, they attracted a paying audience, although it hardly made them rich. After Drury Lane's new manager, Fleetwood, bought out Highmore and took the departed actors back at Drury Lane, 'those golden Times' became only a 'Remembrance'.

Cibber Sends Fielding Packing

Martin Battestin has argued that the 1733 stage mutiny drove Fielding to-ward more aggressive satire of Walpole:

What almost certainly precipitated Fielding's abrupt, though at first largely surreptitious, commitment to the Opposition's cause was the catastrophic turn his once lucrative theatrical career had taken as a consequence of the actors' rebellion at Drury Lane . . . By 9 March [1734] young Cibber and his renegades, whom Fielding had ridiculed on stage in the new [1734] version of *The Author's Farce* and whom he had denounced in the Dedication to *The Intriguing Chambermaid*, had returned in triumph to the Theatre Royal . . . Cibber's triumph would send [Fielding] packing to the Little Haymarket . . . (Battestin 1989: xxi–xxii).

If this is the case, Fielding may have become a mutineer against Walpole because of Cibber Junior's return to the fold. Earlier in their relationship Cibber had performed roles in the premieres of Fielding's *The Mock Doctor, The Modern Husband* and *The Covent-Garden Tragedy.* Fielding later saw Cibber's reign with Fleetwood as a disgraceful development. Writing about young Cibber in 1740, when James Quin was to take over as acting manager at Drury Lane, Fielding recalled (without naming Cibber or other rebels)

> the late disorderly Conduct of the Theatre . . . the Occasion of the many Insults which the Actors have sufferr'd from the Town, as well as the Advantages gain'd over it by its neighbouring Stage [Covent Garden],

and how Drury Lane's owner Fleetwood had earlier

> trusted the Conduct of his Stage to some mean, low Rascal [i.e., Cibber], who was probably bribed by those in an opposite Interest, to excite the Indignation of the Town by raising the Prices, and giving them nothing for their Money (Fielding, 9 September 1740 *Champion*).

Fielding here discredits Theo Cibber's work for Fleetwood, and clearly would prefer to see Quin in charge. He sounds bitterly opposed to all Cibber has done, and predicts in the same column dire consequences

> if, instead of making his best Actor [Quin] his Prime Minister, he [Fleetwood] had conferr'd that Office on some illiterate, shabby Fellow [Cibber] without any other Merit, than that of flattering his Master, and suffering himself to be kicked as often as he pleased.

Fielding did not quickly forgive or forget Cibber's behaviour, judging from the date of this, earlier and later references to the actor.

Falstaff's Arrest

The 1733 mutiny at Drury Lane was propelled in part by actor expectations of better payment and shared decision planning. As noted already, Theo Cibber voiced this sentiment in a letter to John Highmore. He proposed that the rebel actors join together, rent a theatre house, create a 'cooperative— or "commonwealth" . . . and set their own salaries' (Shevelow 163). Davies later recalled that the managers at the time

> had weakly fallen out with the most esteemed of their players, on account of a small advance in salary, which they had demanded; the matter in

dispute, did not, I believe, much exceed 400 [pounds] per annum. The actors revolted, and opened the little theatre in the Hay-market, with some appearance of success (Davies I: 61).

A column in the 7 June 1733 issue of *The Grub Street Journal* reported that the mutineer actors sought

> to have as much Salary as they have now [under Highmore]; to share the Profits at the End of the Season; and to be all Managers as well as [Theo Cibber] himself; to sit equal Judges on Authors, and divide the Tyranny of using them as they please.

The *Journal* commentator disapproved of this move toward a cooperative structure. Ahead of the author of *The Stage Mutineers*, the Grub Street journalist suggested the goals of the rebel leadership were self-serving folly. He compared the actors to the 'drunken sailors' Stephano and Trinculo in *The Tempest*: 'they are all to be Viceroy; Pistol [Cibber] desired only to be Viceroy over them'. This idea (minus references to Shakespeare's play) returned in *The Stage Mutineers* a month later, when Pistol promised Truncheon the rank of General, 'and I am to be General over you'.

> TRUNCHEON: Over me? No, Sir, I'll be Governor in Chief.
> PISTOL: Under Pistol—No otherways, I assure you . . .
> TRUNCHEON: Pistol—We are in the wrong—We should forget a private Quarrel in a publick Cause—We'll divide the Government equally.

The cynical *Grub Street Journal* and *Stage Mutineers* responses to talk about a cooperative acting company were symptomatic of other, larger economic and social practices that kept performers in the position of hired hands or servants, subject to the demands of managers.

A 1732 pamphlet entitled 'A Proposal for the Better Regulation of the Stage' confirms this situation:

> Performers at both Houses [Drury Lane and Covent Garden] are so oppress'd by the Tyranny of their Superiors, so circumscrib'd by mutual Combinations against them; sometimes so badly paid, and, at all Times, so arbitrarily treated, that we are persuaded they are ready for the change, let it take Place when it will, and will rejoice at the Deliverance.

The 'Change' proposed by the pamphlet was a new academy where performers would be 'rewarded with an Increase of Pay, according to their merit' and new management by a committee of shareholders 'annually chosen by the Majority of Votes', with 'every Share entitled to a Vote'

(Loftis 1960: 50–52). (The 'Combinations' mentioned here are not actor associations, but cartel agreements among Patent theatre managers to regulate actor hiring to their advantage.) Theo Cibber and his mutineers were not the first, and not alone, to complain about management's treatment of Georgian actors. The 1732 call for reform was unsigned. Extracts of it were printed in *The Weekly Register*, 5 February 1732, with an introduction by Tim Birch, who said his friend Gentle put the cited pamphlet into his hand. The proposal giving actors 'so arbitrarily treated' and 'circumscrib'd' more voice in their profession was echoed in *The Stage Mutineers* by Pistol's call for his colleagues 'To shake off Chains of Tyranny' by joining his insurrection, and Mrs Squeamish's request for 'a Liberty to supervise my Part, before I determine whether I'll play it or not', although their lines were originally written to be humorously presumptuous (Phillips 1733: 24).

Writing about eighteenth-century employers (not about those who employed actors *per se*), E.P. Thompson noted:

> They clung to the image of the labourer as an *un*free man, a 'servant'; a servant in husbandry, in the workshop, in the house. (They clung simultaneously to the image of the free masterless man as a vagabond, to be disciplined, whipped and compelled to work.) (Thompson 1993: 36).

Actors were free to be unemployed and indigent if they did not comply with management's casting choices and play as cast for low pay in many cases. In *The Stage Mutineers* the rebels plan to join 'an Itinerant Company' if their mutiny fails. But wandering players could be arrested for vagrancy.

When John Gay portrayed a beggar as a playwright with a company of beggar actors in 1728, he was mocking a longstanding prejudice against theatre artists who were seen as no better than vagabonds in some quarters of London. The prejudice took a new turn in November of 1733, when Drury Lane actor John Harper was arrested for the crime of vagrancy. His theatre's manager, John Highmore, ordered the arrest as part of his battle against the actors who had walked out. Harper was a popular performer, particularly appreciated for his portrayal of Falstaff; he was arrested the day he was scheduled to play that role. (Theo Cibber took his place on stage.) In this battle, as in one Shakespeare depicted in *Henry IV*, Falstaff emerged triumphant.

Laguerre's 1733 engraving titled 'The Stage Mutiny' shows Harper dressed as Falstaff among the mutineers, with Theophilus Cibber as Falstaff's companion, Pistol. In Hogarth's use of the same imagery for part of his 'Southwark Fair' print, irrepressible Jack Falstaff and his cohorts stand their ground, even though other actors (not on the banner showing Falstaff and Pistrol) are falling off their fairground stage when it collapses, in an ironic visual reference to Theo Cibber's August 1733 fairground production of *Tamerlane the Great* which advertised 'the Fall of Bajazet'.

Old Jack Falstaff stood his ground in court, too. On stage he may have been a rogue, but in November of 1733, he was judged not to be a vagabond. John Harper was released from gaol after evidence proved that he was 'a freeholder in Surrey, [and] a housekeeper in Westminster'. Several hundred people cheered the actor's release after the trial (Genest III: 405–06). Hume offers some valuable insight into the trial when he notes: 'The issue was not the solvency or domicile of the actors, but whether performing without a licence made them, legally speaking, vagrants' (Hume 176). Harper's residency may have won his release; but the motive behind the arrest was to stop his and other performances in an unlicensed theatre.

As part of the protracted dispute between Drury Lane actors and management lasting from 1733 to 1734, Harper's arrest was one scene from a much longer struggle. Vagabond charges threatened actors again on 29 March 1737, when London's *Daily Post* reported:

> The Actors of the several Theatres are in no small Pain about the present Act depending in the House of Commons call'd the Vagrant Act, for fear of being deem'd Vagabonds; and are therefore perpetually soliciting their Friends for a Clause in their Favour (Scouten Part 3: 654).

Another actor protest against management involved David Garrick in 1743, and a much earlier dispute took place between Drury Lane actors such as Betterton and Mrs Barry, and their manager, Christopher Rich, in 1695. While a few players like Garrick achieved fame and wealth, others found it hard to avoid debtor's prison, and not all of them were freeholders and house owners like Harper. Hogarth's 1738 engraving of 'Strolling Actresses' portrays a wandering stage troupe in which one tearful player may be Clarke. Her autobiography complained of the hardships that accompanied such an itinerant life, into which she fell after censorship forced her sometime employer Henry Fielding our of play production.

The London Merchant Refuses to Pay his Taxes

During 1733 another public outpouring, involving far more citizens than the hundreds who cheered Harper's prison release, took place in response to Walpole's plan for taxation of wine and tobacco. Merchants, traders, and consumers gathered to protest the Excise Bill outside Parliament. Langford writes that on 14 March 1733, 'the day set for the final unveiling of Walpole's project, Westminster was crowded with demonstrators. According to the *London Evening Post*, admittedly not the most impartial of sources, "there was the greatest Appearance of eminent Merchants, and Traders of the Cities and Suburbs of London and Westminster . . . the like not seen in the Memory of Man, in order to apply their several Members [of Parliament] to oppose the new intended Excise on Wines and Tobacco"' (Langford 65). A nineteenth-century engraving of the scene makes it look like a riot, with one man and his poster fallen on the ground as others scurry past. The slogan on the poster, 'Liberty, Property and No Excise Tax', recalls the banner 'Liberty and Property' held by a stage mutineer in Laguerre's 1733 engraving. It also recalls the warning about actors spoken by a Manager in *The Stage Mutineers*: 'They are ready to rebel: One Step more wou'd make 'em all Patriots; Liberty and Property wou'd be the Word, and all the unthinking Fools wou'd join them.' Such outspoken calls for actor freedom might have seemed humorous, if not absurd, to spectators watching *The Stage Mutineers* in 1733, at least when the sentiments were voiced by characters named Pistol, Haughty and Squeamish; the players not on stage, those who had followed Cibber out of Drury Lane, would have taken the slogans more seriously. Here again one rebellion (that of the players) borrowed language from another (the anti-Walpole tax protesters).

The ephemeral battle cries for liberty and property in 1733 briefly met with success that year. They might also be regarded as ancient antecedents of current debates over constitutional rights undermined by money and those who spend it to influence policy in the United States. Since a Supreme Court decision ('People United') sanctioned corporate campaign spending as an exercise of free speech, those who lack money (today's 'indigent' actors) will be heard less, or hardly at all; liberty is no longer synonymous with free speech, only with property when campaign promises (if not elections) become a form of property sold to the highest bidder. 'Liberty is property' might be a more accurate slogan for the current situation.

In his mock-preface to *The Covent-Garden Tragedy*, Fielding joked that the script offered 'No fine Moral Sentences, not a Word of Liberty and Property, no Insinuations, that Courtiers are Fools, and Statesmen Rogues'. His successor and rival satirist (Edward Phillips, probably) had characters mention 'Liberty and Property' in *The Stage Mutineers* without the author seriously supporting these sentiments. Both writers distanced themselves from one of the most popular slogans of the day, while acknowledging its usage. Fielding, as noted in an earlier chapter, subsequently mocked Walpole's tax plan.

Perhaps the playwrights did not want to side with the protesters. In not backing the protest slogan, the authors also would have avoided punishment of the sort that was reported in the 24–27 March 1733 edition of the *St. James's Evening Post*. At the New Theatre in the Haymarket, 'one of the Comedians took the Liberty to throw out some Reflections upon the

Prime Minister and the Excise, which were not design'd by the Author; Lord Walpole being in the House, went behind the Scenes, and demanded of the Prompter whether such Words were in the Play, and he answering they were not, his Lordship corrected the Comedian with his own Hand very severely' (Scouten Part 3: 280). Fielding's work was not on the Haymarket stage on the night of 22 March when the minister's son, Horace Walpole, visited to see the pantomime titled *Love Runs All Dangers* (text never published, author remains unknown). Presumably the dissenting actor improvised remarks critical of the ministry's position. Later anti-Walpole comments became firmly fixed in Fielding's texts, and he too suffered reprisal (from the father, not the son).

Political cartoons and public burnings of effigies of the minister in response to Walpole's tax plan must have disturbed the Minister as well; but he or his son could not publicly beat a whole crowd, or retract a cartoon once it was printed. Beating an actor was not so difficult, and perhaps the satisfaction the minister felt in hearing about that 'correction' backstage in 1733 encouraged him to censor other theatre artists—notably Fielding—who was beaten by Walpole's legislation.

The Laughing Audience of 1733

To avoid 'correction' of other writings, Fielding and the author of *The Stage Mutineers* kept their names out of some satiric documents (journal columns, some plays in Fielding's case) now attributed to them. Several centuries later, W.J.T. Mitchell saw such namelessness as

> a key ideological feature of the Occupy movement [of 2011–13], which insisted on an iconography of non-sovereignty and anonymity, removing the face and figure of the charismatic leader in favour of the face in and of the crowd, the assembled masses' (Mitchell 101).

The faces in the crowds attending *The Stage Mutineers* must have been those of a laughing audience; they kept the play running for twelve performances (a respectable run) in the summer of 1733. While protest events in the twenty-first century are hardly the same as those of the eighteenth, the assembled audience at theatres featuring political satire in the time of Phillips, Fielding and Charke may have gained strength from its laughter as a crowd enjoying the comedy of rebellion.

Fielding's friend William Hogarth paid tribute to 'The Laughing Audience' in a December 1733 engraving with that title; the only scowling face in the picture is said to be that of a critic. One of the laughing faces beneath a large white wig might be Fielding's, watching *The Opera of*

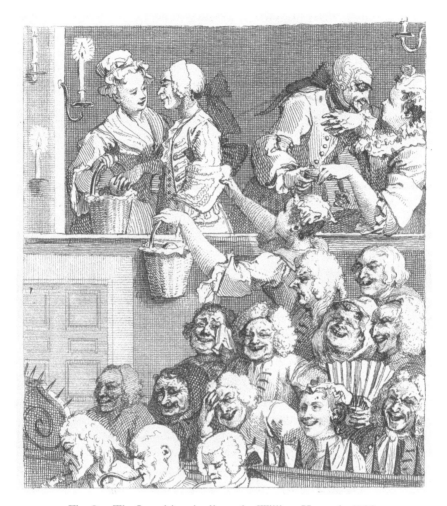

Fig. 8. The Laughing Audience by William Hogarth, 1733.

Operas, a musical version of his *Tragedy of Tragedies*, performed at both Drury Lane and Theo Cibber's Haymarket in November, 1733. Then again, the spectators inside a theatre might be watching *The Stage Mutineers*.

E.P. Thompson in his study of eighteenth-century English dissent refers to

> the ever present resistance of the crowd . . . which stretched at times from small gentry and professional men to the poor, but which appeared . . . to be made up of 'the loose and disorderly sort'.

Henry Fielding, Thompson notes, was aware of different crowds at different entertainments in London:

> whilst the people of fashion seized several places to their own use, such as courts, assemblies, operas, balls, etc., the people of no fashion besides one royal place, called his Majesty's Bear Garden, have been in constant possession of all hops, fairs, revels, etc . . . they seem scarcely to regard each other as of the same species (Thompson 1993: 56–57).

Fielding's theatre satires evidently accommodated both the fashionable and the people of no fashion. His plays drew 'Mobs of Quality', and 'the multitudinous Mob', according to *An Apology for the Life of Mr. T . . . . C . . . . ., Comedian*, and the anonymous author of this document (possibly Fielding himself) notes with mock-regret that 'Mob' enthusiasm for such satire 'made the Minister not a little uneasy' (Mr. T.C. 1740: 92–93). Fielding later praised 'the Mob' in a 4 April 1752 *Covent-Garden Journal* column (discussed more fully in Chapter Nine) for its behaviour inside theatres, and found it 'laudable' for 'Qualities very greatly superior to those who have hitherto, with much Injustice, pretended to look down upon them'.

Theophilus Cibber Without Apologies

The 'mob' laughter of an audience that could make a 'Minster not a little uneasy' required prompting from actors. They too became a 'mob', and threatened the empire of theatre managers in 1733 when Theophilus Cibber incited 'the ever present resistance of the crowd' in his fellow mutineers. He and Fielding shared a gift for public disturbance through their art. But Cibber's 'mob' action benefited him more than other actors involved, as he became the right-hand man of Fleetwood at Drury Lane.

> Theo. Cibber had contrived to insinuate himself so far into the good graces of Fleetwood that he was appointed acting Manager, but Fleetwood some time after finding him an improper person displaced him for [the actor Charles] Macklin (Genest III: 423).

His period of grace did not last.

Had Theophilus, like his father, not been so disagreeable to others, he might be regarded as an early labour organizer. In a sympathetic study of Theo Cibber's stage career, Conrad suggests that the actors who protested at Drury Lane and were locked out by management had right on their side:

If a modern manufacturer locked out his skilled employees because they
were buying stock in his firm and then blacklisted them with the only other
manufacturer who could use their skill, he would be disciplined by his
national association and caricatured as a monster in the newspapers. . . .
(Conrad 64).

Perhaps Theo's protest was three centuries too early. Instead of receiving
praise for his labour activism or his acting, for most of his career Cibber
Junior was known as his father's son, a would-be Colley Cibber. His
nickname of Pistol was a joke; Cibber's portrayal of Falstaff's companion
on stage was acclaimed for comic flamboyance that might have been
inappropriate excess, more revealing of self-enamoured histrionics than
the role Shakespeare wrote for Pistol in *Henry IV* and *The Merry Wives
of Windsor*. Arthur Scouten remarks that Theo Cibber's artistic 'progress
was the most erratic of all, [with the actor] ruining every advantage and
alienating every manager he ever had' (Scouten Part 3: cxxxii). His
ambition exceeded his abilities, perhaps; that seems to be one reason satire
was directed at him in plays by Henry Fielding, Edward Phillips and
Henry Woodward.

When a theatrical caricature of Cibber as Pistol appears in the 1736
Beggar's Pantomime, attributed to Henry Woodward, the situation involves
actresses who compete for the role of Polly Peachum. Pistol vows to publish
a letter favouring one actress—who represents Cibber's wife, Susannah. In
print his 'words are strong, / Not one spelled wrong', promises Susannah's
defender in the scenario. Theo's letter-writing in defence of family matters
was already known to the theatre public by this time. Adding to the Cibber
family presence in Woodward's pantomime was Charlotte Charke, who
performed the role of Pistol. She often portrayed men onstage, and certainly
had insider knowledge about how to represent her brother comically. Poor
Theo had even his sister turned against him by the satirists.

Edward Phillips not only placed a mock-tragic, self-aggrandizing Pistol
in *The Stage Mutineers*, but brought him back again in 1739, for a small role
as a Spaniard, 'a little, shuffling, tricking, strutting, domineering fellow',
in *Britons, Strike Home*, a patriotic afterpiece about Britain's conflicts at
sea with Spain. The enemy nation's Don Superbo Hispaniolo Pistole has
only one speech, but it is full of blustery threats to 'burn, and sink, plunder
and destroy . . . trick, and kick . . . bluster, huff, and swear'. The portrait
suggests Pistole's inspiration, Theo Cibber, was still a target of stage jokes
in 1739.

The Mad House, an unsigned ballad opera performed in 1737, briefly
placed Pistol on the stage as a character confined to Bedlam. In the play
we learn 'the Fustian Rascal had recourse to Mutiny, drew his Sword on
the Dramatis Personae, and behaved like a Madman. We have therefore

brought him hither [to the madhouse] that you may tame him'. The lunatic described here sounds very much like the Pistol portrayed in *The Stage Mutineers*, in Bedlam four years later.

Fielding's feud with the often-mocked actor lasted decades; unflattering references to him were published as early as 1734 in the revised *Author's Farce*, and as late as 25 April 1752. A satiric column Fielding wrote for *The Covent-Garden Journal* refers to 'a huge laced Hat on [a man's head] as big as Pistol's in the Play', an aside that recalls the Georgian engraving of Cibber as stage mutineer in a tricornered hat large enough to fit a swollen head. While not worn by Cibber himself in the 1752 column reference, the hat is said to rest over 'a Wig somewhat disheveled, and a Face which at once gave you a perfect Idea of Emptiness, Assurance, and Intemperance'—a countenance quite fitting for a man wearing Pistol's hat.

All the anti-Pistol humour devised by Fielding, Phillips, Woodward, and others makes it difficult to write favourably about Theo Cibber. But judging from some statements he himself issued, the man tried to make his profession more collegial, more democratic, and more remunerative; even if he did so largely to advance his own standing, or in a lapse from self-interest, he served his colleagues too. He was more of a madman onstage, in plays portraying him, than off.

The son of Colley sounds quite respectable at times in the *Apology* published bearing his initials in its title:

> I found this an admirable Time to put in execution a Design I had plan'd, which was, at a proper Opportunity, to fling off the Yoke, and set up for Masters and Managers ourselves. At one of our private Meetings all were complaining, yet no one proposed a Method of Redress, when I got up from my Chair and thus delivered myself: '. . . If you think you receive Injuries, deliver yourselves from them. If you would not be Slaves, be free . . . You may be the Asserters of the Cause of Liberty. What though your Enemies have got the Patents, you have your own Talents, your own Endowments of Nature, and Acquisitions of Art . . . The Means of Freedom are in your own Possession, which, if you refuse, may you be perpetual Slaves, and be sold like a Herd of Sheep from one purchaser to another' (Mr T.C. 1740: 87–88).

It could be argued that the writer of this speech overestimates the freedom of actors who live in a tightly-controlled labour market. Yet the call to resist a cartel system of management, attributed here to Theophilus Cibber (although he did not write the statement), suggests he was seeking more than his own promotion. The same can be said for a speech delivered by Pistol in *The Stage Mutineers*. The address to his fellow actors, while subtly comic in its context, could almost pass for a declaration of actor independence, and a Brechtian alignment with the discontented:

> . . . We are met
> Like daring Sons of Britain, freeborn Spirits,
> To shake off Chains of Tyranny—Is it resolv'd
> That each in his degree shall share in Empire? . . .
> Whoe'er has ought to claim, now let him speak.

In response to this speech, various characters respond by speaking of their own goals in rebellion. Admittedly, the goals are mostly self-centred and trivial (better costumes, a chance to dance in red shoes, guaranteed roles as Empress and Queen, etc.). The play is after all a farce and not a serious portrayal of a labour union. Any interest Pistol expresses in favour of shared benefits is undercut later, when the character confides to his cohort Truncheon words that betray his deception:

> Ha! Ha! Ha! How we great Men delude the unthinking Many! . . . there is not one of 'em but thinks to have prodigious Power in our future Common-Wealth: But in our Common-Weal, as in all others, a few only will share the Power—I and you, Truncheon, and perhaps another . . .

(The other person mentioned in his aside is Miss Crochet, with whom Pistol flirts.) Calling himself a great man—invoking the phrase satirists associated with Walpole—Pistol becomes a mock-tragedy's villain here, if he was not one earlier. The scene echoes Shakespeare's scene with Trinculo and Stephano; perhaps, as noted earlier, the scene's author read the *Grub Street Journal*'s 1733 comparison of the off-stage mutiny to that play. After Truncheon and Pistol briefly quarrel, Truncheon makes amends by proposing that the two of them 'divide the Government equally'. They then agree on a duopoly a little like that of the two Patent Theatres, Drury Lane and Covent Garden, that virtually agreed to eliminate all the smaller theatres in London.

In the counterfeit autobiography of Cibber, apologist Mr T . . . . C . . . . . claims to have watched the Covent Garden representation of himself in *The Stage Mutineers*:

> A Farce was wrote, and performed, and the Bent of it was to ridicule poor me: Tone of Elocution, my buskin Tread, my Elevation of Countenance, my Dignity of Gesture, and expressive Rotation of Eye-balls. In short, all my Manner was burlesqued, and a Mock-Pomp of Words, which were a Parody of Tragedy Speeches, and Pistol's Bombast, run through the Character. This I will say, this Thing was so well timed, and the Person who mimicked me did it so well, that it succeeded far beyond any the least intrinsic Merit that was in it.

Whoever wrote this passage preserves the comic scene and its efficacy as satire quite well, even as he discounts the merit of the play; the imagery sharply defines Theophilus as a bombastic, unintentionally clownish actor, overblown as Shakespeare's Pistol.

In *The Stage Mutineers*, after Pistol draws a sword to threaten a playwright (the Fielding stand-in, Crambo) who flees, a manager reasons with him:

> Come come Pistol, lay aside the Buskin, and a Word or two in downright humble Prose: This Theatrical Empire is ours. Therefore you and the rest of your Brother Heroes, must submit to the Laws which we in our Wisdom shall think proper to ordain.

Rather than comply with this plea, Pistol attempts to rally actors to his side, and fails as many of them decide to depart with a travelling theatre. The managers then discover they have won a Pyrrhic victory; Pistol has no following and they have no acting company. 'We have conquered indeed, but what have we gained—An Empire without Subjects.' The actors briefly return to sing a song before *The Stage Mutineers* concludes; their dispute with management goes unsettled, the theatre empire left in disarray.

In commentary on the play, Dane Farnsworth Smith asserted that it 'has no originality or literary value' only 'personal and biographical interest' (Smith 169–70). More value can be found in *The Stage Mutineers*, however, when it is seen as a comic depiction of the ongoing struggle over control of 'Theatrical Empire'. In 1733, it mocked the managers and rebel actors of Drury Lane, including the heir apparent to management of his father's theatre, Theo Cibber. Its basis in theatre history makes the farce an unusual and revealing document—one in a series of plays that saw fit to pillory the poet laureate's son and his followers, and inadvertently preserved traces of an actor rebellion against cartel managers.

Pistol's Triumph and Fall, 1733–37

Between 1733 and 1735, Theophilus Cibber had considerable influence on his own theatre group's productions, and then over Drury Lane's repertoire. Owner Charles Fleetwood was busy squandering his wealth, and acquiring gambling debts, which left Cibber virtually in charge of daily operations at Drury Lane in 1734. Theo also had success with his pantomime, *The Harlot's Progress*, based on Hogarth's engravings; it remained in the Drury Lane repertoire from 1733 to 1744.

Genest's 1832 summary of the actual 1733 mutiny and its aftermath reports that when the 'Seceders' rejoined Drury Lane's company, 'the most grave and sensible part of them were already sick of their enterprise, and ashamed of being made dupes of so young and wild a leader as Theo. Cibber' (Genest III: 406). So it cannot be said he won lasting or complete support from his followers. Nor did Theo Cibber's position as Drury Lane's Acting Manager last too long.

Despite such setbacks, Cibber again found himself near the top of the heap in 1737. When Henry Fielding's company at the Haymarket and other small theatres were closed by the passage of the Licensing Act that began in June, Theophilus thrived. Cibber Senior's play, *Love's Last Shift*, could be seen at Drury Lane on 6 September 1737 with Cibber, Jr as Sir Novelty and his wife Susannah Cibber as Amanda. The family dynasty (minus Charlotte Charke) was back in the theatre's brightest candlelight, all the more visible after the disappearance of smaller theatres. The Prince and Princess of Wales watched Theo Cibber's *The Harlot's Progress* performed at Drury Lane on 27 October.

During the fall of 1737, Cibber Junior was continually performing roles at Drury Lane, including his renowned Pistol in Shakespeare's *Henry the Fourth, Part II* (seen at Drury Lane 29 October 1737). Full of himself, and then overreaching his hold later in the season, he had the audacity to portray himself as a comic character (named 'Cibber, a comedian') in a new afterpiece that opened on 26 January 1738. *The Coffee House* by Reverend James Miller was one of the first new plays to be performed 'since the Act of Parliament took Place, obliging all Plays, Farces, etc, to be licens'd before play'd', and it was 'damn'd by the Town' (Scouten Part 3: 699). The condemnation of the play has been attributed to its portrayal of a coffee house that Templegate lawyers in the audience regarded as a slighting depiction of Dick's Coffee House in London. The spectators were loyal to Dick's proprietor, Mrs Yarrow, on whom they felt Miller had based his character, the Widow. Miller's unflattering portrait of her upset the coffee-drinking lawyers at the play's premiere, or so say some accounts. However, these accounts neglect to mention that Theophilus Cibber was portraying—celebrating—himself in *The Coffee House*; this too might have provoked a riot.

Theophilus Cibber Incites a Riot

The leader of the 1733 stage-mutiny against Highmore's Drury Lane management had a reputation as a rabble-rouser and intemperate actor, and lines Miller wrote for him sustain that reputation. In *The Coffee House* the character named Cibber threatens the Widow when she plans to marry her young daughter to a rich old man named Harpie.

CIBBER: What, marry her to Harpie! If thou dare attempt it, I'll bring a
body of playhouse dragoons, all Alexander's army, and demolish thy
citadel for thee.

WIDOW: I defy you, and all your company, Sir. Tho' you are so uppish,
Sir, I have gentlemen enow that will stand to my side, all the reverend
benchers to a man, Sir.

These lines cry out for lawyers in the audience to shout in favour of the
Widow, and shout down Cibber's performance, as they apparently did.
The fact that Theophilus Cibber was 'playing' himself also might have
encouraged spectators to forget that they sat watching actors, and instead
see Cibber as himself, the cad, threatening a stand-in for their woman
friend. In a Pirandellian-style self-reflection, centuries ahead of Pirandello,
the character Cibber comments on his own folly:

. . . the follies we mimick on the stage are apt to become real habits to us . . .
I off the stage as well as on, sometimes play the fop, and sometimes the fool,
and am sometimes sober, and sometimes drunk, now and then have a scant-
ing of wit, but seldom or never a grain of common-sense . . .

Here was another invitation for spectators to join the playwright in
criticizing the notorious actor, to yell agreement as he admitted he
sometimes plays the fool, the fop, and the senseless.

Resentment against Cibber's support of censorship could have been
another source for protest of his performance. The fact that Miller's *The
Coffee House* was one of the first new plays to pass censorship may well have
provoked the audience, particularly when the character Cibber boasted
(using lines Miller wrote for him):

Any part that you please, Sir, I'll try if I can hit it. D'ye want a sage politician,
for instance, with a face full of business, and a head empty of brains?—Why,
I must proclaim, for certainty, what never could happen, and whisper for
secret what never could be known' (Miller 1781: 7).

Here the man who sided with Walpole against satirists felt free to recite his
own (or technically Miller's) mockery of lawmakers, in front of an audience
of lawyers. The temptation to jeer and mock Cibber must have been great.
Whether Miller's play or Cibber's presence on stage, or both, set off
audience protest, Cibber Jr was no longer in command of the stage empire
that evening. And it happened again two weeks later, on 16 February 1738,
when Cibber appeared as the character Julio in another new play by James
Miller. The preface to the 1738 edition of Miller's *Art and Nature* quotes a
gentleman present at the opening saying he 'never knew a Play destroyed

with so much Art' by its 'enemies', 'giving no Quarter to the Parts which they thought would entertain' (Scouten Part 3: 703). While no clear motive for the spectator opposition is recorded by the gentleman observer, it is possible that simply the return to Drury Lane of Cibber in a Miller play was enough to incite more vehement protest from those offended by *The Coffee House*. The stage-mutineer of 1733 was no longer a leader of mutiny within the theatre, but a source of it. For a time in 1738, Cibber had to flee to France to avoid his creditors. Jeers from the lawyers may have given him additional reason to leave the stage. By December, 1738, he was in court, suing his wife's lover, William Sloper, for damages, to pay for the loss of her 'services and assistance' (Nash 1977: 126). His career went off track more than usual. He was back at Drury Lane as an actor again in 1741; but never in his lifetime would he acquire the fame or fortune or the 'theatrical empire' known to his father. His 1744 autobiography, mostly a reprint of letters titled *A Serio-Comic Apology for Part of the Life of Mr. Theophilus Cibber*, includes pitiful accounts of attempts to earn compensation and take the stage again, usually without success.

Cibber and Charke Become Gazeteers

When *The Stage Mutineers* was revived in July 1735 at Lincoln's Inn Fields, it was performed 'with alterations and additions. Written by the author of the comedy' (Scouten Part 3: 502). Again no author's name appeared. As noted earlier, Charlotte Charke performed in the 1735 production; she may have known the author, if he revised while she rehearsed. Her autobiography makes no reference to the play, and only briefly refers to 'a revolt' against Mr Highmore, which she joined with her brother by making 'a decampment' 'to the new theatre in the Haymarket', where her salary was 'raised from thirty shillings to three pounds', and she 'had a very good share of parts' (Charke 1755: 39).

Charke appeared only once as Mrs Haughty in *The Stage Mutineers*. She took another role a week later. On 30 July 1735, Lincoln's Inn Fields opened another anonymously authored afterpiece, *Politicks on Both Sides*. In this new 'Satiric Farcical Ballad Opera' Charke played the role of Gazeteer, and spoke the epilogue (Scouten Part 3: 502). The play was never published, and we can only speculate about its content and authorship. The cast list's whimsical character names (Sir Libel Hothead, Truelove, Fanny Wellplot, Constantia, Squire Caleb, Sir Politick Staunch, as well as Gazeteer) suggest that the play was a topical satire. Here again, the reason for authorial secrecy remains elusive; but a clue can be found in the name of Charlotte Charke's character, 'Gazeteer', which also was the name of the pro-Walpole journal, the *Daily Gazeteer*, to which her brother Theo was a contributor. The first issue of the journal appeared on 30 June 1735, one month before the new play opened. A play with speeches satirizing the new pro-Ministry journal and its writers—or simply referring to them—would have been quite timely. The play's text has not survived, but several unsigned satiric commentaries on the new *Daily Gazeteer* were printed around the same time in *The Craftsman*, and have been attributed to Henry Fielding. Might his satiric responses to the *Gazeteer* have been echoed in lines spoken by Charke's character? By March 1736 she had joined Fielding's troupe, the Great Mogul's Company of Comedians. *Politicks on Both Sides* might have increased his interest in her acting, if her stage character spoke anything like the jokes about *The Daily Gazeteer* printed in Fielding's unsigned column. There he asserted that a Minister can be seen as 'politically defunct' 'when all the Books, Pamphlets, and Papers, written in his Defense, are so far from doing Him any Good, that They serve only to exasperate People the more against Him. And plunge Him deeper in the Mire'. While 'weekly, quartan, and tertian Apologies' have not helped the Minister, wrote the columnist about Walpole, he now seeks a daily gazetteer, and: 'At this rate, We may expect, in a little Time, to see a Morning, a noon, and an Evening Paper, every Day published, in the same glorious Cause' (Battestin 1989: 98–99). Perhaps Charke impersonated a contributor to the *Gazeteer* who resembled her brother. Could her lines have been written by the author of *The Stage Mutineers* (who was altering the 1733 play that week) or Fielding? Or by Charke herself?

Just before the summer season ended, on 5 September, Charke appeared at Lincoln's Inn Fields as French Harlequin in a new play, *The Carnival, Harlequin Blunderer*, which she wrote. The play with songs was never published. A week earlier, at the same theatre, she performed the roles of Pickle Herring in a production of Jonson's *Bartholomew Fair*, and Polly Peachum in *The Beggar's Opera*. Charke evidently had no need to continue as a stage mutineer with so many other roles (including one as author) available that month.

The author of *The Stage Mutineers* who returned to alter his play in July of 1735 might have been Phillips; but that remains questionable, since the primary attribution of his name was made by another anonymous author (possibly Fielding) who wrote Mr T . . . . C . . . . .'s *Apology* in 1740. The continued anonymous authorship of stage satires such as *Politicks on Both Sides* and *The Stage Mutineers* during the summer of 1735 could have been prompted by Sir John Bernard's 5 March 1735 introduction of a 'Bill for restraining the number of playhouses and "regulating" the actors'. This bill would have abolished every small theatre, including Goodman's Fields, the Haymarket, and Lincoln's Inn Fields. It was not a time to flaunt one's identity as a satirist of politicians. According to one source, 'the Bill caused a panic among those actors and managers who would be ruined if it passed Parliament' (Battestin and Battestin, 1989: 184). Their fear was not unwarranted; ruin came in 1737.

Gordon Craig's Lament

The 1733 farewells to an occupation were early but not unwarranted, as actors who were mutineers onstage and off in 1737 found themselves regulated and closed out of the Great Mogul's Company by Walpole's Ministry. 'After 1737', Scouten observes,

> a dramatist would not find another theatre as easily as had Fielding in 1734 ... [and] a group of actors could not secede and set up for themselves, as the Drury Lane players had done in 1733. When such a move was attempted ten years later, with such prominent men as Garrick and Macklin as leaders, the rebels found that there was no place to go (Scouten Part 3: cxlvii–cxlviii)

In one last attempt to relive his days of glory, Theophilus Cibber returned to the Haymarket stage and cast himself in lead roles at the end of the 1754–55 season. He played the mock doctor in *The Mock Doctor*, Marplot in *The Busy Body*, Bayes in *The Rehearsal*, and Brazen in *The Recruiting Officer*, with his sister Charlotte and Mrs Midnight (Christopher Smart) taking other roles in the productions (Scouten Part 4: 489–91). By 1756 he was sadly underemployed again, when he published a list of 110 plays in which he had performed, and declared himself ready for any of his old roles. Cibber was not overwhelmed with offers, particularly since the preeminent theatre manager of the day, Garrick, had dismissed him from Drury Lane in 1755 (Conrad 160). Once more the rebel without a theatre of his own, Cibber accused Garrick of tyranny in a letter complaining that 'in a time of the Abuse of Power, and the unfair Treatment of Men of Genius', it was often more difficult to meet with 'these stage dictators' than to gain admittance to a prime minister. His ally in the ministry, Walpole, was gone. All Theo Cibber could do to restore his reputation was reminisce. He wrote about the past, the glorious years of 1733 and 1734 'when many crowded Audiences spoke loudly in Favour of our attempts'. But his days as a popular rebel, even as a popular topic of satire, had passed. Pistol's occupation was now letter writing, and no one revived *The Stage Mutineers* again in Theophilus Cibber's lifetime, which ended in 1758.

Whether there is a need to revive or even reread eighteenth-century mutineer plays today might be debated. But at least one unacknowledged, perhaps unwitting call for their return was issued in 1908. That year scenic designer and essayist Gordon Craig described early twentieth-century theatre conditions in terms that sound like a short preface to *The Stage Mutineers*:

The English actors have no chance; their system of management is bad, they get no chance of study or experience, and dare not rebel or they would lose their bread-and-butter; so they laugh their life away as best they can, that is to say, grimly (Craig 134).

Without mentioning the discontent of eighteenth-century actors, Craig's complaint suggests the 1733 rebellion needed to be repeated centuries later. A century after Craig's lament, the situation is worse, with many in the profession underpaid, facing debt or demeaning commercial walk-ons, and frequently unemployed. As Scouten said of Garrick and Macklin's peers, so too most contemporary actors could not secede as the Drury Lane players had in 1733, because so few of them have a theatre from which to depart, or a Haymarket they can afford to rent.

Charlotte Charke fared worse than her brother in her later years; but her performance of Henry Fielding's satires continued even after his company dissolved, as we will see in the next chapter.

CHAPTER SEVENTEEN

Charlotte Charke's *Tit for Tat; or, Comedy and Tragedy at War*: A Lost Play Recovered?

> How Brecht pillaged the playbooks of the past and other cultures we know well, and are probably not unduly shocked; the more layers of human time, the more people of all ages who left their traces in the artifact, the richer and the better.
>
> Fredric Jameson, Brecht and Method

More than 300 years after her birth, the eighteenth-century English actress Charlotte Charke (1713–1760) continues to attract attention as an author and as the rebellious, cross-dressing daughter of England's poet laureate. Her 1755 autobiography, one of the first published by an actress, recounts some of Charke's adventures as a puppeteer, single mother, playwright and strolling player arrested for vagrancy. Although she suffered a few scandals and spent time in prison, some of Charke's offences are now viewed more favourably. Her rejection of patriarchy, and her impersonation of men onstage and off, anticipated the refusal of conventional gender roles that continues in our own day.

As an actress Charke anticipated what we now call performance art. She turned her own daily life into an imitation of art; when in prison, she sang songs of the popular stage outlaw, Macheath, as if she was the highwayman herself. Besides performing in Henry Fielding's version of Molière's play, *The Mock Doctor*, Charke became a quack doctor offstage, and compared the two situations in her autobiography, *A Narrative of the Life of Mrs. Charlotte Charke, Youngest Daughter of Colley Cibber, Esq., Written by Herself.*

Charke also played *The Beggar's Opera* roles of Macheath and Polly Peachum onstage, although not both on the same night. One might consider her a Brechtian actress ahead of her time. We have no detailed account of her cross-dressing portrayal of Macheath and other men in other plays (except for the description in Chapter Eighteen); but in taking such roles she unwittingly met Brecht's expectation, noted in *The Messingkauf Dialogues*:

> When it's a matter of sex . . . actors must show something of what an actress
> would bring to the interpretation of a man, and actresses something of what
> an actor [male] would bring to that of a woman.

A man portraying a role would 'hardly have brought out his masculinity
so forcibly' as a woman in the same role, according to the Philosopher in
Brecht's text (Brecht 1965: 76).

John Gay himself experimented with cross-gender acting in *Polly*, his
sequel to *The Beggar's Opera*. Charke may have taken the role in which
Polly Peachum disguises herself as a young man to escape slavery in the
West Indies, when Henry Fielding rehearsed *Polly* in May of 1737. She
was a member of his company and had considerable experience in cross-
dressing. Fielding may have learned something from Charke about female
preferences for male roles, too, but he seems surprisingly intolerant of the
practice in one of his later prose pamphlets. Published anonymously in
1746, *The Female Husband: or, The Surprising History of Mrs. Mary Alias
Mr. George Hamilton*, recounts the career of a cross-dresser and bigamist
arrested after she married a number of women. Perhaps because Fielding
was a barrister by 1746, and the woman under discussion was a criminal,
he depicted Mary's life rather unfavourably. In his playwriting he had
often exposed corruption in high places; here he reproached sham and
illicit behaviour, too, but Hamilton's lifestyle was hardly luxurious, and
Fielding found no humour in the situation. Displaying a different attitude
toward cross-dressing on stage in earlier years, the satirist hired Mrs
Charke to engage in comic impersonations of prominent men, and both
he and she employed cross-dressing for political and social satire. Charke
once appeared on the Haymarket stage with another notable cross-dresser,
Mrs Midnight, also known as poet Christopher Smart, in a 15 September
1755 Haymarket performance of *The Rehearsal*. Mrs Midnight took the
role of the goddess Pallas, and Charke was Prince Volscius (Scouten Part
4: 491). The gender ambiguity in such comedy helped raise doubts about
the probity of those satirized.

Besides performing on stage, Mrs Charke shared with Fielding and
Brecht the practice of adapting eighteenth-century British satires. Fielding,
as noted, adapted Gay's *Polly*, although his version of the ballad opera
never opened. Charke's first and only surviving stage satire appeared
in print as soon as she wrote it. *The Art of Management*, printed in 1735,
was inspired in part by *The Stage Mutineers* of 1733; she drew on her own
experience, too, but the 1733 mutineer play served as an important source
for her satire. (Both texts are discussed in detail in the previous chapter.)
Charke also appears to have adapted one of Henry Fielding's satires in
1743, although she never acknowledged his writing as a basis for her play,
Tit for Tat.

Fig. 9.   The cross-dressed actress with a handkerchief may be Charlotte Charke
in this detail from Hogarth's 'Strolling Actresses Dressing in a Barn'.

We know her lost play, *Tit for Tat; or, Comedy and Tragedy at War*, was staged during a period when Charke was desperate for money to pay debts. She presented *Tit for Tat* at London's James Street Theatre, an unlicensed stage where the new work played once on 16 March 1743, in a performance advertised as a benefit for 'the author, Mrs. Charke'. The author took the lead male role of the rake Lovegirlo, according to Kathryn Shevelow's brief account of the event in her biography, *Charlotte* (Shevelow 304).

No copy of the play's text has been found, but its absence may constitute an important clue to the history of *Tit for Tat*, if Charke chose not to publish because it was originally Henry Fielding's play, not hers. A close reading of documents from the period suggests that she adapted Fielding's satire, *The Covent-Garden Tragedy*, or simply gave it a new title. If she advertised herself as 'the author, Mrs. Charke', for the 1743 production, that was not completely misleading; she had been an author earlier in her life when she wrote *The Art of Management*. The actress known for impersonating men in a variety of 'breeches' and 'travesty' roles assumed the mantle of a male author (Fielding) this time, if she turned his play into hers.

She was no stranger to Henry Fielding's work, having performed with his Great Mogul's Company of Comedians seven years earlier in London. She even performed the role of author in one of his plays—Spatter in *Eurydice Hissed*. Charke also staged *The Covent-Garden Tragedy* with puppets at her own venue, Punch's Theatre, in 1738. Fielding's farce, first performed by actors at the Theatre Royal, Drury Lane on 1 June 1732, featured in its list of characters a rake named Lovegirlo, just as Charke's *Tit for Tat* did according to an advertisement for her production. Charke also would have known the Fielding play because her brother Theophilus Cibber originated the role of Lovegirlo in the 1732 Drury Lane première. (Some aspects of the play are discussed in Chapter Ten.)

Thomas Lockwood notes in his introduction to Fielding's play that it was performed five more times after its opening night debacle, revived at the Theatre in the Haymarket in 1734 as an afterpiece to Fielding's *Don Quixote in England*. Lockwood also reports that Charlotte Charke performed the role of Lovegirlo in a 1742 production of the play at Bartholomew Fair (Lockwood 2007: 347–48). For that performance the play was retitled *The Humours of Covent Garden; or the Covent Garden Tragedy*, which suggests that Charke was already changing the title of the play while performing it. Might her 1742 performance have been revived the following year under the title *Tit for Tat*?

Until the original manuscript of her play is found, one can only speculate exactly what Charke borrowed or wrote in *Tit for Tat*. But if she borrowed from Fielding, and called the work hers for the author's benefit night, it might explain why the script was never published under her name. It was published (with a different title) under Fielding's name in 1732, and sold to the public for one shilling a copy. Charke's debt to Fielding's text might have been noticed by spectators attending the James Street show in 1743; but no objections or reviews survive in print. The James Street Theatre was 'illegitimate' in any case—not a patent theatre like Covent Garden or Drury Lane—and its productions in that respect were illicit. (An unlicensed presentation became more of an offence once the Licensing Act passed in 1737.)

One other connection between Fielding and Charke might be made here. It is unlikely but not impossible that Fielding derived some inspiration for *The Covent-Garden Tragedy* from Charlotte Charke, who knew about rakes, since her husband Richard was a Lovegirlo of the first order—a debauchee without shame—before he left Charlotte for life in the West Indies in 1733. The marriage was a disaster; but as a result of it, Charlotte knew at least one rake well enough that she could portray such a character with confidence on stage. Richard Charke was an associate of another rake, Charlotte's brother Theophilus, whom Fielding knew well—and both men might have influenced the portrait of rakes devised by Fielding, who behaved like a rake himself on occasion.

The subtitle of Charke's play, *The War Between Comedy and Tragedy*, summed up a kind of combat that is rampant in Fielding's play, too, as his dialogue mocks the tragic drama of his era, and wages war against its conventions through parody. The plot of *The Covent-Garden Tragedy* rarely becomes serious or tragic. Two whores employed by Mother Punchbowl argue over which of them deserves payments from Lovegirlo. Jealousy drives one of the women, Stormandra, to seek the death of the rake loved by her rival, Kissinda. Stormandra informs her friend, Captain Bilkum:

> 'Tis War not Love must try your Manhood now,
> By Gin, I swear ne'er to receive thee more,
> Till curs'd Lovegirlo's Blood has dy'd thy Sword.

After the call for war in Fielding's play, Lovegirlo's death by Bilkum's sword is reported by Leathersides, who claims to have witnessed the fight. In fact the rake lives on and returns to the arms of Kissinda.

The duel between the two men constitutes a kind of 'tit for tat'. A second series of blows takes the form of Fielding's parodic blank verse that mocks the tragic and heroic tenor of the brothel conflicts. Here too comedy wars against tragedy. The result is no ordinary tragedy, as the play's prologue warns:

> Our Poet from unknown, untasted Springs,
> A curious Draught of Tragic Nectar brings.
> From Covent-Garden, culls delicious Stores,
> Of Bullies, Bawds, and Sots, and Rakes, and Whores.

Ultimately, the playwright offers a happy ending for the rakes and whores, as they survive their rivalry and embrace one another; it is hardly the upright moral resolution a sentimental eighteenth-century audience would expect. Charke, who spent many days and nights on the margins of society, may have regarded the tragicomic lower depths of the play as her own world, in a play she could call her own.

While critics such as Simon Trussler and Thomas Lockwood perceptively analysed the innovations in Fielding's play, *The Covent-Garden Tragedy* merits more attention as a vehicle for Charlotte Charke. The actress knew from bitter personal experience what the rakes were talking about in the comedy. It could have been her former husband speaking when Lovegirlo said:

> Who but a Fool wou'd marry that can keep a whore?
> What is this Virtue that Mankind adore?

After her own failed marriage with Richard Charke, the actress probably no longer regarded married life as a 'virtue' any more than Lovegirlo did. Charke became a 'Lovegirlo' in another sense. She chose to live with a woman, one Mrs Brown, for a number of years. Portraying a lover of women on stage was appropriate for Charke in this regard, too. With her own preference for a woman partner off stage, Charke would have enjoyed the irony of reciting Lovegirlo's lines:

> Woman! What is there in the World like Woman?
> Man without Woman is a single Boot,
> Is half a Pair of Sheers. Her wanton Smiles
> Are sweeter than a Draught of cool small Beer
> To the scorch'd Palate of a waking Sot.

The comparison of womankind to a drunkard's small beer is not entirely flattering; but the irony of the praise, and the dubiousness of the authority behind the lines might have been increased if an actress (Charke) dressed as a man recited the lines.

To make Fielding's play more her own in 1743, Charke could well have changed not only the title, but also some lines, including the closing couplet. After reuniting the rake with his beloved mistress, the original text had Lovegirlo conclude his victory with an inconsequential announcement:

> From such Examples as of this and that,
> We are taught to know I know not what.

Given the play's mockery of poetic justice and revenge tragedy, Charke could have revised Fielding's last lines to announce:

> From such Examples as of this and that
> We see no need to return tit for tat.

The change would have insured that the text included Charke's play title, and concluded with a final rejection of revenge. Spectators seeking more conventional British justice or praise of virtue could eschew the theatre and go to a courtroom, as Henry Fielding did by entering the legal profession after censorship drove him from the stage. If Charke took over Fielding's play, she also continued his tradition of stage satire, mocked high-flown language and the tragic conventions of her father's generation. In the role of the rake Lovegirlo, the actress would have been able to speak derisively of marriage arrangements and patriarchal roles she rejected in her own life; and the author's benefit night production of *Tit for Tat; or, Comedy and Tragedy at War* might have provided enough money to keep her out of debtor's prison a few more weeks.

The brevity of *The Covent-Garden Tragedy*'s original run (one night), and its few performances between the 1732 premiere and Charke's 1743 use of it meant it would have been unfamiliar to many spectators; it could pass for an almost new play when and if Charke adapted it. Perhaps those who celebrated Charke's three-hundredth birthday in 2013, and still remember her unusual career, will consider staging a few plays—including a newly altered version of Henry Fielding's afterpiece—in her honour. Like Brecht after her, Charlotte Charke may have sensed that some eighteenth-century satires deserve another chance to be heard, which led her to pillage a playbook.

CHAPTER EIGHTEEN

Mrs Charke Escapes Hanging

The author of this diary entry apparently watched Charlotte Charke perform the role of Macheath in the summer of 1734, when The Beggar's Opera *was produced at the Haymarket by Charke's own ensemble, the Mad Company of Comedians. She performed the same role on 26 June 1736 when the Haymarket was under Henry Fielding's management. Charke's cross-dressing in other plays is discussed in Chapters One and Two. Original spelling has been modernized.*

Last evening I had the pleasure of seeing Mrs Charke in breeches perform the role of Macheath. She played other men's roles previously, and I have seen others portray Captain Macheath, Mr Gay's infamous highwayman. But until now I did not fully comprehend the humour of the part. Mr Gay required the actress portraying Polly in his banned sequel to *The Beggar's Opera* to disguise herself and wear breeches. Here, without the author asking for it, her mimicry of Macheath gains considerably from Mrs Charke wearing a man's coat and pants. Vows that no power could tear her from Polly Peachum are thrown into doubt by our knowledge that Macheath is not the man he pretends to be.

In prior showings, beginning with Mr Walker in 1728, Macheath was a man of little honour; but he was a man. A rake and criminal of the first order, the character won sympathy through Polly Peachum's love for him, and the audience's great love for Miss Peachum as played by Lavinia Fenton. Miss Fenton's display of innocence was delectable, nor could all the low life and illicit behaviour of a highwayman tarnish her appeal. Her constancy to Macheath in the face of all his faults gave the rogue a kind of redeeming charm: if he could win her affection, he could not be entirely lost to virtuous behaviour.

With Mrs Charke in the role of Macheath, the tables are turned. The affections of Miss Peachum seem misplaced, her innocence has gone astray, as she mistakes a womanly youth in a red coat and grey wig for her lover and husband. Captain Macheath's words, 'What a fool is a fond wench!' apply to his character now, as well as Polly's. Mrs Charke's Macheath, with his roving interest in women, clearly prefers female company (and a lot of it), as it is less predatory than that of the men around her. Macheath in Charke's skin abandons women as a favour to them; he would not have them live like slaves in his thrall. 'If with me you'd fondly stray', he sings to Polly, and she adds 'over the hills and far away', acknowledging her partner's inclination to rove, but not fully understanding she too will be left.

Mrs Charke brings to the role an added attraction as the daughter of our poet laureate. She lavishes her talents on Mr Gay's popular ballad opera and its music, whereas her father rejected the piece when it was first offered to him at Drury Lane. The claim of immorality that Mr Cibber tendered toward the piece, his fears of its poetic injustice, as Macheath escapes hanging, seem refuted by his daughter's performance of the highwayman role. Her slender, lithe form, even when decorated with a fancy coat and leather leggings, renders her alleged crimes implausible, exaggerated legends attributed to the man by rivals. How could this weak, nay womanly creature be so dangerous to a society that enjoys his company? When Jenny Diver and Suky Tawdry take hold of Macheath's pistols in a tavern, and Miss Tawdry advises him the pistol 'is fitter' for his hand than cards and dice, the women subtly confirm Macheath's mildness, his preference for gambling over more destructive vices. Charke's character would rather sing with a man than murder him. Macheath loves many women, certainly; but here he loves influential men's daughters (Peachum's, Lockit's) especially, as if he had been one himself.

It was hard not to recall her father's aversion to the play, and to his daughter, when Mrs Charke delivered a new prologue writ by her own hand. I copied her words so that I might recite them to the critics later at Ned's Coffee House. (The gentlemen there said Mrs Charke's rendering was far superior to mine.) Wearing a blood red coat and two pistols under her belt, Mrs Charke's Macheath stepped forward and addressed the house thus:

> On other days you've seen me drest
> As a lady, a lowly servant. But my best
> Role's one where I suffer an arrest
> For marrying the women we have all grown
> To love, Miss Polly Peachum, famously known
> For her virtues. A lady no one could disown
> But a cruel father. Such fathers exist,
> Alas, and their daughters cruelly dismissed
> All too often from the house that raised
> Them. He who loves Polly should be praised.
> For Macheath is such an affectionate man
> He marries not once, but whenever he can.

> Who'd fault this fellow for enjoying the bed
> In which again and again he is newly wed?
> The man's not a rake who instead
> Of debauching marries an angel. Sublime
> Surely's his love, and not a hanging crime,
> But judge for yourself, for 'tis now curtain time.

Her voice was not as deep as Mr Walker's, nor as sure as Mr Lacy's; but Mrs Charke was a quick-witted Macheath, quick-footed too, as she danced with divers women in the tavern and sang

> Youth's the season made for joys,
> Love is then our duty,
> She alone who that employs,
> Well deserves her beauty.

Her songs were most favourably received, as she delivered them in a joyful choirboy's voice; so charming a criminal as this Macheath might win over many an innocent listener besides his Polly. 'Tis no wonder some among the clergy fear this entertainment by Mr Gay will distract playgoers from their virtuous ways; but fine playacting is a virtue, too. The new Macheath is rightly pardoned and roundly applauded. His pardon comes from the Queen, the applause from spectators who welcome Mrs Charke's love of daughters in defiance of a hard-hearted father. Surely such love is not a hanging crime.

Now that Mrs Charke has performed the roles of Macheath and Polly Peachum on different nights, we look forward to her performance of both roles in the same show. Mr Gay's scenario might have to be rewritten so the lovers never meet face to face; but that requirement has been met—the two characters never meet without wearing disguises in the playwright's sequel to *The Beggar's Opera*. *Polly* could be performed with Mrs Charke portraying both Macheath the black pirate and his forlorn wife, if only the ban on it is lifted.

CHAPTER NINETEEN

Garrick and Swift's School for Scandal
With a Digression on Yoko Ono

By the time David Garrick produced *Lilliput*, he already was quite successful as an actor and adaptor of plays by Shakespeare and Jonson. But he had written only four plays of his own, if *Lilliput* is counted as the fourth. Pedicord and Bergmann, the editors of Garrick's complete plays, include *Lilliput* as one of the artist's own plays in their list of the Garrick canon. At least one other early stage text, *Lethe* (1740), can be called a satire, with its debts to Aesop and Aristophanes. The author might have become more of a stage satirist had critical and public response to *Lilliput* been more favourable. As it turned out, Samuel Foote and not Garrick became known as the period's pre-eminent satirist after Fielding. Some critics call Foote the English Aristophanes. But for a few weeks beginning 3 December 1756 Garrick was the Georgian theatre's Jonathan Swift. With *Lilliput* he brought episodes from Swift's great novel to the stage, and provoked a small controversy. Its seventeen performances led two Garrick biographers to judge the play 'moderately popular,' even if the London premiere 'enraged a critic for the *Theatrical Examiner* (1757)' (Stone Jr and Kahrl 215).

The primary source for Garrick's one-act afterpiece was *Gulliver's Travels*; but his depiction of contemporary mores within a Swiftian tale may also have been inspired by Dr Johnson, who wrote an updated report on Lilliput and attributed it to Gulliver's grandson in 1738. In Johnson's account the grandson expressed surprise that Lilliput's laws and constitution 'so nearly . . . resemble our own', meaning England's. Garrick also had his characters live in a Lilliput that resembled England, as he reported new details on events introduced in Swift's original account. *High Life at Lilliput*, as Garrick's play was titled before it was shortened to *Lilliput*, drew on chapters five, six and seven of *Gulliver's Travels*, Part I, and featured an adult actor, Astley Bransby, as the giant Gulliver among a large population of smaller folk all portrayed by children. The casting of 100 children to represent Lilliput's population, and placement of innocent youth in scenes of infidelity disturbed one critic; but the youthful hoard would have made Gulliver look more mature as well as larger than his captors.

Garrick's text briefly, mildly verges on political commentary, when the adulterous Lady Flimnap, having agreed to a truce with her husband, predicts that in the future he will have 'as little regard for me as [he, Lord Flimnap has] for the business of the nation'. Lord High Treasurer Flimnap is more interested in extramarital affairs than his nation's business affairs. So is his wife. In the contentious disrespect Garrick displays toward upper-class profligacy, his satire becomes acerbic and Brechtian, showing what Jameson has termed 'Brechtian aversion to respectability in general' and 'antisocial energies' that have a counterpart in Garrick's mockery of Georgian high life (Jameson 187–88).

As in John Gay's ballad opera inspired by Swift (who suggested the genre of 'Newgate pastoral' to the man writing *The Beggar's Opera*), in Garrick's social satire too a 'great' man meets an undaunted woman. The greatness of Garrick's Gulliver is first of all physical; he lacks the 'great' influence on law exerted by the criminals in Gay's play, but Gulliver inspires another form of excess. His large features attract Lady Flimnap, whose huge ambitions the play confirms in its epilogue, where the actress playing the role asks: 'Was it not Great?—A lady of my Span / To undertake this monstrous Mountain Man?' She answers her own question: 'The Prudes I know will censure, and cry, Fie on't! / Prepostrous sure!—A Pigmy love a Giant! / Yet soft—no Disproportion Love can know. / It finds us equal, or it makes us so.' The half-serious epilogue proved to be prophetic; a prudish critic for the *London Examiner* did censure the play, and described its first production as 'petite, trifling, indecent, immoral, stupid' and scandalous. The marital infidelity within the satire was no more indecent, probably less so than other Georgian stage portraits of unhappily married men and women; but its use of a child to depict the unfaithful wife of Lord Flimnap was exceptional.

Lady Flimnap's desire exceeds her physical capacity to an extent that her monstrous, comic pursuit might be compared to the erotic dreams of Ben Jonson's Sir Epicure Mammon. Garrick's lady is smaller, and says less than Mammon; but like him she is an overreacher who fails to achieve her desired consummation. The gargantuan dream here is articulated by a tiny person, dwarfed by the size of the man she courts. The physical disparity between Lady Flimnap and Gulliver in the original tale accentuates its grotesque aspects more palpably than her advances would on stage with a child in the role. A Hogarth sketch, with a woman inches high standing at the feet of a giant man, might best convey the satiric dimensions of the incongruity. Hogarth's portrait of Tom Thumb for the frontispiece to the 1731 edition of *The Tragedy of Tragedies* (shown in Chapter Twelve) comes close, but Thumb is not as small as Lady Flimnap would have to be. Garrick must have known the popular Fielding text, and perhaps its performance with a child in the title role inspired his decision to cast children as Lilliputians. Other companies of child actors had been called 'Lilliputians' too, notably one with Garrick's friend, the actress Peg Woffington. While they were said to be children, at least one of these actors was a teenager. Jane Pope, a Garrick company member whose birthdate is known to be 1742, was fourteen years old when she portrayed a man in *Lilliput*.

The prologue to *Lilliput* was delivered by Henry Woodward, a fine comic actor (and an adult) who briefly spoke as a 'conjurer'. With his 'magic ring and taper wand' he promised to transport the audience to a country in which 'giant vices may in pygmies dwell'. Praising the actor on another, later occasion, Davies said 'the moment he spoke, a certain ludicrous air laid hold of his features, and every muscle of his face ranged itself on the side of levity. The very tones of his voice inspired comic ideas' (Davies Volume I: 265). Woodward's opening assurance to spectators at *Lilliput* that 'To you these little folks have no relation' surely would have had the opposite effect of a disclaimer, especially if parents of the child actors sat in the audience.

Jonathan Swift Takes the Stage

Despite enough audience support to warrant a respectable run, the press critic mentioned earlier found the play as scandalous in 1756 as an affair by Lady Flimnap with Gulliver might have been in Swift's day. Recital of Garrick's lines by children was regarded as corruption of the innocent. With the youngsters speaking about passionate affairs and contemplating adultery, the production itself became immoral—or so the *Examiner* claimed: 'To debauch the minds of infants, by putting sentiments and glances in their Breasts and eyes, that should never be taught at any years.'

The play anticipates these objections. Gulliver himself objects to the behaviour of Lady Flimnap, then flees from the lady and Lilliput. That does not eliminate all thought of adultery, however, as Lady Flimnap's husband, an incorrigible rake and Lord High Treasurer, continues to enjoy the promise of extramarital affairs. (Lord Flimnap may have represented Robert Walpole in Swift's novel; by the time Garrick staged the play, Walpole was no longer alive, and Lord Flimnap's character would not have been an instrument of topical satire.) The playwright hardly endorses rakishness or attacks political corruption in these scenes, but he devotes enough attention to the extramarital affairs of Lord and Lady Flimnap to make his afterpiece a smaller (Lilliputian) version of other plays in the period that featured fops, rakes and flirtatious ladies. The false, malicious accusations against Gulliver spread by Lady Flimnap after he declines her overtures might warrant giving Garrick's play the subtitle of *Swift's School for Scandal*. *Lilliput* anticipated Sheridan's *School for Scandal* by some twenty years, and previewed ideas later expressed in the prologue Garrick wrote for Sheridan's great comedy in 1777. That prologue begins by observing:

> A School for Scandal! Tell me, I beseech you,
> Needs there a school this modish art to teach you?

Lilliput too was a kind of prologue to Sheridan's play.

Details of the modish behaviour in Garrick's play were first introduced by Gulliver himself, in a brief denial he makes in Part I, Chapter VI of *Gulliver's Travels*. Referring to the wife of his Lilliputian nemesis, Lord Flimnap, the title character writes that he was:

> . . . obliged to vindicate the Reputation of an excellent Lady, who was an innocent Sufferer on my Account. The Treasurer took a Fancy to be jealous of his Wife, from the Malice of some evil Tongues, who informed him that her Grace had taken a violent Affection for my Person, and the Court Scandal ran for some time that she once came privately to my Lodging. This I solemnly declaire to be a most infamous Falsehood, without any Grounds, farther than that her Grace was pleased to treat me with all innocent Marks of Freedom and Friendship. I own she came often to my House, but always publickly, nor ever without three more in the Coach, who were usually her Sister, and young Daughter, and some particular Acquaintance . . .

Gulliver's Offences Enlarged

Swift's Lilliputians charge Gulliver with a number of offences. The worst of these is not adultery, but extinction of a palace fire by use of the only liquid available at the time—his own urine. Garrick makes no reference to this episode. The Lilliputians in Swift's novel also blame Gulliver for not destroying every man, woman and child in the enemy country of Blefuscu; for entertaining enemy ambassadors; and comforting if not joining forces with the enemy. The accusations drive Gulliver to take refuge in Blefuscu, a flight that confirms suspicions against him; but Gulliver flees primarily to avoid trial and punishment, including his blinding. Garrick's play adds attempted adultery to the list of offences by amplifying Swift's brief references to Lady Flimnap's passion.

Before the Lady expresses her passion in the play, the topic is introduced by an epistolary preface attributed to an author with the initials W.C. W.C.'s letter, printed in the 1757 edition of the play text, states that he heard the story about Lady Flimnap from Mr Jacob Wilkinson, 'an old Gentleman, who was formerly a Haberdasher at Redriff [where Gulliver lived in England], and an Intimate of Gulliver's'. W.C.'s style, borrowed from Swift's own, suggests a continuity of sources if not of authorship. The letter preceding the play's scenes focuses on the source of the Lady Flimnap scandal, and reports that haberdasher Wilkinson said Gulliver protested:

> . . . . Upon his Death-Bed, that tho' he was a great Traveller, and a Writer of Travels, he never published but one Falsehood, and that was about Lady Flimnap. He acknowledged, that notwithstanding his Endeavors to justify her Innocence in his Book, she had really confessed a Passion for him, and had proposed to elope with him, and to fly to England.

The letter previews the episode, but also creates a fictive, pseudonymous authorship for the play. Garrick, like Swift, does not take credit for writing this tale about Gulliver; the first edition of *Lilliput* lists the famous actor's name only as author of the prologue delivered by Woodward at Drury Lane.

The plot previewed by W.C.'s letter is supplemented in Garrick's play by revealing stage directions that physicalize the relationship between Giant and Lady. Lady Flimnap in private conference with the 'Monster' Gulliver admits she does not pay much attention to her children and husband, and then she adds:

LADY FLIMNAP: . . . . Had I been an English Lady, perhaps I might have seen an Object that might have raised my Affection, and even persuaded me to live at home. [*Looking at him and sighing.*]

GULLIVER [*aside*]: In the name of Queen Mab, what is coming now! Sure I have not made a Conquest of this Fairy.

LADY FLIMNAP: What a prodigious fine Hand your Lordship has!

GULLIVER: Mine, Madam! 'Tis brown sure, and somewhat of the largest.

LADY FLIMNAP: O! My Lord, 'tis the nobler for that—I assure you, that it was the first Thing about your Lordship that struck me—But, to return—I say, my Lord, had I been happy enough to have been born—bred—and married in England, I might then have been fond as I am now sick of Matrimony. [*approaching tenderly*]

GULLIVER [*retreating*]: Perhaps your Ladyship has taken some just Aversion to our Sex.

LADY FLIMNAP: To one of it I have—my Husband—but to the Sex—Oh no! I protest I have not—far from it—I honour and adore your Sex when it is capable of creating Tenderness and Esteem.

CAPT. LEMIUELGULLIVE^R

Splendide Mendax Hor.

Fig. 10.   Portrait of 'Gloriously False' Lemuel Gulliver. Artist unknown.
'Lemiuel Gulliver' not quite accurately spelled or spaced.

As Gulliver retreats from the tiny lady, who probably attempts to caresses his hand 'tenderly', he asks in an aside, 'What can I possibly say to her, or do with her?' This question can be read as an indication of Gulliver's surprise at the situation, and his inability to accept her proposal, or, for those choosing to imagine mutual sexual attraction in the lines (as the *Examiner* critic did), these words suggest Gulliver would have an affair with the Lady, if only he could figure out how to manage it.

Spectators of the scene might also wonder at this point where the encounter is heading. An actor who wants to disclose Gulliver's own secret desires could read a welcoming note instead of disapproval into his aside on Lady Flimnap: 'What a profligate Morsel of Nobility this is!' But the disparity in sizes of the two characters makes intimacy of certain kinds difficult, if not literally crushing and fatal to the diminutive woman who so immodestly praises Gulliver.

Lady Flimnap openly admits that she has 'imprudently' made her private visit, and 'A married Woman [such as herself] . . . ought not to visit a Gentleman . . . And yet, such is my Weakness, I have visited a Gentleman'. The lady also says that she would be tempted to leave Lilliput and accompany Gulliver elsewhere if asked. Gulliver in another aside sees that he is 'in a fine Situation—She certainly wants to elope with me'. (This plan could lead to another version of Garrick's later comedy, *The Clandestine Marriage*, if followed through.) When Gulliver raises questions about the 'Disproportion' of size between them, Lady Flimnap rather boldly answers that 'Love is a great Leveller, and I have Ambition—and I think if I made no Objections, your Lordship need not'. Gulliver declines the proposal.

Readers of the play can only speculate how the lady would consummate her desire if given the opportunity. Some grotesque physical humour remains undiscovered in her understated sexual fantasy. If in fact the woman is only six inches high, a full-fledged affair between the giant and the Lilliputian would require physical feats of balance, poise, restraint, and special acrobatic acts beyond the gifts of most circus artists, unless the relationship remained limited to the lady's sighs, walks across Gulliver's brown and prodigious hand, and praise of his 'tenderness and esteem'. If Lady Flimnap ever viewed any of Gulliver's other appendages besides his nose, arms, and hands, particularly on the infamous night he exposed his privates to douse the fire in the palace, that is not revealed; such sights are left unarticulated by the playwright, who may have regarded the entire encounter as a scene of tenderness and esteem innocent enough to have a child portray Lady Flimnap. But the *London Examiner* found this part of the play, the physical encounter between large man and small woman (or girl) particularly disturbing: 'The question of Gulliver, in answer to the infant lady's gross addresses, is horrid, if we allow an audience a common share of delicacy, *what should he do with her?* And what the devil does it mean?' The full question asked by Gulliver in Garrick's text is: 'What can I possibly say to her, or do with her?' The answer might vary according to the stage director's and actor's choices. Ultimately, however, the giant does not esteem the Lady.

Onstage at Drury Lane, when the play first opened, the disparity in size between Gulliver and Lady Flimnap would not have been insurmountable, with a girl and adult facing each other. The girl portrayed by Miss Simpson was underage (although her exact age is not recorded), and talk of an affair might have been more scandalous, less comic and grotesque, than if she was merely six inches tall. If Garrick's production called on a young girl to caress an adult actor's hand during their encounter, that is hardly a scandal by modern standards, though it no doubt upset *The Examiner* critic. Even today if the play showed no more than hand-holding, it might be called sexually exploitive, as a girl around the age of ten is required to make a pass verbally at an adult, and admit to dreams of an illicit affair with him.

A Brush with Yoko Ono's Fly

The *London Examiner* critic no doubt would have been appalled by a contemporary variant of Swift's and Garrick's satire in Yoko Ono's film, *Fly* (1970). Her cinematic documentation of a small winged insect flitting across the body of a naked woman portrays another grotesque and comic form of intimacy between disproportionately sized creatures. Pausing on the woman's breast, near a huge nipple, the fly looks tiny but magisterial; the insect is in charge, as the woman has been instructed not to move. The film has an odd counterpart in *Gulliver's Travels*, when Gulliver in Brobdingnag is a tiny man besieged by enormous summer flies: 'odious Insects, each of them as big as a Dunstable Lark'. The insects continually hum and buzz about his ears, and sometimes 'fix upon [his Nose or Forehead]'. Ono's cinematic close-ups of a nude woman, showing her body from a fly's perspective, also recall Gulliver's sighting of a young nurse's naked breast in Brobdingnag. The once giant adventurer, now insect-sized, sights a hill of flesh: 'It stood prominent six Foot, and could not be less than sixteen in Circumference. The Nipple was about half the Bigness of my Head. . . .' Both these situations confirm George Orwell's comment on Gulliver's voyage to Brobdingnag, 'the essential manoeuvre is the same, i.e., to make the human being look ridiculous by imagining him as a creature six inches high' (Orwell 2008: 293). In the case of the Ono film, the human being shown in camera close-ups becomes a giantess, not a miniature; the imagery startles and amuses as the woman passively allows the tiny fly to roam with impunity, much as in Swift's novel the miniscule Lady Flimnap cavorts in the hand of her beloved giant, free from the dangers of being swatted or crushed to death during her amorous tour of a body part. Ono's film has more in common with Surrealism than Epic theatre; but it should be noted that in the 1960s she often performed with the Fluxus group of artists and musicians including George Brecht. In that sense if no other, some of Yoko Ono's scenarios shared aesthetic tenets with Brecht. There is also a kind of distancing effect built into the scenes where a human body, be it Gulliver or Ono's recumbent woman, attracts a tiny visitor, and suddenly becomes a gigantic sex object.

In rejecting Lady Flimnap's tiny overtures, Gulliver proves he is no rake. He declines the lady's advances on the grounds that he is a married father of six children. As far as Flimnap is concerned, that is no reason to desist. 'Have not I a Husband and as many Children?' she replies. Gulliver next pleads 'want of Birth and Education', lack of breeding in 'High Life', and the 'love of his Wife and Children', as reasons for his inability to the match the lady in her great passion. Clearly his English upbringing has not prepared him for philandering in Lilliput. Just as clearly he has not read or seen the plays of Colley Cibber or his contemporaries, which might have prepared him.

Gently turned down by the love of her life, Lady Flimnap turns against Gulliver, avowing she has cast her affections 'upon a Monster, a married Monster, and who, still more monstrous, confesses a passion for his Wife and Children'. Cured of her own passion by his rejection, she falsely accuses Gulliver of having 'own'd a violent Passion' for her. Her words of affection are attributed to Gulliver, upon which Lady Flimnap's husband draws his sword, prepared to fight with the offending giant. In Garrick's play the accusation and the threats following it, rather than any charges of treason or incontinence made against the giant, lead him to flee the Lilliputians.

Garrick's focus on the lady's advances almost turns Swift's story into a comic, miniature version of *Phaedra*, the classic drama where a woman's illicit passion leads to the punishment of the young man she loves. In *Phaedra*, too, a monster plays a role — as he arises from the sea to kill the innocent man Phaedra loves. Here the innocent man (Gulliver) takes to sea — wading across it to refuge in the neighbouring nation of Blefuscu. His escape is reported but not shown toward the end of Garrick's play.

Child's Play

Garrick's *Lilliput* was first performed as an afterpiece to *The Orphan, or, The Unhappy Marriage*, and would have constituted a second play about marriage. It had seventeen performances, a decent run for an allegedly indecent play. Perhaps spectators attended because the objections to it intrigued them, or because their children performed among the hundred youngsters in the cast. Garrick's motives for casting children (who were paid for their work) can only be guessed, but he may have chosen not fewer than a hundred children because:

(1) They were smaller in size than the adult actors, and in that regard were closer to Lilliputians. In one favourable response to the 1756 production of *Lilliput*, a *London Chronicle* critic wrote: 'It was agreeably, to the place where the Scene was supposed to be, acted by Children.'

(2) As noted earlier, companies of child actors had previously been employed for a number of other satiric plays. Decades before Garrick wrote his *Lilliput*, children called 'Lilliputians' appeared on London and Dublin stages. They performed Gay's *Beggar's Opera* within a year of its 1728 opening. Evidently the popular ballad opera became even more pleasing to the public—or won new audiences—through novel casting of children in the roles of Macheath, Polly Peachum, and others. The actress Charlotte Charke managed a Lilliputian company for three performances at the Little Theatre in the Haymarket in London in July 1736. No complaints about Gay's play or Charke's stage directions corrupting the innocent survive; it seems the public's love of child actors overrode questions about immorality in those efforts. References to great men (such as Walpole) within Gay's play would have had extra comic resonance when spoken by youngsters. The use of child actors might even have won approval for its revival of a practice applauded in the age of Ben Jonson, since Jonson was popular again in the eighteenth century.

(3) Garrick may have wanted to train and educate a future generation of actors, and started their training at a young age. A Latin epigram from Juvenal's first satire prefaces the published text of *Lilliput*, and its Latin: 'Eadem cupient, facientque MINORES', might be translated: 'Our descendants will desire and act the same as we do.' This could mean that children in the play would grow up to act as Lord Flimnap and his wife do, or as Garrick and his theatre company behave: they faced a choice between a future as rakes and flirts, or as gifted stage artists with a post-Swiftian sense of humour. One of Garrick's child actors, Miss Jane Pope (1742–1818), is better known because her career continued into adulthood. She portrayed Mrs Candour in the 1777 Drury Lane premiere of Sheridan's *School for Scandal*. The author's invocation of Juvenal also suggests that the Roman poet, along with Swift, inspired him to view the foibles of his contemporaries through satire. The displeased critic of the *London Examiner* offered a related statement on education, when he asked: 'Where is the instruction, or even tolerable language, to gild the dirt over? O tempora! O mores!'

The peace agreement reached between Lady and Lord Flimnap toward the end of Garrick's play may also have disturbed the *Examiner* critic, although he didn't say so. Lord Flimnap grants his wife permission to follow her inclinations, and she promises not to disturb his romantic adventures. Today this might be called an open marriage, although Lord Flimnap's statement to his wife that she may 'fall in Love when you please with either Man or Monster' hints at something abnormal about their morality. Their appetites know no bounds, and receive none. 'We scorn restriction', in Lord Flimnap's words. The tenor of the agreement is not entirely different from other Georgian comedies about illicit affairs, such as Fielding's *The Modern Husband* or Garrick and Colman's *The Clandestine Marriage*.

A tentatively posed source of marital disputes and larger wars surfaces during the play's mob scene. One man in the mob speculates that in Gulliver's homeland people are so 'brave and free . . . you may quarrel whenever, or with whom ever you please . . . they never mind Laws, if they are brave and free'. The second mob speaker remarks: 'La! What a Slaughter an Army of such Men-Mountain would make!' It is doubtful Garrick fully agrees with the mob's admiration of such bravery and slaughter, or with Lord Flimnap's declaration of liberty, given the grotesque situations through which he mocks and undermines them.

Antisocial and improper behaviour might have surfaced not only in the tryst between Lady Flimnap and Gulliver, but also in scenes featuring the 'mob of Lilliputians' portrayed by children. Fewer than a dozen characters speak in the play, so it is difficult to say exactly where Garrick placed the other ninety children trained for his production. The scene that calls for 'a mob of Lilliputians' has only two of them ('First Mob and Second Mob') speak; many other youngsters might have trouped onstage 'huzzaing', as the stage directions ask. One in the mob ('First Mob') refers to Gulliver's 'strange country' of England, where 'the Children are as big as we are', a self-referential joke dependent on the size of the actors. The mob watches the arrival of Gulliver in Lilliput's capital city of Mildendo. They hear the giant request that anyone who wants to see him should not 'run over my Face, nor put their Lances into my Nose, or shoot their Arrows into my Eyes', acts that might be committed by a mob of youths. The traveller almost seems to be inviting trouble with those lines, and again when he looks at the large assembly of little men and women before him and declares: 'Everything is in Miniature here but Vice, and that is so disproportioned, that I'll match our little Rakes at Lilliput, with any of our finest Gentlemen in England.' Garrick's audience might have enjoyed this joke at their own expense—it was as close as the play came to flattering the audience.

The playbill for the Drury Lane production suggests another use for the crowd of children, when it announces the play will 'conclude with a

Dance by the Lilliputians'. Augustin Noverre served as the unlisted choreographer, perhaps, since he performed a number of times at Drury Lane, and taught dance to a number of children, including those of Garrick's friend, William Windham II. Garrick may have employed most of his troupe's youngsters in a celebratory dance following Gulliver's escape and Lord Flimnap's concluding lines:

> Let low-bred Minds be curb'd by Laws and Rules,
> Our higher Spirit leaps the Bounds of Fools;
> No Law or Custom shall to us say nay;
> We scorn Restriction—Vive la Liberté.

A dance of low standing but not low-bred Lilliputians could show leaps of feet as well as 'Higher Spirit leaps', and choreographed expressions of liberty.

If *Lilliput* were revived today, with children performing all the roles but two, a contemporary audience probably would take exception to the production's antiquated language rather than its morality, and find modern child actors insufficiently trained in the art of reciting eighteenth-century dialogue without a Garrick to train them. The play itself now can be viewed as a historical curiosity, antic testimony from an era when Swiftian satire adapted by Garrick still could generate a small scandal, and call upon a critic to defend the public against the play's antisocial energies. Perhaps it would fare best today as an animated cartoon illustrated by Robert Crumb (who turned part of Boswell's diary from the same period into a comic strip discussed in Chapter Twenty-one). If the cartoon is screened on a Saturday morning, at an hour suitable for children, with the Garrick text intact, parents as well as children might be led to wonder anew about the unusual humour and morality of this Georgian play.

Brecht Praises Garrick's *Hamlet*

One of the many writers who discussed David Garrick's acting without seeing it was Bertolt Brecht. Writing on Charles Laughton's role in *Galileo*, Brecht noted that: 'we seem to have lost any understanding and appreciation of what we may call a *theatrical conception*: what Garrick did, when as Hamlet he met his father's ghost' (Brecht 1964: 163). Faint praise, but praise for Garrick nonetheless. Although he did not see Garrick perform the role, Brecht could have read a number of reports on Garrick's Hamlet, notably the eyewitness account published by the German scientist and Anglophile Georg Christoph Lichtenberg. Lichtenberg vividly described the actor's responses when 'confronted by the ghost'. He witnessed the scene in which Garrick's Hamlet:

> staggers backward three or four paces. His knees knock together . . . His hat falls to the ground . . . The mouth gapes open . . . [he stands] suddenly petrified by the terror from which he was endeavouring to escape.

More important as the possible source for Brecht's appreciation of the scene's 'conception', Lichtenberg is 'certain' that the 'wondrous grace of manner and movement' 'has cost [Garrick] long self-training and careful study of the best types of high breeding in the best society of London' (Lichtenberg 1871: 75). This detailed account would have let Brecht see Garrick's theatrical conception as the result of prolonged and careful preparation. 'Those who make [stage art] work hard to give the impression that everything just happens', Brecht notes after his reference to Garrick, but in fact such art is the result of labour, 'the process of manufacture'. His main example of such conception is Laughton's rehearsal for the title role in *Galileo*. Brecht saw Laughton employ a 'system of performance-and-repetition' in which 'psychological discussions were almost entirely avoided' (Brecht 1964: 165).

Acting before the age of psychological realism, Garrick too developed a system of 'performance-and-repetition' in rehearsal. Call it an early

Brechtian attitude toward role-playing. Thomas Davies mentioned
Garrick's careful preparations for Hamlet in his 1780 biography:

> To venture half prepared, as some imprudent actors have done, to represent
> a variety of characters, was not Mr. Garrick's practice. He examined well his
> strength before he undertook any arduous task . . . He had prepared himself
> for the able discharge of this task [the role of Hamlet], by having very care-
> fully acted it in Ireland.

Lith. de Ducarme.

GARRICK.

Tragédien Anglais.

né en 1716, mort en 1779.

(Rôle d'Hamlet.)

Galerie Universelle.   Publié par Blaisot.

Fig. 11.   Ducarme's Portrait of David Garrick as Hamlet in his wig.

The Prince of Denmark role was tested and premeditated. One Brechtian 'gesture' of fright physicalized by Garrick took the form of a special wig designed so that Hamlet's hair would rise at the sight of his father's ghost. His wired wig pioneered the mechanical reproduction of fright. Judging from a portrait of Garrick in his hair-raising wig, and other poses he held on stage as well as in artists' studios, the actor did not personally have to feel an emotion deeply to show it. He manufactured his gestures and voice with a mastery that Brecht later summarized (although not referring to Garrick) in a discussion of Epic acting: 'On those occasions when the recipient is observing coldness it is just that he has encountered the mastery without which it would not be art at all' (Brecht 1964: 236).

Garrick also let the ghost in *Hamlet* speak almost all the lines Shakespeare wrote for him—a change from earlier, cut versions of the text—making part of the scene new to those in the audience who had watched it before. He took a few of the ghost's words and gave them to Hamlet, so that the prince said 'O horrible, most horrible'. Through his theatrical conception Garrick insured that the audience would see and hear Prince Hamlet's fright (Stone Jr and Kahrl 1979: 274). 'Faced with irrational practices, his reason is utterly impractical', Brecht noted of Hamlet. Although not referring specifically to the irrationality of the ghost scene, Brecht's view of the play supports Garrick's conception of the encounter (Brecht 1964: 202). The fright that Garrick's Hamlet generated in conversation with his father's ghost was first seen in Dublin during the summer of 1742. Curiously, that was also the first and only summer of Garrick Fever.

Garrick Fever

The epidemic known as Garrick Fever arrived in Ireland when the actor performed at Dublin's Theatre Royal. Garrick had already won consider-able praise on the London stage, where he first appeared as Richard III in 1741. But his reception in Dublin was warmer in several respects, not least among them that of the summer weather. In a Dublin theatre crowded with spectators, excitement over the actor's stage talent combined with excessive heat led to what Thomas Davies calls an 'epidemical distemper which seized, and carried off great numbers'. Davies does not indicate the exact number of those carried off by the distemper, but episodes of discomfort and death contracted in Garrick's presence were numerous enough to be 'nicknamed the Garrick fever', according to Davies.

By now many volumes have been written about David Garrick's life, art, and his contemporaries; but remarkably little detail can be found about the exact nature of the 'Garrick fever' that broke out in Dublin. The fever did not spread to England upon Garrick's return there, as far as we know, although Garrick continued to be an exceedingly popular actor. It would seem that other factors besides exceptional summer heat contributed to the Dublin-based ailment. According to Percy Fitzgerald, the Dublin Theatre Royal's boxes and galleries 'were crammed', and the stage itself although 'cramped and small' 'was often oddly enough crowded with strangers, who were scarcely to be distinguished from the performers' (Fitzgerald, 122). The management must have sold every seat, and added more. The crush of spectators around Garrick probably did not cause fainting fits and fatal illness in itself. Clothing worn by spectators and actors alike in the summer heat might have added to their discomfort, with corsets, petticoats, ornate hoop dresses, long men's jackets and powdered wigs increasing the temperatures of those who wore the fashions of the day onstage and off. Most likely of all, the infectious illness that carried off spectators was carried into the crowded theatre by spectators already ill, but unwilling to forgo seeing the great actor, even if attendance spread their discomfort inside the theatre, and worsened their own health in the heated, crowded setting.

It would be injudicious to dismiss all these contributing factors, and single out Garrick himself as primary carrier of the fever. If he was as gifted as his contemporaries assert, the actor could have spread a fever of excitement through his performances, but it was probably not lethal. Most of the time, Garrick's art enlivened theatrical life, and left his audiences pleased and applauding. His *Richard III* had been a sensation at London's Goodman's Fields. The 1742 Dublin visit introduced a new audience to that play and others featuring Garrick's crowd-pleasing stage manners. More versatile, subtle and modulated than the bombast and ranting for which some of his colleagues were known, Garrick's acting won acclaim in Dublin for roles that included Captain Plume in *The Recruiting Officer* (with his sometime mistress Peg Woffington as Silvia), the title role in *King Lear*, and Marplot the comic bungler in Centlivre's *The Busy Body*. In Dublin he also inaugurated his first public performance of *Hamlet*, with Mrs Woffington in the role of Ophelia. Perhaps he thought of it as a safe place to try out the role, removed from the box office pressures and critics of London.

One detail in Percy Fitzgerald's account of the Dublin *Hamlet* suggests another condition conducive to Garrick fever: namely, the ease with which his audience could be disturbed by theatrical artistry. Fitzgerald writes that Garrick's version of *Hamlet* 'left out every word that could shock a modest ear' (Fitzgerald 124). Presumably Garrick knew he had 'modest ears' in the Dublin audience, and that led to his caution with the text of *Hamlet*. Since he performed the role at the end of his Dublin season, he could have learned earlier that his spectators were sensitive to language. Had some of the bawdy scenes in *The Recruiting Officer* offended first? Had they contributed to the fever? Fitzgerald calls Garrick's censorship of *Hamlet* 'remarkable and almost courageous behaviour', but it was not courageous to expurgate the play, although it might have been remarkable. In any case, Shakespeare's words were probably not what caused spectators to faint or fall down in Dublin, even if delivered with unfamiliar cadences.

Besides generating heat in an already warm theatre, Garrick's acting conferred upon Dubliners the prized benefit of witnessing a famous artist live and in person, direct from London. (Some of them were dying to see him.) As his career progressed, Garrick became adept at promoting himself offstage. He didn't have to rely solely on acting to raise his artistic standing, and instead of a 'fever' he generated publicity. He posed heroically for a portrait by Gainsborough and prints by Hogarth. He honoured Shakespeare at Stratford's 1769 Jubilee as if the Bard was a personal friend. He became manager of the theatre at Drury Lane, and hired and cast actors there to his own advantage. The 'fever' that had erupted in Dublin gave way to other, more temperate sensations that Garrick created for his audience in the years to follow.

Nearly 200 years after Garrick fever arrived in Ireland, the French poet and stage director Antonin Artaud wrote an essay in *The Theatre and Its Double* suggesting that effective theatre could infect its audience like a plague, although rather than kill spectators, such theatre 'disturbs the senses' repose' (Artaud 28). Artaud's modern, twentieth-century perspective on theatre has only a little in common with Garrick's art and his fever. The Frenchman discusses a malady more extreme and devastating than distemper. But he too envisioned theatre as an event wherein actors affect their audience's physical condition.

'Garrick fever' also gave rise to a humorous nineteenth-century one-act play by J.R. Planché. Titled *The Garrick Fever*, Planché's farce portrays a provincial Irish town where expectation of Garrick's performance in *Hamlet* leads townspeople to mistake a roving actor for the great tragedian. Initially they acclaim the impostor's performance of the Shakespeare role although — or because — the man hardly can be heard amid the noise of the admiring crowd:

> MAJOR: Did you ever hear such acclamations— such a hububoo of applause, in your born days?
> LADY O: At his entrance, of course.
> MAJOR: At his exit— at the end of his ghost scene, and all through it as well. Devil a word in twenty could you hear for the shouting. They've got the Garrick fever, my lady, badly, and a noisy disorder it is.

After a brief period of admiration, in which few people can hear him, the inebriated impostor faints, and his career as Garrick comes to an end. Planché wrote the play in 1839, nearly a century after the fever first broke in Dublin. He commemorated Garrick's first appearance in Ireland with a parody of it, as if to confirm that personages of great importance appear twice in history, first in tragedy, the second time as farce. In Garrick's case, the actor himself performed both tragedy and farce when he first appeared in Dublin. Today the fever that accompanied him in 1742 returns primarily as a topic of interest to historians and museum curators. The 'hububoo of applause' for him and his imitators can no longer be heard. But the discussion of Garrick's acting continues. That he was an 'early Brechtian' actor will be argued further in the next chapter.

CHAPTER TWENTY-ONE

A Portrait of the Artists as
Beggar's Opera Disciples
Including David Garrick, Epic Actor

From Hogarth to Crumb

When Macheath escaped hanging in John Gay's first ballad opera, few could have imagined how long and how illustriously he would live on in the annals of graphic art—criminal art, if you will—as well as dramatic literature. His crimes paid repeatedly, insofar as later artists sold them to the public in engravings, oil paintings, and comic strips. Hogarth returned to the scenes of Macheath's crime and captivity more than once. William Blake and Robert Crumb followed after him.

Hogarth 'excelled not only in exhibiting the coarse humours and disgusting incidents of low life, but in exhibiting the vices, follies and frivolity of the fashionable manners of his time', Hazlitt observed in one of his lectures (Hazlitt 203). The fashionable manners of his time included watching *The Beggar's Opera*, which could be done by purchasing a ticket to the playhouse at Lincoln's Inn Fields or purchasing a black and white print. One black and white print depicting Captain Macheath standing alone can be seen in a plate Hogarth engraved for the series, *A Harlot's Progress*. A harlot named Moll keeps a jar of medication for venereal disease atop the framed portrait of her hero, the Captain.

Another Hogarth depiction of Macheath, a colourful oil painting, shows the highwayman wearing leg irons inside Newgate Prison. (A detail from Blake's copy of this portrait can be found in Chapter Three.) Except for the leg irons, Macheath looks much like the men in the theatre audience (also depicted by Hogarth) watching Polly's endeavour. Clearly this was a 'fashionable manner of the time'. Hogarth painted six versions of this picture, and all six were welcomed by grateful art patrons.

When Brecht wrote *The Threepenny Opera* he looked not only at Gay's text, but also period illustrations. He wrote: 'The English drawings of The Beggar's Opera . . . show a short, stocky man of about forty with a head like a radish, a bit bald but not lacking dignity. He is emphatically

J. Ellys Pinx.   J. Faber Fecit

If Wit can please, or Gallantry engage,   **Mr. Walker**   The Fair in Troops attend his sprightly Call,
Macheath may boast he justly charms ŷ Age,   in the Character of   Nor longer doat upon an Eunuch's Squall;
A second Dorimant; like him in Fame,   **Cap.ⁿ Macheath**   Well pleas'd they blush & own behind ŷ Fan,
The Fop's Example & the Ladies Flame.   His Voice, his Looks, his Actions speak a Man.

Fig. 12.   A 1728 portrait of actor Thomas Walker as Macheath with
a radish-shaped head. Engraved by John Faber after John Ellys.

staid . . .' Since Hogarth's Macheath wears a hat and a wig in prison, as does actor Thomas Walker in the Faber engraving, Brecht must have been imagining some of the attributes he observed. He assumed only bald men wear wigs, perhaps, or looked at a different picture from the two just mentioned. Macheath's head could be construed as radish-like in these two pictures, where the bewigged highwayman looks stocky, and not heroic if that means tall and handsome. The described image suited Brecht's own view of Macheath—developed in his revision of Gay's play—as a business-man who dreams of owning a bank. His prowess, Brecht suggests, is more financial than sexual or homicidal. In fact, he prefers to avoid bloodshed, and wears white kid gloves; if his hands are dirty or bloodied, the gloves will hide it.

Robert Crumb also must have looked at Hogarth's depiction of Macheath before drawing his own eighteenth-century portraits in a 'Klassic Komic' version of Boswell's London diaries. James Boswell imagined himself to be Macheath, and a scene illustrating Boswell's reference to the highwayman was drawn by Crumb as part of a comic strip. The criminal who almost lost his life in 1728 entered the world of 'underground comics' in 1981, when Boswell's impression of Macheath surfaced in R. Crumb's black and white illustrations titled 'Excerpt from Boswell's London Journal, 1762–1763'. The drawings first appeared in *Wierdo*, a Last Gasp Eco-Comic issued in Berkeley, California in Fall of 1981. The comic book pages were subsequently reprinted in *The Complete Crumb*, Volume 14 (2000), an edition that in 2013 was displayed among older engravings and memoirs in Yale University's Lewis Walpole Library exhibition on 'Young James Boswell in London, 1762–1763', curated by James Caudle, Associate Editor of Yale Editions of the Private Papers of James Boswell. It was a pleasure to see works by Hogarth, Rowlandson and Crumb in the same display, inside a library dedicated to eighteenth-century literature and the papers of Sir Robert Walpole's son, Horace. (Another exhibition featuring the visual tributes to Macheath and Polly Peachum should be planned for 2028, the tercentenary of Gay's play. The hastily wed couple deserve to be celebrated for staying together for 300 years.)

Perhaps Crumb is our age's Hogarth, and it is quite appropriate to display his Boswell imagery in the same room as Hogarth's 'Royal Sport' Pit Ticket and Rowlandson's 'A Brace of Blackguards', as was the case at the Lewis Walpole Library. Within American art history, Crumb has been acknowledged as a master of graphic arts, a pioneer in the alternative culture of the 1960s and beyond. Some of his art portrays sports and blackguards of a more recent variety than Macheath, notably an oily playboy and entrepreneur resembling Donald Trump on the cover of 'Hup' comics, and talking animals like 'Fritz the Cat', as unsavoury as any human counterparts.

If Crumb is a Hogarth for our time, Boswell belongs to the same generation in one regard: his 1762–63 diaries were not published until 1950. (They were undiscovered until the 1920s.) That may be the reason they survived or avoided expurgation by earlier editors. The racy details of Boswell's London escapades, which clearly intrigued Crumb, were suddenly available to American readers in the 1950s. *Life* magazine celebrated the newly published volume of Georgian gossip when it surfaced. Hogarth never had the opportunity to read these pages of Boswell's; they were written a few years after the period when the artist devised his finest serial engravings, such as *A Rake's Progress* (1734), which anticipate comic strip serialization. Crumb's drawings based on Boswell's confessions might be subtitled 'The Literary Rake's Progress', as they portray the famous biographer of Samuel Johnson courting an actress, contracting venereal disease from the woman, and then recovering. The young London diarist also compares himself to the rake Macheath in this illustrated story, and does so while physically entwined with two young women.

Commenting on the Boswell comics in an interview, Crumb confessed that, in devising his graphic story, as well as one about Krafft-Ebing and another based on Sartre's novel *Nausea*:

> the idea was to do classic comics like the old American 'Classic Comics' that were out in the 50's when I was a kid. . . . There are a lot of things going on in Boswell's diaries but there were a couple of contradictions that I wanted to bring out. In all those literary things that I did, I saw something comic in the characters that was probably not intended to be there in the original. . . . Boswell . . . with his pretensions to being a cultured gentleman while he was compulsively going out and looking for prostitutes in the park every night. He gets venereal disease and he's lamenting about what a dismal proposition it is and how he won't be able to take his walks in the park anymore, funny without being humorous (Mercier 27–29).

In a discussion of Crumb's Boswell, D.K. Holm notes,

> Crumb does a remarkable job of evoking 18th Century London, and his likenesses are close to his subjects while still having the Crumb flavor. . . . The women in the story are viewed through Boswell's eyes and id, and yet Crumb found here a sympathetic subject who appeared to share with the cartoonist an affection for large-rumped women (Holm 88).

Crumb's Boswell adaptation, its affinities with Hogarth's style, and its departure from the American Classic Comics format of the 1950s, have already been discussed in fine detail by scholar Will Pritchard in *Eighteenth-Century Studies*. Pritchard observes that 'visual quotations underscore

Crumb's affinities with Hogarth and hint at his desire to associate himself with his satiric predecessors' (Pritchard 296). That includes Hogarth's un-varnished portraits of women as merchandise, and men as their pleased traducers.

Boswell in the Age of Post-Freudian Angst and Fetishism

The comic strip artist's affinity for aspects of eighteenth-century sensi-bility, his gift for evoking the visual wit of Hogarth, as well as Rowlandson and Gillray, while maintaining his own 'Crumbian' sense of post-Freudian angst and fetishism, deserve high praise. Regrettably, he completed only one comic strip about the period—the one on Boswell. It is not hard to imagine him doing other stories adapted from Swift, Fielding, or Gay.

Although it constitutes only a fragment of his work, Crumb's homage to the highwayman Macheath displays the comic strip artist's preoccupations as well as Boswell's. Crumb devotes just two of his twenty-two panels to Boswell's admission that he 'thought himself Captain Macheath' while he disported himself with two young women in a secluded tavern room. The anal penetration portrayed by Crumb is not mentioned by Boswell, and seems more connected to Crumb's own fascination with 'big ass' women than anything in Macheath's prior history. (One of Crumb's other creations is 'Big Ass Comics'.) Besides showing Crumb's sexual fantasy, one of his panels about Boswell contemplating Macheath includes a funny asterisked note, '*FROM "THE BEGGAR'S OPERA"', that lets modern comic readers know where Captain Macheath first appeared. The comic book artist briefly becomes a theatre historian. (If only more theatre historians drew comic strips, the field might attract younger readers.)

Fig. 13.   Boswell comparing himself to Macheath in Crumb's illustrations based on the 1762–63 diary. © R. Crumb.

Dialogue and narration accompanying Crumb's drawings quote the London journal in which Boswell several times compares himself to the popular stage character. Boswell's identification with the highwayman seems to have influenced his behaviour, not just surfaced in his diary writing, as Crumb suggests in his illustration of the 19 May 1763, entry. Here the diarist describes himself in the company of two young girls in a room above the Shakespeare Tavern. 'I toyed with them and drank about and sung "Youth's the Season" and thought myself Captain Macheath; and then I solaced my existence with them, one after the other, according to their seniority' (Boswell 1950: 264). Crumb reprints these lines in his comic. The note already quoted explains the source of the song, *The Beggar's Opera*, where Captain Macheath in a tavern (like Boswell) carouses with several women and then sings

> Youth's the season made for joys,
> Love is then our duty.
> She alone who that employs,
> Well deserves her beauty.
>
> Let's be gay,
> While we may,
> Beauty's a flower, despised in decay.
>
> Let us drink and sport today.
> Ours is not tomorrow.
> Love with youth flies swift away.
> Age is nought but sorrow.

The song offers a variation on 'Gather ye rosebuds while ye may', with a possible autobiographical reference to the author John Gay; but nothing in the singing or Boswell's reference to it suggests the explicit sexual activity Crumb depicts. In *The Beggar's Opera* a dance between Macheath and prostitutes accompanies the song. Perhaps the traditional staging of the scene, with Macheath engaging several women at once, led Boswell to imagine himself as the stage character while he 'toyed' with two women. Crumb quotes more of the confession Boswell made about his encounter with the duo: 'I was quite *raised*, as the phrase is: thought I was in a London tavern, the Shakespeare's Head, enjoying high debauchery after my sober winter.' The diary editor, Frederick Pottle, reads Boswell's reference to his 'high debauchery' as evidence that he engaged in a 'genteel ceremony', which might rule out the sodomy Crumb depicts; the graphic artist's imagery makes the debauchery—high or low—quite apparent with its display of naked breasts, posterior, and physical exertions. The two frames could almost be titled 'Before' and 'After', as the first shows the threesome smiling and toasting one another while their sexual encounter begins; the second frame shows their fatigue as the 'ceremony' reaches its climactic conclusion. The contrast between the two scenes adds some humour not present in Boswell's own narration. (Hogarth also created a 'Before' and 'After' seduction scene; it was more 'genteel' than Crumb's.)

Charlotte Charke's Prison Songs

The actress Charlotte Charke also sang selections from *The Beggar's Opera* in an extratheatrical setting comparable to Boswell's. For Charke a prison cell, for Boswell a tavern, recalled Macheath's adventures, and became a location suitable for performance of his songs. Without question the songs and behaviour of Macheath had a lasting impact on Boswell and on Charke, who played several roles (Polly Peachum, Jenny Diver, Macheath) from Gay's ballad opera on stage before she sang in a prison cell. Boswell knew the ballad opera well, and had previously asked about Gay when he met the Duke of Queensberry, a patron of the playwright. In his diary he notes that he told the Duke 'that from reading Mr. Gay's writings, I had taken an affection to his Grace's family from my earliest years', meaning the Duke's support of Gay when he was refused permission to stage the play *Polly*, and other support, endeared Queensberry to Boswell early in his life. (Support shown for Gay by the Duke and Duchess of Queensberry is discussed more fully in Chapter Five.)

The association by Charke and Boswell of their own lives with Macheath's prison and tavern scenes almost supports eighteenth-century objections to Gay's play made on the grounds that it would corrupt its spectators, lead them to a life of crime or debauchery. But that is not quite accurate; both Boswell and Charke are already (respectively) in tavern debauchery and prison confinement when they begin to sing Macheath's songs. If Gay's play does anything for them, it provides an aesthetic frame; they see themselves as comic and theatrical figures, celebrants and 'genteel' performers rather than criminals or mere rakes. And in fact, neither Charke, arrested for vagrancy as an actress, nor Boswell, hosting two women in a tavern room, committed an offence comparable to Captain Macheath's hanging crimes.

Understanding Pottle's Footnotes

In a footnote to his 1950 edition of *Boswell's London Journal, 1762–1763*, Frederick Pottle wrote: 'In one way or another the figure of Macheath dominates the entire journal' (Boswell 1950: 251–52). Pottle's note is curious, since Boswell makes only two specific references to Macheath in the diary, which covers a two-year period. He rarely mentions the highwayman's name in 300 pages. If the figure of Macheath is so dominant, in Pottle's view, why does the editor say so only in a footnote? Could it be Pottle who is dominated by the figure of Macheath?

The footnote accompanies a 3 May 1763 entry in which Boswell records a visit to Newgate prison, and sees inmate Paul Lewis in chains. He observes that the prisoner

> was called Captain; was a genteel, spirited young fellow. He was just a Macheath. He was dressed in a white coat and blue silk vest and silver, with his hair neatly queued and a silver-laced hat, smartly cocked. An acquaintance asked him how he was. He said, 'Very well' quite resigned. Poor fellow.

That is the extent of the second, and only other explicit reference to Macheath in the journal.

In another footnote Pottle notes that the actor West Digges 'was especially captivating in the part of Macheath in *The Beggar's Opera*', and that Digges 'had long been Boswell's ideal of manly bearing and social elegance' (Pottle 1950: 44). Here Pottle, not Boswell, suggests Digges's Macheath inspired the diarist. Will Pritchard, writing about Crumb and Boswell in *Eighteenth Century Studies*, at one point confirms Pottle's view that there are 'many moments when Boswell imagines himself as Macheath from *The Beggar's Opera*', but he offers no more evidence than Pottle to persuade readers that Macheath's character haunts Boswell. Instead Pritchard explores the question of theatrical behaviour raised by such references to Macheath: 'in Crumb's hands it [playing Macheath] looks less like plausible self-fashioning than grotesque self-delusion. At this moment and throughout the comic Crumb refuses to grant his subject any self-possession or self-control; this refusal is reinforced by the perpetual expression of idiotic glee that his Boswell wears' (Pritchard 296).

For all the vivacity of Boswell's references to Macheath, the figure of John Gay's highwayman hardly 'dominates the entire journal', or Crumb's comics, or not obviously so; it requires some speculation to fathom what Pottle meant when he wrote that footnote, and why Pritchard echoed it. The editor wrote his introduction and notes to the journal in 1950, about entries that had never before appeared in print. Pottle's notes introduce a new, private side of Boswell's life to scholars and the general public. Part of that private life might be called the author's youthful adventures, often sexual escapades described in confessions of promiscuity. Dr Johnson did not approve of such sexual adventures once he knew the young man's penchant for them. They reflect a sense of prowess and risk-taking that also could be attributed to Macheath, although there is a difference; the

WALKING UP THE HIGH STREET.

Mr. Johnson and I walked Arm in Arm up the High Street to my House in James Court: it was a dirty night: I could not prevent his being assailed by the Evening effluvia of Edinburgh. — As we marched along he grumbled in my Ear "I smell you in the dark."

Vide Journal p. 13.

Fig. 14.   Boswell and Johnson in Rowlandson's 1786 etching.

ballad opera is a comic portrait of human foibles, and those foibles include Macheath's tendency to pursue women even when it endangers him and leads to his arrest. Gay suggests (and Brecht also, in his version) that jail, a death sentence and near self-destruction are the price paid for Macheath's sexual indiscretions. Polly Peachum's father wants the criminal arrested because he kept her from marrying a rich, respectable man whose wealth and status would benefit his whole family. By comparison, Macheath's other crimes seem petty to Jeremiah Peachum. So Macheath gets a death sentence for seducing and marrying Polly. All Boswell gets for his Macheath-like indiscretion is gonorrhoea and a lot of scholarly attention after 1950.

The dominance in the diary that Pottle attributes to Macheath may be related to a larger force in Boswell's life: London's theatre, its plays, actors and actresses. It is not 'self-fashioning' or 'self-delusion' or Macheath so much as an attraction to theatre that Boswell's diary reveals throughout.

Boswell and the Theatre; Mr Digges and Mrs Lewis

The genesis of Boswell's social disease deserves further attention in this regard, since it involves an actress, and beyond that, the attractions theatre life had for the diarist. Not just Macheath's debauchery or song, but freedom of expression in the theatre and its greenrooms initiate Boswell's interest in Macheath and an actress named Louisa. A 14 December 1762 diary entry describes Boswell's new paramour as 'a handsome actress of Covent Garden Theatre', and notes that when admitted to see Louisa: 'She was in a pleasing undress and looked very pretty'. He agrees to meet her for tea two days later, then visits one Mr Love and discusses the actor Digges. Theatre was very much on his mind that day, although Boswell makes no reference to roles played by Louisa, also known professionally as Mrs Lewis. (Pottle in a note informs us she played the Queen in *Hamlet* at Covent Garden on 27 September 1762, and Mrs Ford in *Merry Wives of Windsor* on 20 October. She appears to have taken no part in *The Beggar's Opera* that season.)

Her stage roles interest the young visitor less than her state of undress backstage; but Louisa's sexual attraction and her attraction as an actress intersect when the diarist confesses, on 18 January 1763: '. . . most courageously did I plunge into the fount of love, and had vast pleasure as I enjoyed her as an actress who had played many a fine lady's part'. The theatre was a fitting place for a diarist to begin his affair. Much as Louisa is first seen in 'undress', Boswell's diary displays his private life, and becomes his private theatre, a space where he rehearses and reviews highly charged scenes. He plays the lead role in minor scandals, mooing like a cow from his theatre seat at one performance (not featuring Louisa), in other scenes indulging himself with women, drink, and wanderings around London. After he meets Dr Johnson, some of Boswell's enthusiasms appear to be redirected to literary discussion and the pleasures of philosophy, although he enjoyed those earlier in his career, too. Dr Johnson generally declines to show great enthusiasm for actors, even his friend David Garrick. Actresses in undress unsettle Johnson, and he avoids them. Ultimately Johnson himself, not Boswell, takes centre stage in the young man's writing.

Boswell's theatre visits and his brief assumption of the Macheath role may be linked to his London journal observation 'that we may be in some degree whatever character we choose' (Boswell 1950: 47). He says this with regard to his own acquisition of 'a composed genteel character very different from a rattling uncultivated one which for some time past I have been fond of'. The prospects of transformation appeal to him. That said, he is not seeking to be Macheath every night. His critics may share with Boswell a gift for making him 'whatever character we choose', but such talent also is exercised by actors, and by an actress such as Mrs Lewis.

His Macheath-like escapades in an affair with Louisa first thrilled Boswell; it was, after all, as physically close to theatre life as he could get. The episode then left him deeply depressed when he learned he had contracted venereal disease; his own review turns quite negative, as it were. Crumb, honing in on this episode while leaving out many others, also focuses our attention on the roles actors and their transformative art play in Boswell's life.

Though Boswell refers to Gay's highwayman twice, critics such as Pottle and Pritchard are the ones who cast him in a Macheath role that 'dominates' the diary; such a preference, if it existed in his own lifetime, was not a known, widely proclaimed or publicly shared role, but rather a secret identity, kept to himself, a private fantasy prior to the publication of his journals in 1950. His 'theatre career' went largely uncredited and unreviewed for centuries. (Rowlandson did portray Boswell mooing like a cow in the theatre, but that etching was published in June 1786, long after the journal entries were written and left unpublished.)

Boswell offered another, more sceptical view of *The Beggar's Opera* later in his *Life of Johnson*. There he wrote that Dr Johnson in his *Life of Gay* was decisive

> as to the inefficiency of 'The Beggar's Opera' in corrupting society. But I have ever thought somewhat differently; for, indeed, not only are the gaiety and heroism of a highwayman very captivating to a youthful imagination, but the arguments for adventurous depredation are so plausible, the allusions so lively, and the contrasts with the ordinary and more painful modes of acquiring property are so artfully displayed, that it requires a cool and strong judgment to resist so imposing an aggregate; yet, I own, I should be very sorry to have 'The Beggar's Opera' suppressed (Boswell 1831: 453).

Boswell here makes no reference to his own 'youthful imagination' captivated by the highwayman. It is almost as if he had two different identities: one as Boswell the biographer and companion of Dr Johnson; the other as young Boswell, the secret admirer of Macheath.

David Garrick, Epic Actor

That Boswell had two or more identities, some kept private in his diary, some public, is consonant with a theory of acting that he published in a 1770 essay. He wrote:

> . . . my notion is that [a player] must have a kind of double feeling. He must assume in a strong degree the character which he represents, while at the same time retains the consciousness of his own character.

> A player is the character he represents only *in a certain degree*; and therefore
> there is a distinction between his being what I have said, and his being the
> character he represents in the full sense (Boswell 1929: 15–16, 18).

Here we have Boswell as an early Brechtian, espousing an acting theory
that anticipates Brecht's Epic theatre theory by nearly two centuries.
Brecht would later propose

> that the actor appears on the stage in a double role, . . . from which this way
> of acting gets its name of 'epic' . . . that [the actor] is actually there, standing
> on the stage and showing us what he imagines [the character portrayed] to
> have been (Brecht 1964: 194).

The fact that both Boswell and Brecht were intrigued by Gay's Macheath,
and adapted the character for their own purposes, may have had something to do with their similar theories of acting. Macheath himself seems
capable of double or multiple feelings, having acquired at least four wives,
and in Gay's sequel to *The Beggar's Opera* disguising himself as a black-
faced pirate whom Polly Peachum fails to recognize. His ability to change
and keep some of his life secret could be part of what appealed to diarist
James Boswell. What else was the unpublished diary but a secret, second
version of his life?

Images of an 'Epic' actor 'standing on the stage and showing us what
he imagines to have been' (to quote Brecht again) also can be seen in
eighteenth-century portraits. Hogarth, Reynolds and other painters
framed prominent actors in striking, highly theatrical poses. The acting of
the period lent itself to this kind of portraiture, especially in Garrick's case.
As Peter Thomson observes in an essay on Garrick: 'The whole framing of
the action on the eighteenth-century stage declared artifice, and Garrick
placed himself within that frame' (Thomson 2000: 91).

It is regrettable that Garrick never played the role of Macheath—at least
for our purposes, it would have enhanced the theory about his 'early Brechtian' acting. Boswell lamented that Garrick had not written something on
acting, and said so in his essay 'On the Profession of a Player':

> I heartily wish that Mr. Garrick would give us an Essay on that subject [of
> character portrayal]; as he is so fully master of it, and writes with precision
> and vivacity . . . We would read an Essay by Mr. Garrick on the art of acting,
> as we do Xenophon and Caesar, or the King of Prussia, on the art of war.

Garrick published a short unsigned treatise on acting in 1744, but either
Boswell overlooked it, or he did not know that Garrick wrote the piece
which mocked his own portrayal of Macbeth. 'Would Mr. Garrick give us

the Essay which I have here figured, it would add much celebrity to his profession', professed Johnson's biographer (Boswell 1929: 16). Then Boswell proceeded to write the essay he wanted for Garrick, or at least started it in the same piece of 1770. First he quoted Samuel Johnson arguing that: 'If, sir, Garrick believes himself to be every character that he represents, he is a madman and ought to be confined. Nay, sir, he is a villain, and ought to be hanged.' Responding to Johnson's concerns about actors like Garrick wholly identifying with the characters they portray, Boswell proceeds to offer his own view, which finds him (as quoted already) saying that

> a player is the character he represents only *in a certain degree*; and therefore there is a distinction between his being what I have said, and his being the character he represents in the full sense of the expression.

This early expression of Epic theatre theory stems from Boswell defending Garrick against Dr Johnson's accusation; the biographer's understanding of how an actor assumes a role suggests Garrick could have been one of Brecht's followers, or vice versa, without knowing it.

The fact that modern writers have not seen Garrick on stage, as Johnson and Boswell did, does not deter new testimony on Garrick's Brechtian qualities. Noting that Diderot published his *Observations on Garrick* in 1770, a recently published textbook observes: 'Diderot's cool-headed, self-manipulative actor [i.e., Garrick] might be compared to the ideal actor of Meyerhold and Brecht in the twentieth-century' (Williams 2006: 243). Brecht may well have read Diderot on Garrick, too; he knew the Frenchman's writings well enough to propose the founding of a Diderot Society in 1937 (Brecht 1964: 106). Perhaps Boswell knew Diderot's thoughts on Garrick, also; although he does not quote the Frenchmen in his 1770 essay, both published writing on Garrick that year.

While Boswell makes no reference to Macheath or John Gay in his essay on acting, it is tempting to trace his theory of 'double feeling' back to his youthful impersonation of the highwayman in London. John Gay's fictive character may have influenced the lives of many eighteenth-century spectators, those at the theatre and those who saw Macheath in prints by Hogarth or other artists. As noted earlier, some critics of the original production paid tribute to the character's effect on the public by denouncing the play as an immoral influence. Swift acknowledged its capacity to affect public behaviour, too; but he praised the play for that reason, and pseudonymously argued in *The Intelligencer* that Gay's ballad opera 'will probably do more good than a thousand sermons'.

In the 1728 'A Key to the Beggar's Opera in a Letter to Caleb Danvers, Esq.', a critic complains that the work is 'an undeniable Mark of a vitiated Taste and a degenerate, licentious Age, which delights in seeing Things of the greatest Importance turned to Ridicule . . . And [has made theatres] the popular Engines for conveying not only Scandal and Scurrility, but even Sedition and Treason through the Kingdom'. These objections to *The Beggar's Opera* appear to have been part of a hoax; 'A Key' was first printed in *The Craftsman*, a journal unfriendly to Walpole and approving Gay's political satire. (Goldgar 69–70)

The negative phrases just quoted can also be read as ironic praise, acknowledgement of the satire's successful ability to foster 'delight in seeing Things of the greatest importance turned to ridicule'. That and the play's alleged 'Licentiousness' won Macheath a following that included Boswell and Brecht. The anti-hero's ability to trespass across the boundaries of socially acceptable behaviour, to abandon 'genteel' and 'proper' manners for something more private and anarchic, might have appealed to the gentlemen (Boswell, Brecht) and even the lady (Charlotte Charke) who followed him to their delight in their own theatrical ways, *to a certain degree*. Boswell's Macheath, and Crumb's depiction of Boswell imagining himself as the rake Macheath, can be seen as celebrations of that 'double feeling' experienced by an artist portraying someone else while not entirely forgetting himself or his own time and place. It was a feeling Crumb may have enjoyed when fusing his confessional comic strip sensibility (the one that led to his 'Dirty Laundry' series of self-portraits) with Boswell's biography. The same 'double feeling' may have been experienced by Brecht when he adapted *The Beggar's Opera* in 1928 and discovered his own affinity with earlier, eighteenth-century Brechtians, John Gay, Jonathan Swift and William Hogarth.

CHAPTER TWENTY-TWO

Walpole in America

England's first Minister, Robert Walpole, never visited America; but his country estate, or parts of it, travelled to San Francisco in 2014 and stayed through February 2015. The San Francisco Legion of Honor museum exhibition titled 'Houghton Hall, Portrait of an English Country House' celebrated the residence built for Walpole in 1722, a time when he held considerable political power and influence. Houghton Hall furnishings designed by William Kent, along with paintings and sculptures purchased in Italy, Sèvres porcelain from France, and other luxury items in the house once served as 'magnificent testimony to [the minister's] new position in government', and aimed 'to present Sir Robert Walpole as a man of culture and learning', according to a statement from the Legion of Honor's curators.

The exhibition endeavours to replicate the house's eighteenth-century glorification of the Great Man, but the glory of the estate and the man who owned it has faded. The gold punch-bowl still glitters, the carved white marble bust of Zeus remains immaculate; but the replicated rooms look like hoary and incomplete stage sets. The Minister's library is represented by a few antique books and two-dimensional bookshelves painted on a flat. Glass cases full of china and tureens stand in for the dining hall. The dressing room holds a few once-noble costumes. These settings, such as they are, accommodate spectators who walk around the rooms; but the main actor hardly puts in an appearance. Walpole can be seen in a few oil portraits. We learn much more about his silver wine coolers, his Italian artworks, and his favourite armchair, than about the man who acquired them.

Robert Walpole was more attracted to foreign arts and crafts than those made in England, judging from the variety of Italian, French, Dutch and Chinese artefacts on display. In the 1720s England's foreign holdings and commerce were expanding, and it is understandable that the first resident of Houghton Hall would want to display cultural treasures from abroad in his country house. These are the spoils of international trade and colonization, as well as political corruption. Some Englishmen might have been disturbed by the Velazquez portrait of Pope Innocent X, who wears a bright red cap and robe; the papacy had opponents in Britain. Perhaps famous foreign artists (as long as they were not critics of the Minister) were exempt from such prejudice. In any case, Walpole filled his house with artefacts and art representative of empires older than his own, with some exceptions of local colour. At the Legion of Honor, reconstructed dressing room walls are covered by faded English tapestries depicting seasonal activities such as sheep-shearing and unabashed hog-butchering complete with a pool of blood. Some of Kent's gilt wooden furniture also was made in England.

The exhibition includes more recent art, John Singer Sargent paintings, a few Gainsborough portraits, and other works acquired by the minister's descendants, notably the Seventh Marquess of Cholmondeley, who currently resides in Houghton Hall, the family's Norfolk manor home and who permits this show to honour his estate.

While scant attention is devoted to the details of Sir Robert's career (as opposed to his luxurious property), small hints of his misconduct surface. One sentence in a wall caption admits that the first Minister's 'rise to power was not without mishap', due to his brief imprisonment in the Tower of London in 1712 when he was 'found guilty of corruption'. Discourse on corruption later in his career would have taken up too much space, perhaps, so no reference is made to the 1720 South Sea financial scandal through which Walpole rose to power, or the rise of opposition to his policies or the creation of anti-Whig anti-Walpole satires by Swift, Gay, Fielding and Hogarth. The great man's mistresses receive one sentence and no portraits. The fact that Walpole was in debt for £50,000 when he died in 1745 is briefly noted without any explanation of the debt's origin. (He 'burnt the bills' recording such costs, according to one wall caption.)

That the minister liked to have gold around him is evident not only in the gilt wooden furnishings, but also in two John Wootton oil portraits in which Sir Robert wears a gold-trimmed blue hunting costume. The lavish outfit must have impressed hounds and foxes alike. Clearly this imagery of the well-dressed sportsman was more acceptable to the minister than was William Hogarth's 1726 print, *The Punishment of Lemuel Gulliver*, also titled *The Political Clyster* (not shown in the Legion), of which neither his estate nor the museum curators would approve. According to Ronald Paulson, Hogarth's print inspired by Swift's satiric travelogue 'is about an England in decline', and the grotesque punishment of Gulliver shown 'is overseen by a First Minister' who could be Walpole. He and a clergyman give an enema to 'a heroic and harmless Gulliver while ignoring the rats devouring their children' (Paulson 1973: 173).

One painting by Hogarth is included in the Houghton Hall exhibition: a 1732 oil showing the Cholmondeley family, including Walpole's daughter

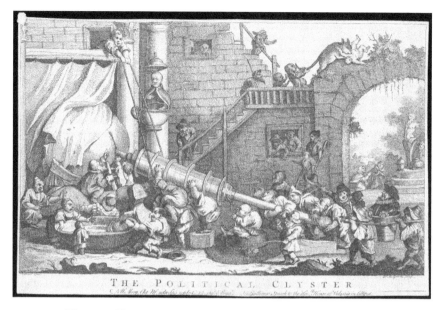

Fig. 15.   Hogarth's portrait of Walpole and Lemuel Gulliver.

Mary, who had married George, Third Earl of Cholmondeley. By the time the Earl commissioned the painting his wife had died; she still appears, with angels flying over her head, in the company of her husband and children. It is a respectful and engaging portrait, slightly surreal as the angels hover above Mary. Large, full bookshelves fill the background to suggest a learned if widowed household. By 1732 the painter was successful enough to win a commission from a relative of the first Minister; evidently the 1726 Gulliver print and other satires did not deter the Earl from paying for a Hogarth.

Hogarth and the Minister shared an interest in some stage plays which might have provided an excuse for inclusion of other paintings or prints in the Legion show. The artist produced six oil versions of a scene from John Gay's *The Beggar's Opera*, and designed an engraving based on Henry Fielding's *The Tragedy of Tragedies*, both plays attended by Robert Walpole. He saw the plays and later had his government censor their authors. But he is touted as a man of culture and learning here, not an opponent of free expression, and none of his theatre visits is mentioned in the exhibition. Hogarth's satires can be seen elsewhere in America, notably in Yale's Center for British Art and the Lewis Walpole Library, but not in Walpole's Californian house.

Sir Robert once hired Hogarth, according to the art historian Paulson. When goldsmith Paul de Lamerie needed an engraver to create a salver bearing the Great Seal of England in 1727, Paulson contends that Walpole 'personally selected Hogarth [as engraver] to ensure his future silence', buying the young artist's favour after recognizing 'that Hogarth was potentially the most dangerous graphic satirist of the age' (Paulson 1971: 174). This patronage receives no mention in the Legion of Honor, as the silence Walpole purchased seems to continue.

Ironically, while the Legion's stage set reconstructions of the Walpole family library, dressing room, bed chamber, and china shelves feature wares from other nations, a separate permanent display elsewhere in the museum features beautiful, witty porcelain tureens, tea cups and plates manufactured in England at the end of Walpole's lifetime. Colourful and realistic images of flowers, vegetables and insects on the Chelsea porcelain created between 1745 and 1769 attest to the ingenuity and superb craft of English artisans. The Chelsea dishes on display have nothing to do with the Houghton Hall exhibition; that might be seen as a favourable attribute, almost like being in a salon of the refused.

The invention and humour of artists who opposed Walpole and his policies, or were excluded from his country house, deserve a counter-exhibition paying tribute to socially critical and popular art of the Augustan and Georgian periods. Paintings and engravings, political cartoons, ceramics, the stage plays and prose satire of Swift, Gay and Fielding, inspired by the corruption and abuses of wealth and power under Walpole's rule could be shown alongside other works (such as poet laureate Colley Cibber's insipid tributes to power) that supported the first Minister and his allies. Walter Benjamin's contention that cultural treasures are inseparable from imperial conquests and triumphal processions at the expense of the oppressed could be illustrated by this alternative exhibition's eighteenth-century art. Walpole's empire and his legacy were more troubled, and led to greater creativity and artworks than the luxurious items from Houghton Hall suggest.

Oppositional works that engage in debate over a national leader's activities might not appeal to the wealthy benefactors who sponsored the Houghton Hall tribute. But the brief reference to Walpole's dying £50,000 in debt deserves more explanation, as does the story of how the first Minister acquired so much money to buy and furnish his mansion. His lengthy control of government from 1721–42 depended on his use of bribery to secure a Whig majority in the House of Commons (Jeffares in Swift 1992: 214). And his corruption, eloquently discussed and graphically illustrated during his lifetime, but not in the Legion of Honor, inspired some notable satiric theatre, poetry and print-making.

In 1729 one of the Minister's most ardent critics, Jonathan Swift, wrote a poem asking what condition can be worse than 'submitting still / To Walpole's more than royal will', when the leader 'comes to drain a beggar's purse; / He comes to tie our chains on faster, / And show us, England is our master; / Caressing knaves and dunces wooing, / To make them work their own undoing' (Swift 1992: 145).

This Anglo-Irish poem on Walpole's 'more than royal' rule admitted the author's 'hate / [for] Both kings and ministers of state' with candour that would not win Swift an invitation to Houghton Hall. But an invitation is no longer necessary; at least through February of the current year, for a small price (no fee at all on first Tuesdays of the month) anyone can walk into the Minister's library and dressing room, or rather replicas of them—stage sets holding framed portraits, precious punch bowls, velvet-covered and gilded chairs—enough material culture to persuade visitors the man was wealthy and acquisitive. All that is missing is the history behind the scenes.

CHAPTER TWENTY-THREE

The Future of Eighteenth-Century Brechtiana
Polly Exonerated

For release to the press
12 December 2028_
London

Three centuries after a ban was placed on John Gay's ballad opera, *Polly*, Prime Minister David Hare announced that amends will be made to the author and his work, through official revocation of the ban and a posthumous award of knighthood to Mr Gay. 'We're also giving him an Olivier Award for the play', Hare said.

Standing next to the PM at 10 Downing Street, Miss Cate Blanchett, the film actress who currently serves as director of the National Theatre of Great Britain, said she planned to take the title role in Gay's play during its revival at the National later this month. (Miss Blanchett refused to answer a question about her age, saying that an actress should be able to portray women of different ages and different centuries.)

Polly was first staged in a censored version in 1777, and no Prime Minister before Hare is known to have praised the play. Acclaimed for his own playwriting before his election as PM in 2020, Hare today made favourable reference to *Polly*'s criticism of British colonialism, slave trade, and usurpation of native people's lands. 'It also contains humour and some lovely songs', he remarked. Miss Blanchett, standing at Hare's side, then sang Air XXVII from *Polly* with lyrics about the 'coward tribes' who 'to power and grandeur rise' by 'tricks and disguise'.

'I'm glad there's no reference to me in it', said the Prime Minister as he joined Miss Blanchett in a refrain of the lyrics. The NT Director also announced that the poet laureate, Caryl Churchill, has been asked to write a sequel to *Polly*, to show what became of the ever popular Miss Peachum after she was rescued from pirates and befriended by West Indian natives in Gay's second instalment of the story.

Miss Churchill stepped forward and revealed that her new play will show

Macheath had not been hanged (as was hinted at the end of the banned episode), 'but reprieved again. He returns to London and moves into the banking profession, much like Brecht's Macheath in *The Threepenny Novel*. Polly becomes Minister of Finance and gives her husband a three billion dollar subsidy. We're far beyond an opera for beggars now.'

CHAPTER TWENTY-FOUR

Conclusion:
The Future Promise of an Earlier Age

The first one to propose that Brecht's plays were part of a 'Historic Line of the Epic Theatre' was Brecht himself. He saw the historic line of development moving 'from the Elizabethan drama via Lenz, Schiller (early works), Goethe (*Götz* and both parts of *Faust*), Grabbe, Büchner. It is a very strong line, easily followed' (Brecht 1972: xiii). The line of German authors sketched in his summary was explored more fully by later writers, notably Max Spalter in *Brecht's Tradition*, Hans Mayer in *Bertolt Brecht and the Tradition*, and Ralph Manheim and John Willett, whose translation was just quoted.

The list of English language playwrights in the 'Historic Line of the Epic Theatre' might start with Marlowe and Shakespeare, whose plays Brecht adapted; but it also could include Farquhar, Gay, Fielding, Charke, Swift and Garrick, whose names he did not place on his list. In making a case for post-Elizabethan British Brechtian theatre that precedes Brecht, or anticipates his Epic theory and practice, the essays here have focused on a special group of eighteenth-century texts. Not all plays produced in the period would fit the bill. Nor did Brecht necessarily know all of the plays discussed in this volume. They could not be called Epic until after Brecht developed the vocabulary to allow it; but their 'Epic' characteristics existed before his plays and theory were written.

Brecht once noted that the structure of Epic theatre plays did not present 'a single inevitable chain of events', and the same may be said of the 'Historic Line of the Epic Theatre'. He did not set out to follow or fall in with a 'historic line'.

> This way of subordinating everything to a single idea, this passion for propelling the spectator along a single track where he can look neither right nor left, up nor down, is something the new school of playwriting must reject (Brecht 1969: 44–45).

Brecht agreed to adapt John Gay's ballad opera only after Elisabeth Haupt-mann showed him her translation, and producer Aufricht commissioned the new work. Initially Brecht would have preferred to work on a differ-ent play, but Aufricht rejected his first choice. The playwright was hardly subordinating everything to renewal of eighteenth-century satire in 1928. Despite audience eagerness to see *The Threepenny Opera* after it opened, Brecht took his time before he adapted another English eighteenth-century text (Farquhar's) in 1955. At that late date in his life, he asked assistants at the Berliner Ensemble to report on other English plays from the period that might be staged (as noted in the Introduction). The Epic characteristics of such plays may have attracted his interest; if we look at other plays from the Augustan and Georgian eras as he might have, with an eye toward adapting them, they already look Epic and Brechtian in some respects.

My colleague Peter Thomson wondered if readers of this book would conclude that Brecht influenced John Gay, and that *The Threepenny Opera* can be seen as a source for *The Beggar's Opera*. (Brecht himself once claimed he wrote *The Beggar's Opera*, as noted at the start of Chapter Fifteen). How far from Brecht's Epic theory and practice are these eighteenth-century artists, if we remove the criterion of chronology in our measurement, and see Brecht's 'spectre' haunting the theatre before and after his arrival on the German stage? Rather than take a strictly chronological and geographic approach to history, or see a single author as originator of the practices considered here, *Eighteenth-Century Brechtians* views stage history as a series of episodes that reflect on each other, and through which (as Michael Wilson suggested to me) we can move backwards as well as forwards. By reducing the authority of chronology and individual authorship, considering Brechtian theatre as a practice and art renewed and linked by reutilizations—not timeless but repeatable with variants, as gestures are quotable by actors in Brecht's view—we might well come to a new understanding of the radicalism of Gay and Fielding. The repertoire of plays that are Brechtian can be enlarged, seen not simply as those texts he wrote and adapted, but also those with Epic theatre characteristics that existed prior to his development of new terms to describe such plays. The situation may be analogous to Aristotle's arrival in Athens after many tragedies had been written. He incisively catalogued the defining characteristics of 'tragedy' in his *Poetics*, and Greek tragedies are often analysed in his terms today; but their tragic structures existed before his arrival. It is not as if Aeschylus or Sophocles set out to write a tragedy that conformed to Aristotle's definition, or chose to stand in a 'historic line' of Aristotelian drama.

It almost goes without saying that Gay and Farquhar did not set out to write Brechtian or Epic plays. But an early Epic sensibility has been noted in their plays as well as Fielding's *Historical Register for the Year 1736* and

Pasquin, where a play within the play is subject to on-stage commentary, adjustment and disruption, if not actor mutiny (which occurs in *The Stage Mutineers* and *The Art of Management*). These plays had Epic traits before the genre was described by Brecht, and they represent an alternative to Aristotelian concepts of drama. Fielding seems to have consciously rejected ancient Greek poetics through his mockery of 'the precepts of Aristotle' in the preface to *The Tragedy of Tragedies*; in doing so, he anticipated Brecht's later rejection of age-old dramatic conventions.

The point here is not to forget chronology or existing documentation, but to observe the future promise of an earlier age's political and satiric theatre, to reconsider its innovations from a Brechtian perspective, which in turn changes the way we see Brecht. The two periods (before Brecht and after) differ in many ways. But components of their theatre and aims of their playwrights share what Walter Benjamin in his theses on history termed a 'constellation' of events, recurrent artistic and political concerns embodied on stage by military recruiters, would-be bankers, cross-dressers, beggar kings, naïve daughters and rebellious actors. In these characters and their theatrical expression of views Brecht also explored, the 'past has a claim' on later developments, which represent a revived chance 'in the fight for the oppressed past' (Benjamin 1968: 254, 263). Fredric Jameson provides an example of this second chance for Gay's satire after quoting Brecht's Peachum and his view of the world as 'a miserable place' where 'people are rotten':

> It is a generalization which the spectacle of Peachum's own business tends to corroborate, along with all the other surroundings of Macheath's existence, with the possible exception of the highwayman himself, who exhibits a certain contagious energy in the midst of this truly eighteenth-century dreariness.

Along with the 'eighteenth-century dreariness' and 'moments . . . already present in Gay's original version' that he finds revived in Brecht's 1928 play, Jameson finds a difference, a modern attitude in the German author's 'delight in surprising and redramatizing the very inner and outer work-ings of capital, the schemes of the businessmen, (not excluding Peachum's own . . .)' (Jameson 185–87).

Brecht, Gay and other satirists considered here took delight in drawing on oppositional politics for their responses to repressive authority, inordinate wealth and corruption. They wrote at different times, but their presentation of self-reflexive and political satire through theatre hasn't merely happened in the past. It happens, it continues in the present tense of live performance on stage; it recurs in 1728, 1729, 1737, 1928, 2014, whenever their plays are re-staged, rewritten, and inspire new plays, from

The Beggar's Opera to Kneehigh's 2014 adaptation of Gay titled *Dead Dog in a Suitcase (and other love songs)*. The names of the writers and actors change, the plays change too. To paraphrase Benjamin again, a new Henry Fielding or John Gay (instead of Benjamin's Messiah) might enter our theatre at any time; but until that time, the original imagery and dialogue of Fielding, Gay, and Brecht, their humour, social visions and inventions as embattled artists who preceded us, prepare us to abet and applaud the arrival of their successors.

'A sequel to a Play is like more last words. 'Tis a kind of absurdity', says the Poet at the beginning of John Gay's *Polly*; and yet that is only the beginning of his sequel to *The Beggar's Opera*. Gay's 'last words' in *Polly* were not allowed to be spoken on stage in his lifetime. But his eighteenth-century scenes and the 'absurdity' of speeches by Gay's characters were heard later, and the songs of Macheath, Polly Peachum, and Jenny Diver were sung anew, in one sequel with lyrics by Brecht, other versions by Dario Fo, Vaclav Havel, Wole Soyinka, and Kneehigh's Carl Grose. It is another absurdity that 'last words' could be heard so many times, in so many sequels; and yet the last word has not yet been heard.

Eighteenth-Century Brechtians:
A Timetable of Events

1701	War of Spanish Succession begins, lasts until 1713. British recruits needed.
1706	George Farquhar, former army recruiter, writes *The Recruiting Officer*.
1708	Whig Parliament member Robert Walpole becomes Secretary at War.
1712	Walpole impeached for corruption as Secretary at War, found guilty, sent to Tower of London.
1714	Death of Queen Anne. George I becomes King.
1715	John Gay's *The What D'ye Call It*, a tragi-comical-pastoral farce, raises some doubts about soldiers going to war.
	Walpole becomes First Lord of Treasury, Chancellor of the Exchequer.
1720–21	South Sea Company scandal, stock prices plummet, Gay loses a fortune.
	Walpole thrives on the crisis, becomes known as first Minister. He stays in control of government until 1742 despite growing opposition from satirists.
1726	Swift in London publishes *Travels into several Remote Nations of the World* under the name of Lemuel Gulliver.
1727	King George I dies, George II ascends to throne. Georgian drama continues.
	Walpole still rules.
1728	*The Beggar's Opera* by John Gay opens at Lincoln's Inn Fields on 29 January. Its satire is viewed as an attack on Walpole. The author's sequel, *Polly*, is submitted to the Lord Chamberlain and banned by 12 December.
	Hogarth paints his first oil portrait of a scene from *The Beggar's Opera*. Five more versions will follow between 1728 and 1731; it sells well.
1729	In Dublin Swift publishes *A Modest Proposal For preventing the Children of Poor People From being a Burthen to their Parents, or the*

Country, and For making them Beneficial to the Publick. He does not sign his name to it.

1730   *The Author's Farce* by Henry Fielding opens at the Haymarket on 30 March. *Tom Thumb*, an afterpiece by Fielding, opens at the Haymarket on 18 April.

Ally of Walpole, author Colley Cibber appointed poet laureate on 3 December.

1731   *The Tragedy of Tragedies*, revised version of *Tom Thumb*, opens 24 March.

The London Merchant by George Lillo opens with Theophilus Cibber in lead role and Charlotte Charke as Lucy on 22 July.

1732   *The Covent-Garden Tragedy* by Henry Fielding lasts for one night (1 June) at Drury Lane with Theophilus Cibber in the role of Lovegirlo.

1733   *The Stage Mutineers* attributed to Edward Phillips opens at Covent Garden on 27 July after actors led by Theophilus Cibber protest Drury Lane management policies and are locked out. Charlotte Charke joins her brother Theo in the move to another playhouse, the Little Theatre in the Haymarket.

Walpole's plan for an excise tax is defeated after widespread protest.

John Gay's third ballad opera, *Achilles*, published posthumously.

1734   Charlotte Charke manages the Mad Company of Comedians at the Haymarket, and performs the role of Macheath in a version of *The Beggar's Opera* on 3 June. On the same day she performs the role of Pistol, for which her brother Theo was known, in *Humours of Sir John Falstaff*, an adaptation of Shakespeare.

1735   Charke's play on actor mutiny, *The Art of Management; or, Tragedy Expell'd*, opens on 24 September in the Great Room at the York Buildings.

1736   Fielding forms The Great Mogul's Company of Comedians, opens *Pasquin* at the Haymarket on 5 April and *Tumble-Down Dick* on 29 April.

1737   *The Historical Register for the Year 1736* opens at the Haymarket on 21 March, one of numerous popular political satires Fielding produces at this theatre. Fielding's *Eurydice Hiss'd; or, A Word to the Wise* opens at the Haymarket on 1 April. Charke takes male roles in both plays.

The Licensing Act for censorship is implemented in June. Fielding's theatre closes, he enters Middle Temple to study law on 1 November.

1738   Swift publishes *A Collection of Genteel and Ingenious Conversation* under the pseudonym of Samuel Wagstaff. A version of it is staged at Drury Lane in 1740.

1739   Charke stages *A Rake's Progress* and other puppet plays at Punch's Theatre.

1740   *Lethe; or, Esop in the Shades* by David Garrick opens at Drury Lane on 15 April.

Colley Cibber publishes his *Apology* and soon after *An Apology for the Life of Mr T . . . . C . . . . ., Comedian* appears, claims to be the autobiography of Cibber's son Theophilus.

Polite Conversation, based on Swift's dialogues, plays at Drury Lane on 23 April.

1741   David Garrick, billed only as 'a Gentleman', performs title role of *Richard III* for the first time at Goodman's Fields, 19 October. He is acclaimed.

1742   Charlotte Charke performs lead male role in *Humours of Covent Garden; or, The Covent Garden Tragedy*, at Bartholomew Fair, 26 August.

1743   *Tit for Tat* performed as a benefit for the author Mrs Charke, New Theatre at James Street, 16 March. Text of the play is not published.

1747   David Garrick becomes a manager at Drury Lane, acts, writes and selects plays.

Samuel Foote opens his popular satire on theatre, *The Diversions of the Morning or, A Dish of Chocolate*, at the Haymarket on 27 April.

1748   Fielding becomes a Justice of the Peace in Westminster and performs puppet plays at Madame de la Nash's Breakfasting Room. Also writes novels.

1756–57   David Garrick's *Lilliput* performed at Drury Lane seventeen times.

1763   On 9 May James Boswell visits Newgate prison and regards one prisoner as 'a Macheath'. On 19 May, Boswell in his diary compares himself to Macheath.

1928   Brecht and others adapt Gay's *The Beggar's Opera*, retitled *The Threepenny Opera*. It opens in Berlin on 31 August.

1933   Brecht has to flee Germany after the Nazis take control of the government.

1949   Berliner Ensemble opens on 12 November, with Brecht now living in Berlin.

1950   Boswell's *London Journal, 1762–1763*, is published for the first time.

1955   Brecht and others adapt Farquhar's *The Recruiting Officer*, directed by Benno Besson at the Berliner Ensemble. The play opens on 19 September.

1956   Brecht and Elisabeth Hauptmann attend *The Threepenny Opera* at Milan's Piccolo Theatre in February. On 4 July Brecht publishes a letter to the West German Bundestag opposing compulsory military service and war. Before he dies on 14 August, he helps prepare the Berliner Ensemble for a tour that includes London performances of *Mother Courage* and the Farquhar adaptation, *Trumpets and Drums*.

Bibliography

Artaud, Antonin, *The Theater and Its Double* (New York: Grove Press, 1958).

Avery, E.L. 'The Craftsman of July 2, 1737 and Colley Cibber,' in *Research Studies of the State College of Washington* (Pullman, Washington: June 1939) 90–103.

Bateson, F.W., *English Comic Drama 1700-1750* (New York: Russell and Russell, 1963).

Battestin, Martin with Ruthe Battestin, *Henry Fielding: A Life* (London: Routledge, 1989).

Battestin, Martin (ed.), *New Essays by Henry Fielding* (Charlottesville: University Press of Virginia, 1989).

Beckett, Samuel, *Happy Days* (New York: Grove Press, 1961).

Benjamin, Walter, 'Theses on the Philosophy of History' in *Illuminations*, trans. by Harry Zohn (New York: Schocken, 1968).

——, *Understanding Brecht*, trans. by Anna Bostock (London: New Left Books, 1977).

Borges, Jorge Luis, 'Kafka and his precursors', in *Everything and Nothing* (New York: New Directions, 1999).

Boswell, James, *Boswell's London Journal, 1762–1763*, ed. by Pottle (New York: McGraw Hill, 1950).

——, *Boswell's Life of Johnson*, ed. by Crocker (London: 1831).

——, *The Life of Samuel Johnson*, Volume I. (London: J.M. Dent, 1923).

——, *On the Profession of the Player: Three Essays* (London: Elkin Mathews & Marrot, Ltd. 1929).

Brecht, Bertolt, *The Threepenny Novel*, trans. by Desmond Vesey (New York: Grove Press, 1956).

——, *Poems on the Theatre*, trans. by John Berger and Anna Bostock (London: Scorpion Press, 1961).

——, *Seven Plays*, trans. by Eric Bentley (New York: Grove Press, 1961).

——, *The Threepenny Opera*, lyrics by Eric Bentley, book by Desmond Vesey (New York: Grove Press, 1964).

——, *Brecht on Theatre*, trans. by John Willett (New York: Hill and Wang, 1964).

——, *The Messingkauf Dialogues*, trans. by John Willett (London: Methuen, 1965).

——, *Manual of Piety (Poems)* trans. by Eric Bentley (New York: Grove Press, 1966).

——, *Trumpets and Drums*, trans. by Rose and Martin Kastner, in *Collected Plays, Volume 9* (New York: Vintage, 1972).

——, *Poems 1913–1956* (London: Methuen, 1976).

——, *The Threepenny Opera*, trans. by Ralph Manheim and John Willett (London: Methuen, 1979).

——, *Conversations in Exile*, adapted by Howard Brenton in *Theater* (New Haven: Yale School of Drama, 1986).

——, *Letters 1913–1956*, ed. by John Willett, trans. by Ralph Manheim (New York: Routledge, 1990).

——, *Writing the Truth: Five Difficulties*. (1935). Online at *www.autodidactproject. org/quote/brecht1.html*

Breton, André, *Anthology of Black Humor*, trans. by Mark Polizzotti (San Francisco: City Lights, 1997).

Charke, Charlotte, *The Art of Management* (London: W. Rayner, 1735).

——, *Narrative of the Life of Mrs. Charlotte Charke* (London, 1755).

Cibber, Colley, *An Apology for the Life of Colley Cibber* (London, 1740).

Cibber, Theophilus, *Dissertations on Theatrical Subjects* (London: Griffiths, 1756).

Collier, John Payne, *Punch and Judy: A Short History with the Original Dialogue* (New York: Dover, 2006).

Conrad, Lawrence H., *Theophilus Cibber on the London Stage: 1703–1758* (Ann Arbor, MI: University of Pennsylvania Press, 1960).

Cross, Wilbur, *The History of Henry Fielding*, Volume One (New Haven: Yale University Press, 1918).

Davies, Thomas, *Memoirs of the Life of David Garrick, Esq.* (London: Printed by the author, 1780).

Davis, Herbert, *Jonathan Swift* (New York: Oxford University Press, 1964).

Davis, Mike, *Be realistic: Demand the impossible* (Chicago: Haymarket Books, 2012).

Denning, Michael, 'Beggars and Thieves' in *John Gay's The Beggar's Opera*, ed. by Harold Bloom (New York: Chelsea House Publications, 1988).

Derrida, Jacques, *Spectres of Marx* (London: Routledge, 1994).

Dobrée, Bonamy, *English Literature in the Early Eighteenth Century 1700–1740* (Oxford: Clarendon Press, 1959).

Dorris, George, 'The Projector, the Mock Mason and Miss Littlewood' in *Modern Drama*, Volume 18, issue 3-4 (Toronto: University of Toronto, December 1973).

Double, Oliver and Michael Wilson, 'Brecht and cabaret' in *The Cambridge Companion to Brecht*, ed. by Peter Thomson and Glendyr Sacks (Cambridge: Cambridge University Press, 2006).

Dryden, Robert, 'John Gay's Polly: Unmasking Pirates and Fortune Hunters in the West Indies', *Eighteenth-Century Studies*, vol. 34, no. 4 (2001), pp. 539–557.

Eddershaw, Margaret, *Performing Brecht: Forty Years of British Performances* (London: Routledge, 1996).

Farquhar, George, *The Recruiting Officer* (Lincoln: University of Nebraska Press, 1965).

Fielding, Henry, *An Apology for the Life of Mr. T . . . . C . . . . .*, *Comedian* (attributed to Fielding, James Ralph co-author) (London: Mechell, 1740).

——, *Works, Volume 3: Plays* (London: Bickers and Son, 1903).

——, *The Female Husband and Other Writings* (Liverpool: Liverpool University Press, 1960).

——, *The Covent-Garden Journal*, ed. by Gerard Edward Jensen (New Haven: Yale University Press, 1964).

——, *The Historical Register for the Year 1736* (Lincoln: University of Nebraska Press, 1967).

——, *Tom Thumb and the Tragedy of Tragedies*, ed. by L.J. Morrissey (Berkeley: University of California Press, 1970).

——, *The Criticism of Henry Fielding*, ed. by Ioan Williams (New York: Barnes and Noble, 1970).

——, *Plays: Volume II, 1731–1734*, ed. by Thomas Lockwood (Oxford: Oxford University Press, 2007).

——, *Plays: Volume III, 1734–1742*, ed. by Thomas Lockwood (Oxford: Oxford University Press, 2011).

Fitzgerald, Percy, *The Life of David Garrick* (Ann Arbor: Plutarch Press, 1971).

Foote, Samuel, *The Nabob* (London: W. Lowndes, 1795).

Friedman-Romell, Beth H., 'Breaking the Code: Toward a Reception Theory of Theatrical Cross-Dressing in Eighteenth-Century London', in *Theatre Journal*, vol. 47 no. 4 (Baltimore: Johns Hopkins University Press, 1995).

Fuegi, John, *Brecht: Chaos, According to Plan* (Cambridge: Cambridge University Press, 1987).

Fuller, John, Introduction to *Dramatic Works of John Gay* (Oxford: Clarendon Press, 1983).

Garrick, David, *Lilliput* (London: Paul Vaillant, 1757).

——, *The Plays of David Garrick*, Volume 2, ed. by Pedicord and Bergmann (Carbondale: Southern University Illinois Press, 1980).

Gay, John, *Polly* (London: self-published, 1729) (printed for the author).

——, *Plays* (London: J. and R. Tonson, 1760).

Genest, John, *Some Account of the English Stage*, Volumes III and IV (Bath: H.E. Carrington, 1832).

Goldgar, Bertrand, *Walpole and the Wits* (Lincoln: University of Nebraska Press, 1976).

Grose, Carl, *Dead Dog in a Suitcase (and other love songs)* (2015). Unpublished text loaned by the author. Originally staged by Kneehigh in England.

Harcourt, Bernard, 'Political Disobedience' in *Occupy: Three Inquiries into Disobedience* (Chicago: University of Chicago Press, 2013).

Haskell, Barbara and Hanhardt, John, *Yoko Ono: Arias and Objects* (Salt Lake City: Peregrine Smith Books, 1991).

Hazlitt, William, 'On the Work of Hogarth' in *Lectures on the English Comic Writers* (New York: Dolphin, Doubleday and Company) (no date).

Hightower, Jim and Phillip Frazer, 'The plutocrats who bankrolled the GOP Primaries', *The Hightower Lowdown* (Langhorn, PA: June 2012).

Hogarth, William, *Engravings*, ed. by Shesgreen (New York: Dover, 1973).

Holdsworth, Nadine, *Joan Littlewood* (London: Routledge, 2006).

Holm, D.K., *The Pocket Essential – Robert Crumb* (Herts: Pocket Essentials, 2003).

Hume, Robert D., *Henry Fielding and the London Theatre 1728–1737* (Oxford: Clarendon Press, 1988).

Jameson, Fredric, *Brecht and Method* (London: Verso, 1988).

Kenner, Hugh, *The Counterfeiters* (New York: Anchor Press, 1973).

Kernan, Alvin, *Printing, Technology, Letters & Samuel Johnson* (Princeton: Princeton University Press, 1987).

Kott, Jan, *Shakespeare Our Contemporary* (New York: Anchor, 1966).

Langford, Paul, *The Excise Crisis: Society and Politics in the Age of Walpole* (Oxford: Clarendon Press, 1975).

Lawrence, Frederick, *The Life of Henry Fielding* (London: Arthur Hall, Virtue and Co., 1855).

Lichtenberg, Georg Christoph, quoted in *Old Criticism on Old Plays and Old*

Players in *The Living Age*, Vol. 109, ed. by Eliakim Littell and Robert Littell (Boston, 1871).

Loftis, John (ed.), *Essays on the Theatre from Eighteenth-Century Periodicals* (Los Angeles: Augustan Reprint Society, 1960).

——, *The Politics of Drama in Augustan England* (Oxford: Clarendon Press, 1963).

Marx, Eleanor, letter quoted in *The Portable Karl Marx* (New York: Penguin, 1983), p. 50.

Marx, Karl, *The Eighteenth Brumaire of Louis Bonaparte* (New York: New World, 1963).

——, *Capital, Volume One*, trans. by Ben Fowkes (New York: Random House, 1976).

——, *Capital, Volume Three*, trans. by David Fernbach (New York: Random House, 1981).

—— and Fredrick Engels, 'The East Indian Company—Its History and Results' in *Articles on Britain* (Moscow: Progress Publishers, 1971). pp. 174–82.

McCrea, Brian, *Henry Fielding and the Politics of Mid-Eighteenth-Century England* (Athens: University of Georgia Press, 1981).

Mayer, Hans, 'Bertolt Brecht and the tradition', in *Steppenwolf and Everyman*, trans. by Jack Zipes (New York: Thomas Crowell, 1971).

Mercier, Jean-Pierre (ed), *Qui a peur de Robert Crumb: Who's Afraid of Robert Crumb* (Paris: Cmp. Magnac, 2000).

Miller, James, *The Coffee-House, A Dramatick Piece* (London: Harrison & Co., 1731).

Mitchell, W.J.T., 'Image, Space, Revolution' in *Occupy: Three Inquiries in Disobedience* (Chicago: University of Chicago Press, 2013).

Morton, A.L., *A People's History of England* (New York: International Publishers, 1968).

Nash, Mary, *The Provoked Wife: The Life and Times of Susannah Cibber* (Boston: Little, Brown and Company, 1977).

Nicoll, Allardyce, *The Garrick Stage* (Manchester: Manchester University Press, 1981).

O'Brien, John, *Harlequin Britain: Pantomime and Entertainment 1690–1760* (Baltimore: Johns Hopkins University Press, 2004).

Orwell, George, *The Lost Writings of George Orwell*, ed. by West (Westminster, Maryland: Arbor House, 1985).

——, 'Politics vs. Literature: An Examination of Gulliver's Travels' in *All Art Is Propaganda*, ed. by Packer (Orlando: Harcourt, Inc., 2008).

Paulson, Ronald, *Hogarth: His Life, Art, and Times* (New Haven: Yale University Press, 1971).

——, *Popular and Polite Art in the Age of Hogarth and Fielding* (Notre Dame: University of Notre Dame Press, 1979).

Pearce, Charles E., *Polly Peachum: The Story of Lavinia Fenton and The Beggar's Opera* (New York: Benjamin Blom, 1968).

Pedicord, Harry William, *The Theatrical Public in the Time of Garrick* (Carbondale: Southern Illinois University Press, 1954).

Perkin, Harold, *Origins of Modern English Society* (London: Routledge, 1969).

Phillips, Edward, *The Stage Mutineers* (London: Richard Wellington, 1733). (No author's name on title page.)

Planchê, J.R., *The Garrick Fever* (New York: Robert De Witt, 1839).

Porter, Roy, *English Society in the 18th Century* (New York: Penguin, 1991).

Pritchard, Will, 'New Light on Crumb's Boswell' in *Eighteenth-Century Studies*, vol. 42, no. 2 (2009).

Reed, Peter, 'Conquer or Die: Staging Circum-Atlantic Revolt in "Polly" and "Three-Finger'd Jack"', *Theatre Journal* (Baltimore: Johns Hopkins, 2007) pp. 241–58.

Sanders, Bernie, *The Speech* (New York: Nation Books, 2011).

Scouten, Arthur H. (ed.), *The London Stage 1660–1800, Part 3: 1729–1747, Vol. I and II* (Carbondale: Southern Illinois University Press, 1960).

——, *The London Stage 1660–1800, Part 4: 1747–1776, Vol. I and II* (Carbondale: Southern Illinois University Press, 1962).

Shaw, G.B., *Plays Pleasant and Unpleasant* (New York: Brentano's, 1905).

Shevelow, Kathryn, *Charlotte* (New York: Picador, 2005).

Smith, Dane Farnsworth, *Plays about the Theatre in England from* The Rehearsal *in 1671 to the Licensing Act in 1737* (London: Oxford University Press, 1936).

Spalter, Max, *Brecht's Tradition* (Baltimore: Johns Hopkins University Press, 1967).

Stead, Phillip John, *Mr. Punch* (London: Evans Brothers Limited, 1950).

Steele, Richard, *The Theatre*, ed. by John Loftis (Oxford: Clarendon Press, 1962).

Stone, Jr. George Winchester, and George Kahrl, *David Garrick: A Critical Biography* (Carbondale: Southern Illinois University Press, 1979).

Swift, Jonathan, *Polite Conversation*, adapted by James Miller, handwritten MS in Huntington Library, California (1740). (Copy provided by University of California Berkeley Library.)

——, *A Compleat Collection of Genteel and Ingenious Conversation*, introduced and edited by Eric Partridge (New York: Oxford University Press, 1963).

——, *Gulliver's Travels*, ed. by Greenberg (New York: Norton, 1970).

——, *Oxford Authors*, ed. by Angus Ross and David Woolley (Oxford: Oxford University Press, 1984).

——, *Selected Poems*, ed. by Norman Jeffares (London: Kyle Cathie Limited, 1992).

Thompson, E.P., *The Making of the English Working Class* (New York: Vintage, 1966).

——, *Customs in Common* (New York: The New Press, 1993).

Thomson, Peter, *On Actors and Acting* (Exeter: University of Exeter Press, 2000).

——, *The Cambridge Introduction to English Theatre, 1660-1900* (Cambridge: Cambridge University Press, 2006).

——, Personal correspondence with the author (2013).

Tynan, Kenneth, *Curtains* (New York: Athenaeum, 1961).

—— (ed.), *The Recruiting Officer, National Theatre Production* (London: Rupert Hart-Davis, 1965).

Völker, Klaus, *Brecht Chronicle* (New York: Seabury Press, 1975).

Weber, Carl, interview with the author (Palo Alto, 30 June 2013).

Willett, John (ed.), *Brecht in Context: Comparative Approaches* (London: Methuen, 1984).

Williams, Gary Jay (ed.), *Theatre Histories* (London: Routledge, 2006).

Williams, Raymond, *Culture and Materialism* (London: Verso, 1980).

Zizek, Slavoj, *First as Tragedy, Then as Farce* (London: Verso, 2009).

Index

CPSIA information can be obtained
at www.ICGtesting.com
Printed in the USA
BVHW04s0452200818
524675BV00002B/6/P